Images of Memory

Images of Memory

On Remembering and Representation

Edited by Susanne Küchler and Walter Melion

SMITHSONIAN INSTITUTION PRESS   *Washington and London*

For Herbert L. Kessler

Library of Congress Cataloging-in-Publication Data

Images of memory : on remembering and representation / edited by
    Susanne Küchler and Walter Melion.
        p.   cm.
    Rev. and expanded versions of papers originally presented at a
symposium on the relation of mnemonic functions to pictorial
representation, organized by the Program in Art History and
Anthropology.
    Includes bibliographical references and index.
    ISBN 1-56098-027-3
    1. Memory—Social aspects.   2. Pictures—Psychological aspects.
3. Cognition and culture.   4. Art and anthropology.   I. Küchler,
Susanne.   II. Melion, Walter S.   III. Program in Art History and
Anthropology (Johns Hopkins University)
BF378.S65I43   1991
306.4'7—dc20   90-22943

British Library Cataloging-in-Publication Data is
available.

Manufactured in the United States of America.
95 94 93 92 91
5 4 3 2 1

∞ The paper used in this publication meets the
minimum requirements of the American National
Standard for Permanence of Paper for Printed
Library Materials Z39.48-1984.

Contents

WALTER MELION AND SUSANNE KÜCHLER

Introduction: Memory, Cognition, and Image Production

Premises

The essays in this volume comprise revised and expanded versions of papers originally presented at a symposium on the relation of mnemonic function to pictorial representation, organized under the auspices of the Program in Art History and Anthropology, funded by the National Endowment for the Humanities and based at The Johns Hopkins University. The symposium topic—memory, cognition, and image production—evolved from premises central to the program, which was established to encourage interdisciplinary discussion, and specifically to reconcile two categories of artifact, the ethnographic and the artistic, subjecting them to both anthropological and art-historical modes of inquiry. The manifold aim was to discern the interpretative models presupposed by these categories, and ultimately to engage them in dialectic.

For example, an anthropological account of a bark painting from Northeast Arnhem Land, the sort of object traditionally displayed in an ethnographic setting, would interpret the object by positioning it within networks of social exchange and determining how its circulation affirms kinship or articulates land rights. The bark painting's meanings would arise from an analysis of its functions—the practical uses of bark, and the ritual uses of painted bark: to invoke dream time and to sustain contact with the dead by the community. Absent from this account would be the painting itself—detailed description of its visual properties and intensive investigation of the categories of pictorial interest that engender those properties and are articulated by them.[1]

By contrast, an art-historical account of a biblical story painted by

Rembrandt, the sort of object displayed in museums of fine art, would focus on its formal properties, its generic status as history, and its place within the market for images prevailing in the Netherlands in the seventeenth century. This account would be characterized by a reluctance to situate possible meanings outside the work itself, to embed it within social networks, or to trace the hierarchies of kinship established by its circulation.[2]

The alternative that we propose would encourage the interpenetration of anthropological and art-historical concerns. The bark painting would be treated, perhaps privileged, as a mode of pictorial representation informed by historically and culturally specific pictorial categories such as "dullness" or "brilliance" and requiring interpretation of the relation of beholders to images.[3] This relationship would be understood to function on several cognitive registers, ranging from perception through the conversion of visual experience into metaphors for other kinds of social and cultural experience. The painting by Rembrandt would be treated in terms of its functions in the marketplace, and the ways in which Rembrandt tried to redefine the artist, the workshop, and the work of art itself by inventing a new kind of marketable commodity over which he could retain control.[4]

The Program in Art History and Anthropology offered a forum in which participants could exchange methodologies, exploring the theoretical implications of this exchange. It soon became apparent that anthropologists and art historians shared basic assumptions about the possibility of transmitting images between generations. Anthropologists referred to this transmittability as the maintenance of social cohesion, while art historians referred to the preservation of paradigms, invoking the process of canon formation. Fundamental questions were raised, however. What makes transmission possible? How does imagery mediate and even enable the process of transmission? And what do we mean by transmission?

It seemed to us that these were questions about memory, the process about which the phenomenologist Edward S. Casey has written, "We have forgotten what memory is, and can mean; and we make matters worse by repressing the fact of our own oblivion."[5] There are three main permutations of the connection between memory and image transmission. One might argue initially that memory enables the transmission of images: regardless of the material in which the images are inscribed, that inscribing presupposes reference to a stored fund of images. The second permutation qualifies this formulation: one might argue that memory does not so much enable transmission as it is itself enabled by transmission. This formulation disputes the notion that memory is a discrete function preceding image production; instead, memory is defined as a process precipitated and shaped by the relaying of visual information. The third permutation takes this assertion one step further: one might argue that transmission itself is a mode of memory, that memory is a dynamic process informed by the cognitive experiences through which images are fashioned. This collection of essays tests these hypothetical constructions by inquiring into the ways in which Western and non-Western cultures conceive and deploy memory in the production of images.

Our three permutations involve a shift from a passive notion of memory as a place where visual data are stored to be tapped when necessary to an active notion of memory as a process correlative to and coincident with image production. The attempt to conceive of memory in active terms is a relatively recent philosophical project. The prevailing philosophical treatment of memory is grounded in the discourse of Plato and Aristotle, both of whom visualize memory as a storage receptacle from which images can be retrieved at will. For Plato, memory contains, or rather withholds, epistemic knowledge with which it has been imprinted by divine agency. Dialectical inquiry is a mode of recollection through which we incite awareness of the knowledge we already possess. Aristotle describes memory differently, seeing it as the human function through which information is retained. He takes information to be perceptually and cognitively based, and presumes therefore that individual experience shapes memory. Ultimately, both Plato and Aristotle believe that memory can be tapped; it is activated through processes of philosophical inquiry but does not itself generate those processes.

Frederic Bartlett, Piaget, and others have queried this philosophical model, calling attention to the ways in which experience constantly reshapes recollection.[6] They offer accounts that problematize the threshold between recollection and experience, showing that the experience of recollection and the recollection of experience are reciprocally engaged. Contemporary alternatives to the Platonic and Aristotleian discourse of memory have been primarily psychological, neurological, and phenomenological. In art history and anthropology, however, fields in which the study of images plays a central role and representation should be a central issue, the problem of memory has been neglected. The notable exception has been Frances Yates, whose *Art of Memory* traces the history of mnemonic pedagogy, chronicling its transformation from rhetorical technique to hermetic art.[7] Describing memory as the storage of visual images, Yates herself subscribes to the mnemonic models propounded by Plato and Aristotle.

What has yet to be attempted is an account binding mnemonic functions to processes of representation. While Yates refrains from asking what is involved in the translation from mental images to pictures artificed by the hand, Bartlett and other cognitive psychologists leave ambiguous the place of images in the formation of the schemata that organize memory. Again we might ask what memory, being comprised of these schemata, has to do with image production.

Gregory Bateson's *Naven* remains the most sympathetic attempt to demonstrate the mutually informing links between cognitive habits and mnemonic practice. Bateson studied the valorization of memory within the Iatmul cultures of Papua New Guinea, proposing that the pursuit of memory promotes and maintains cultural formation in all its fullness and complexity.[8] His ethnography shows how visual and kinesthetic performance engages memory, but it marginalizes a whole range of sculpted artifacts that are themselves engaged in the culture's mnemonic practice.

The essays in this volume share Bateson's assumption that memory is actively constructed as a social and cultural process. We take image production to be the locus of the heightened interplay of mnemonic process and cultural formation. Our ultimate aim is the elaboration of an alternative discourse of memory, alternative that is, to the long tradition of discourse originating with Plato and Aristotle. As Yates has shown, the conception of memory as a passive vessel or a tablet waiting to be inscribed has provided and continues to provide a historically valid model. But Yates does not acknowledge that this model is culturally specific. It facilitates an understanding of Leonardo da Vinci's exploration of the physiology of memory but has little relevance to the painting practice of late Ming dynasty cognoscenti, who articulated networks of solidarity by circulating consensually admired images.[9] Nor does this model help us to explain the ways in which Zairian popular painting generates an alternative social memory of the colonial past, disseminating an unofficial political history.[10] By attending to the ways in which image production and mnemonic construction are socially and culturally specific, we hope ultimately to arrive at a cross-cultural theory of memory.

Social and cultural specificity derives from a community's cognitive habits. As the cultural historian Michael Baxandall has argued, pictorial manner consists of the interplay between the beholder's visual skills and the pictorial properties that engage those skills. Perspective construction, as it was formulated by Florentine masters in the fifteenth century, plays on the merchant-buyer's commercial ability to gauge complex spatial volumes. Narrative pictorial construction stimulates the neo-Latinist's familiarity with the linguistic structure of the Latin period. The elaborate arabesque ornamentation of German sixteenth-century limewood sculpture satisfies the desire for calligraphic flourish inculcated in German commercial schools.[11] Baxandall's term for the cognitive skills that generate images and in turn are exercised by them is the *period eye*. His notion of the constituents of visual culture emerges from the work of Sir Ernst Gombrich on perception. Gombrich's famous formulation of the interaction between "making and matching" problematizes the connection between the processes of perception and cognition.[12] He argues that the painter makes patterns that invite the beholder to project remembered images upon them. The perception of images involves therefore the recollection of visual experience. Gombrich refrains from asserting, however, the inseparability of perceptual and cognitive processes, a nexus he suggests but cannot prove. One might discern Baxandall's historical project to be the disclosure of this very link. Gombrich and Baxandall point the way to a historiography of art that aims to position culture historically by reference to cognition.

In her work on Dutch art of the seventeenth century, Svetlana Alpers binds image production even more closely to a cognitive model. She demonstrates the pertinence of Keppler's optical model of eyesight to the descriptive format and function of much Dutch art of his time. Keppler argues that there is no such thing as unmediated perception of nature; rather, the eye represents nature, and vision is itself a mode of picturing, just as picturing is, as Alpers notes, the representation of visual experience. Cognition, perception, and image production intersect in Alper's argument, for to know the world in this visual culture assumes trust in the commonality of seeing and picturing.[13]

In different ways, Alpers, Baxandall, and Gombrich all show how the discourse of art must invoke cognition. Their work, Alpers's and Baxandall's especially, recalls in turn the theoretical example of the anthropologist Clifford Geertz, who has attempted to position the experience of art within a socially specific discourse of culture. Image production is not one of Geertz's central concerns. His relevance to cultural historians such as

Alpers and Baxandall originates in his notion of the symbolic structures of which religious experience consists. Baxandall's "period eye," for example, functions something like Geertz's symbolic structures, which are at once passive and active, allowing the individual to process the flood of sensory impressions as well as shape them into coherent experience.[14]

The anthropologists Pierre Bourdieu and Dan Sperber provide alternative theories of symbolic structuring, which ground these structures within the modality of cognition.[15] Bourdieu invokes the concept of *habitus,* by which he means the internalized structures that enable the activities, beliefs, aspirations, and world view that coordinate a community. The habitus structures but is also structured by these coordinating practices. Sperber opposes the notion that symbolism is a fixed mechanism facilitating the process of social communication. Rather, symbolism is itself a process inextricably linked to other autonomous cognitive processes, the perceptual and the conceptual. Bourdieu and Sperber, and to some extent Geertz, rely on linguistic models of symbolic construction. The essays in this volume explore the relevance of these linguistic models to the making and viewing of images. Like Alpers and Baxandall, we hope to establish the degree to which these models can be pertinent to image production.

The move from verbal to visual formulations must involve the study of physical properties—the materials worked by the hand and the constraints imposed on the hand by the body. We might address the relation of cognition and memory to materials and the hand by framing an observation. Positioning the hand on a metal plate to be engraved or before a panel to be painted valorizes that hand, positing it as the potentially meaningful center of gravity, source of action, and even locus of social identity. To posit the hand in this way is to project upon it precisely the symbolic structures articulated by Sperber and Bourdieu. In turn, the hand at this critical moment justifies these structures by implementing them. The hand and the body of which it is an extension reify the structures that inform cognition. The question then, as posed in this book, is how to articulate this relationship between symbolizing and artificing.

Our concern with the hand poses equally urgent questions about memory and image production. Just as we have argued that memory is neither simply the trace of past experience nor the means through which that experience is retained as knowledge, so too we must argue that images do not simply derive from a fund of stored impressions. Memory may enable image production, but it is neither prior to nor discrete from the artificing functions of the hand. By the same token, the hand, when it inscribes an image on a material surface, is precipitating memory, shaping and consolidating it. The image documents this complex interplay between recollection and handiwork, and it is this juncture we address.

The image documents another juncture, for the act of inscribing has a dual purchase; it shapes memory by literally shaping materials. We can better see the essential relationship between memory and the physical properties of the image by rehearsing a number of descriptive categories. We might invoke the durability and permanence of a painted image or the durability and permanence of memory. The ephemerality of certain images and the risk of their erasure complement the process of forgetting. Durability and loss are potential in every image, while recollecting and forgetting are functions intrinsic to memory. The Platonic and Aristotleian models of memory, which isolate it as a discrete mental property, cannot encompass this fundamental connection between memory and the material properties of image production. In this book we aim to suggest how mnemonic processes are indivisible from the material act of representation.[16]

Our discussion of materials, which grew out of our concern with the hand, has brought us full circle to memory. It seems appropriate now to state the premises that underlie the essays assembled here. In particular, there are four that emerged as common denominators. First, memory is socially and culturally constructed, and recourse to the processes of construction must mediate the understanding of memory, especially the understanding of its embeddedness in active processes of cognition and image production. Second, memory operates through representation. Images do not simply encode prior mnemonic functions, but rather posit a dynamic of mnemonic processing. Images engender modes of recollection as much as they are determined by them. Third, modalities of recollection are historically based, and the project of understanding is a historical one. Fourth, forgetting and recollecting are allied mnemonic functions. Forgetting can be the selective process through which memory achieves social and cultural definition.

In order to test the hypotheses marshalled above, we explore in the following section two historically and culturally specific examples of the affinities between memory, cognition, and image production. These examples come from our own research on Netherlandish and New Guinean visual cultures.

Two Case Studies

Hendrick Goltzius

Hendrick Goltzius, active in Haarlem between 1575 and 1617, and famed in his time as an unexampled draftsman and engraver, is marginal to the art historical field as it is presently constituted. Yet he seemed to his contemporaries to have transformed the way in which images could be memorialized and to have made possible the allied processes of canon formation and historical construction, processes through which emerged a regional history of art. Goltzius's claim to such a reputation rests in the perfection of his *burin-hand,* by which his admirers, specifically his biographer Karel van Mander, mean two things: the hand with which he held the burin, the tool the engraver pushes into a copper plate to score it with an image; and the signature lines, swelling and tapering gradually along their semicircular ambit, that imprint the image when the plate is run through a press. The Dutch term for such lines was *handelingh,* that is, "rendering," and a categorical distinction was made between *handelingh* and *print,* that is, the printed picture engendered by rendering.[17]

We can grasp these terms by looking closely at a self-portrait executed in pen and ink in 1588, just as Goltzius was consolidating his reputation as the greatest delineator of his age (fig. 1).[18] By examining this and several other works on paper, a medium privileged above painting on canvas by his Dutch contemporaries, we can come to understand how he deployed his distinctive *handelingh* to lay claim to the processes of memory and cognition. Ultimately, the activation of these processes by rendering images on paper came to involve for Goltzius the dismantling of self.

I have referred to the drawing of the extended hand as a self portrait because it is inscribed with Goltzius's name, and because it was his hand that was apostrophized by contemporaries and came to stand for the executive skill of which it was the source. The drawing is itself disembodying, for it detaches the hand from Goltzius's body; taut and outstretched, the veins distended by exertion of some sort, the hand asserts its self-sufficiency, filling the sheet to the exclusion of the arm and body to which it should be attached. The hand is poised as if manipulating a burin, steadied on the work surface by the thumb and forefinger while the extended middle and ring fingers guide the burin's spine and blade. The absence of the burin itself, or rather its implied presence, was dictated by the peculiar history of Goltzius's right hand (pictured here as it would

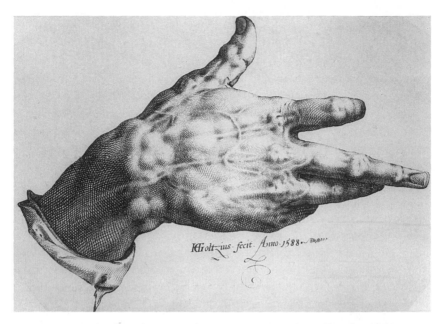

Figure 1. Hendrick Goltzius, *Goltzius's Burin-Hand (Study of a Right Hand)*, drawing, pen and ink, 1588, 229 × 328 mm. The Teylers Museum, Haarlem, Netherlands.

appear in a mirror and portrayed by his left hand, with which he drew). In his "Life of Goltzius," published in 1604, Karel van Mander recounts how as a child the master had burned both hands. The right hand had been improperly bandaged so that the sinews conjoined and the hand could not be fully opened, and he had trained himself to engrave with this lame hand.[19] Through the art of engraving, Van Mander suggests, Goltzius converted his liability into an asset. Conversely, the drawing shows how the hand calls for the burin, its deformation in perfect and permanent conformation with the tool for which it is always ready. The condition of disfiguration is here the precondition of Goltzius's art.

The drawing of the hand invokes the burin in a second way, since it is rendered with pen and ink in imitation of the linear register perfected in Goltzius's engravings. The drawing turns a paradoxical conceit, constituting the hand out of the very *handelingh* of which the hand is the originating source. An engraving of 1586, *Mucius Scaevola* from a series of eight Roman heroes, exemplifies the rendering that is appropriated by Goltzius's pen (fig. 2).[20] The burin models and enlivens the warrior's body by hatching regularly spaced lines whose length, direction, and shape correspond to the figure's contours. Double- and triple-hatching articulate intensifying degrees of shadow, while highlights consist of reserved zones of uncut plate. Goltzius mediates the transition from dark to light by varying the weight of the burin as it inscribes concentric arcs, cutting swelling and tapering courses that invite the eyes to circumnavigate the figure. In his "Life of Goltzius," Van Mander declares that the series's true subject is the heroism of the engraver's hand, whose confident dexterity neutralizes the Romans' deeds, turning their valor into the thematization of the engraver's valorous *handelingh*.[21] This print is a particularly potent example of Van Mander's claim, since Scaevola demonstrated his courage by willfully disfiguring his right hand with fire.[22] In Van Mander's account, the print displaces the virtue of that disfiguring act onto the engraver's hand, valorizing the burin above the sword. The drawing of Goltzius's hand in turn disarms the hand to show that even without the burin it stands alert; moreover, the drawing is a portrait of the burin-hand in two senses, for it portrays the engraver's hand and does so by representing the engraver's *handelingh*. Goltzius describes his hand to picture rendering and mobilizes rendering to honor his hand.

What entitles the burin-hand to such homage, eliding portraiture into a depiction of rendering and the hand? The answer lies in the kind of imitation that this burin-hand made possible. Van Mander again gives access to Goltzius's accomplishment when he writes, "From his earliest years he sought not only to imitate the beautiful and varied forms of nature, but also to accustom himself to portraying the varied manners [Van Mander uses *handelinghen*] of the best masters."[23] It was this imitative project that his contemporaries believed him to have consolidated in his engravings of the 1580s and 1590s. By perfecting the linear means that we have seen distilled in the drawing of his hand, Goltzius could lay claim to an expanded range of pictorial manners. He could adjust the network of flourished arcs to imitate the graphic works of Netherlandish and Italian masters. More importantly, the flexibility of his signature strokes authorized the imitation of the Italian pictorial manner as it was exemplified in the canonical paintings of the Venetian, Lombard, Florentine, and Roman schools. On the one hand, the ease with which he could turn his strokes, using flexion to suggest the rotation of notional spirals, seemed ideally suited to the depiction of the basic unit of the Tuscan and Roman manners—the *figura serpentinata* or human figure mobilized by the symmet-

Figure 2. Hendrick Goltzius, *Mucius Scaevola* from *The Roman Heroes*, engraving, 1586, 353 × 232 mm. By courtesy of the Warburg Institute.

rical rotation of all its parts around a spiraling central axis. On the other, the layering of graduated hatches and the concomitant build-up of different densities of ink seemed ideally accommodated to the *colorito* that was fundamental to the Lombard and Venetian manners—the elaboration of color and tone and the description of surface textures based on the visible laying on of pigments.

It would be difficult to overestimate the potential of Goltzius's burin-hand. Through the *handelingh* of his prints, he could show control of the *handelinghen* of the entire range of regional schools, inserting himself as a maker of images in the manner of whatever master he chose to imitate. Through the circulation of his reproductive prints, he could broadcast information about selected masters, canonizing them by designating their art worthy of imitation, multiplication, and dissemination. The key word here is *selected,* for it was his prerogative, and by extension the prerogative of the local visual culture of which he was a part, to decide whose work would be codified and enlarged through the execution and circulation of engravings.

Those Netherlanders who aimed to articulate what was distinctive about the native visual arts, and who felt that this could be accomplished through the formulation of a literate response to images—humanists such as Abraham Ortelius in Antwerp and Domenicus Lampsonius in Liège, informed collectors such as Bartholomeus Ferreris and Jan Mathijsz Ban, and critical historians such as Karel van Mander—saw in Goltzius the means through which they could control the project of canon formation, wresting control from such supremely gifted but ideologically biased historians as Giorgio Vasari in Florence.[24] Through the medium of reproductive prints, the North could gather and publicize its own canon, developing an authoritative tradition of pictorial paradigms by positioning masters within a historical construction that would encompass the fifteenth and sixteenth centuries. In this way the North could demonstrate that its visual culture was different from rather than subsidiary to that of Italy.

Implicit in this conviction of cultural authority was an assumption about memory: the vividness and precision with which Goltzius could imitate *handelingh* would inscribe mnemonically the essentials of pictorial manner. This assumption involved a fundamental shift in the preferred conveyers of memorable visual information. Up to this time, the primary method through which information about images had been replicated and purveyed had been rhetorical, specifically the use of *ekphrases,* the advanced rhetorical technique of description that aimed to incite in the listener or reader the response generated in the beholder by the experience of looking at images.[25] Goltzius provided the visual means that supplanted such textual modes of representation. His extraordinarily high reputation arose out of the belief, expressed and necessitated by his reproductive prints, that optical experience best served to relay images and the pictorial representation of prior images would confer upon them canonical status.

To illustrate this point, and demonstrate the urgency with which it was felt, we can look at the circumstances surrounding the publication of a seminal Jesuitical work, the *Evangelicae Historiae Imagines* of Hiero-nymo Natali,[26] which are extremely revealing and worth examining in detail.

In the summer of 1585, Father Ludovicus Tovardus, acting on behalf of the Jesuit order in Rome, initiated a complex series of negotiations with Christophe Plantin, head of the most distinguished publishing house in Antwerp and factor for the Jesuits in Flanders. Tovardus commissioned Plantin to hire an engraver who would reproduce accurately and quickly the 153 doctrinally sound illustrations drawn by Bernardo Passero for Natali's book. Prompted by Loyola himself, Natali had extracted narratives of the key events chronicled in the gospels, from the Annunciation to the Last Judgment. In the Jesuit edition of the *Imagines*, these extracts were to be reduced to numbered subtitles accompanying the images, which were to carry the primary burden of narration. The *Imagines* were therefore the full manifestation of the Gregorian dictum that "pictures are the book of the unlettered," for they established a standardized repertory of biblical events from which the central doctrines of faith could be promulgated worldwide. Through reproductive prints, the *Imagines* could colonize the world, fulfilling more vividly than sermons or texts the Jesuits' proseletyzing mission.

It was therefore incumbent on Plantin to find an engraver whose burin-hand would realize the mnemonic functions vested in the *Imagines*. Both he and Tovardus hoped above all to enlist the services of Goltzius, who had only recently established an independent workshop in Haarlem. Informing their efforts is the presumption that Goltzius alone possessed the equipment suited to the task in hand. He was offered unparalleled perquisites: he would be expected to cut heads and hands himself, but could delegate all other work to collaborators of his choice; he could name his price for the project on a lucrative per-figure basis (lucrative because the

images were to be crowded but small); and if he would agree to complete
the project in Antwerp, where he could coordinate his efforts with the
Jesuits' publisher, Plantin, he would be relieved of all provincial and city
taxes.[27]

In spite of Plantin's persistent offers, Goltzius ultimately refused the
commission. He had several grounds for doing so: the Jesuits had not
agreed to provide a paid trip to Italy; they had annoyed him by contacting
competing master engravers; he was profitably engaged in the production
of documentary picture books such as *The Funeral of William of Orange,*
engraved and published under his supervision; he was committed to the
execution of a varied series of demonstration plates after drawings by
Bartholomeus Sprangher, in which he aimed to test his reproductive facility; and he was loath to work after so extensive a series of uniform models.
Even after his final refusal, the Jesuits persisted, and only late in 1586 did
they begin to search seriously for another engraver, finally securing the
services of the Wiericx family in Antwerp. The Jesuits' desire to procure
Goltzius and their refusal to consider Italian engravers underscore his
incontrovertible hegemony over the production of reproductive prints.
Tovardus and Plantin had tried to elicit from him the promise that he
would mark all the finished plates of the *Imagines* with either his name or
his monogram. Such marked plates would carry the guarantee of absolute
faithfulness to the original, compounded with a standard of workmanship
that would ensure that the image would be vividly remembered.

It is telling that the uniformity of the modelli prompted Goltzius to
decline the commission, since the series for which he achieved his greatest
acclaim, the *Early Life of the Virgin* published in 1594, consists of six
plates, each of which distils the pictorial manner of a canonical northern
or Italian master.[28] Van Mander tells us that these prints legitimized his
claim to the epithet *Proteus.*[29] Like Proteus, who could camouflage himself
by changing form at will, Goltzius subsumed his hand into the pictorial
manner of the masters selected for imitation. These prints, Van Mander
alleges, changed the very nature of the reproductive enterprise, for they
imitated pictorial manner itself, distilling *handelinghen* rather than copying
prior images. In the *Rest on the Flight* in the manner of Federigo Barocci,
for example, Goltzius implements the painter's characteristic male and
female types in a typical configuration, but most impressively he captures
the quality of grace that seemed Barocci's categorical imperative (fig. 3).
Grazia or "grace" is a multivalent term that implies ease of execution: the

PRÆCVRSOR DOMINI LACTANTIS AB VBERE MATRIS   QVEM PRÆCOGNOVIT SALIENS VTERO ABDITVS, HVNC ET
BLANDITVR PVERO PVER, ET COLLVDIT AMICE,   INDICE MONSTRAVIT DIGITO CRESCENTIBVS ANNIS

Figure 3. Hendrick Goltzius, *The Holy Family with the Infant St. John the Baptist*, also known as *The Rest on the Flight*, or *The Holy Family under a Tree*, engraving, 1593, 460 × 350 mm. The Baltimore Museum of Art: Garrett Collection BMA 1946.112.12050.

unforced and ingenuous smile on the Virgin's face; the family's liberty of unstrained movement; and the fluency with which the eyes follow the passage of the burin's strokes, circulating evenly from form to form, unchecked by contours. The print invites us to commit to memory the *grazia* of Barocci, instilling it in an unprecedented image resulting from the confluence of the engraver's and the painter's hands.

Van Mander tells us that this and other plates from the series came from the vivid impressions with which Goltzius returned from Italy in 1591. In the *Rest on the Flight* he imitated his memory of Barrocci's pictorial manner, and Van Mander avers that the series resulted from his dissatisfaction with verbal resources.[30] The experiences he had attempted to describe in words after his return he could more fully realize through engravings. It is as if the *Early Life of the Virgin* recapitulates the substitution of prints for *ekphrases* that we invoked earlier as one of Goltzius's crowning achievements. What the *Rest on the Flight* calls to our attention then is neither a prior image, for this image is newly invented, nor the virtuosity with which he has conjured Barocci, for the virtuosity consists paradoxically in the dismantling of all traces of Goltzius's personal manner. Rather, we are asked to attend to *handelingh* itself, which is here the concretization of a mnemonic process, engaged and expressed by the act of engraving. Goltzius has activated his burin-hand because his memory of *handelinghen* is so pressing. Conversely, the action of his burin-hand has triggered a recollection so powerful that it transforms the execution of the plate into the invention of a new work that seems as if by Barocci. The power of the print is its ability to obscure the threshold between a reproductive and an originating act. The beholder is expected to operate at this threshold; like the engraver, we are to memorize the *handelingh* that he has appropriated so thoroughly it seems to have appropriated him.

I am arguing, on the basis of Van Mander's formulation, that the images in the series of the *Early Life of the Virgin* are schematizations of memory coeval with the representation of *handelingh*. Like the drawing of Goltzius's burin-hand, which characterizes him as the agent of engraving but refuses to figure him, these prints efface their maker, or rather testify to his ability to elide himself into the memory of those masterworks whose manner he enacts. The Dutch term for images fashioned in this way is *uyt den geest* or "from the mind," by which is meant "from the memory of things seen." The term designates the process by which images are executed from the memory of intense visual experiences.

Coextensive with *uyt den geest* is the allied term *nae t'leven* or "after life," which designates the production of images from immediate visual impressions. An engraving executed with the modello in sight or a landscape drawing rendered while the draftsman views the scene would have been termed *nae t'leven*. The two terms are inextricably bound. To be convincing, the work done *uyt den geest* must seem to display the vividness and specificity of work done *nae t'leven*. By the same token, the production of an image *nae t'leven* will inscribe in memory the visual experiences translated onto paper; the act of translating from sight to image converts the axis of seeing and recording into a process of memorization.[31]

The burin-hand that worked *uyt den geest* in the *Early Life of the Virgin* could also be applied to work *nae t'leven*. In the print of *The Farnese Hercules*, engraved in the 1590s but published only posthumously as part of an incomplete canon of antique effigies viewed by Goltzius in Rome, two spectators gaze up at the figure, cuing us to the fact that the print was executed *nae t'leven* (fig. 4). Goltzius means by this that he engraved the plate while looking at a drawing that had been executed while he actually studied the statue. His procedure combined views taken from two vantage points, in order to give maximum visual information while ensuring the accuracy of the drawing. From a sufficiently distant site, he recorded the effigy's contours; he then traced them onto a second sheet on which, after moving much closer, he recorded musculature and other surface details. This relay of images, each done *nae t'leven*, positioned the print squarely within the category of works done after life.[32]

A more sweeping argument arises from the print, however: rendering, and specifically the burin-hand exemplified by this engraving, can represent the cognitive act of knowing the world through the agency of attentive sight. The figure's musculature is articulated by lines that rise from its right side on a diagonal defined by the lines of sight of the depicted viewers. Their viewpoint determines the orientation of Goltzius's lines, which are coextensive with their gaze. (One might add that he is here self-effacing once again, for he subsumes his gaze into theirs.) If to render this effigy has involved recording the optical passage of the eyes along its surface, then looking at the print involves the realization that our looking rehearses the engraver-beholder's own. Our cognition—our increasing awareness of the statue's pose, its tension in rest, its surface articulation, and its iconography (the apples of the garden of the Hesperides, clutched in the figure's left hand, indicate that he has completed the cycle of twelve

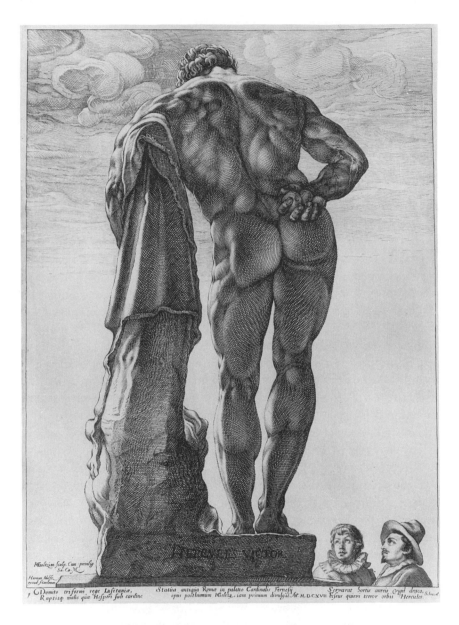

Figure 4. Hendrick Goltzius, *The Farnese Hercules*, engraving, ca. 1595, published 1617, 405 × 294 mm. By courtesy of the Warburg Institute.

labors)—renews a prior act of beholding, or to put it in terms more suited to Goltzius's self-effacing project, appropriates his prior experience, eliding it into the present of our own.

That the print thematizes cognition itself is made apparent by the way it compels us to acknowledge the threshold between rendering and representation, *handelingh* and its pictorial outcome. Every line has been deeply and cleanly scored, so that its passage is clearly visible, even in areas of double- and triple-hatching. As our eyes travel the patterns of circulation mapped out by these lines, we are constantly made aware that information about the body arises from the conversion of linear into representational means, just as we are always aware that description consists of the action of the burin-hand. That conversion of linear networks into representation, along with the allied process which recognizes that representation devolves upon lines, foregrounds cognition, identifying it as the crucial faculty on which the print's legibility depends. Goltzius employs a second device to emphasize the process of cognition: the disjunction between the stasis of the figure at rest and the linear flexion that mobilizes our eyes. He relies on our cognitive skills to disclose the stilled figure of Hercules from the optical courses motivated by rendering.

We have been examining two kinds of engraving promulgated by Goltzius in the 1590s. In reproductive prints executed *uyt den geest* he reifies memory by constituting his burin-hand as the recollection of pictorial manner. In prints done *nae t'leven,* he documents visual experience by harnessing his burin-hand to the description of things seen. In the late 1590s, he and his collaborators enlarged upon the cognitive value of the burin-hand in a remarkable series of prints recording the strandings of whales on the Dutch coast near Haarlem. These prints have a different purpose from the ones we have studied so far. Executed *nae t'leven,* they mediate the observation of nature rather than art, offering the means through which nature may be apprehended and constituted as knowledge. In closing with the history of their execution, I aim to show how Goltzius came to believe in the transparency of his burin-hand. By *transparency,* I refer to his conviction, asserted through his collaborators, that his burin-hand could focus our attention on nature, while stripping it of any interpretative overlay. It is as if he had effaced himself altogether, casting his burin-hand as the mirror of nature, from which all distorting imperfections had been erased. The images of beached whales argue that prints purify the cognition of nature by allowing unmediated access to it.

Goltzius inaugurated the series with a large pen-and-wash drawing done *nae t'leven* of a sperm whale stranded on the Dutch coast at Berkheij between Scheveningen and Katwijk on 3 February 1598 (fig. 5).[33] The prints that followed, among the largest and most technically ambitious published in Haarlem and Amsterdam, were executed by Jacob Matham and Jan Saenredam, engravers who had assimilated Goltzius's burin-hand and were affiliated with his Haarlem workshop. By deferring to them, Goltzius was again proving himself to be a latter-day Proteus, multiplying the agents of his burin-hand to deny its singularity and deflect attention from himself. By 1600 he had ceased engraving altogether, continuing the publishing functions of his reproductive print workshop but delegating the implementation of his burin-hand to his stepson Matham. Matham shared Goltzius's *handelingh* with masters who established workshops in other Dutch towns: Jan Muller in Amsterdam, Jan Saenredam in Assendelft, and Jacob de Gheyn II in The Hague. It would be fair to suppose that Goltzius

Figure 5. Hendrick Goltzius, *The Whale Stranded at Berkheij (Katwijk) on 3 February 1598*, drawing, pen and red-brown ink, washed in red-brown and gray, and heightened in white, 1598, 296 × 437 mm. The Teylers Museum, Haarlem, Netherlands.

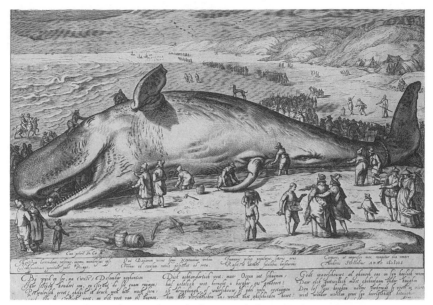

Figure 6. Jacob Matham, *The Whale Stranded at Wijck aan See on 19 December 1601*, engraving, 1601, 310 × 425 mm. By permisssion of the Trustees of the British Museum.

could cease to engrave because his burin-hand, having achieved such circulation, had multiplied beyond the compass of himself.

Goltzius's drawing is reportorial in function; it describes the animal, the topography of the site, and the behavior, dress, social rank, and trades of the throngs of onlookers who gather from neighboring communities to view the whale. Later in 1598, Jacob Matham executed a large engraving after this drawing; the engraving was published by Goltzius in the same year. In 1601 Matham drew, engraved, and published the whale beached at Wijk aan See on 19 December. In 1602 Jan Saenredam likewise drew, engraved, and published a beached whale, this time stranded at Beverwijk (fig. 6). Goltzius's drawing established the format and function of this series, which shares the *handelingh* of prints like *The Farnese Hercules*.[34]

Matham's prints juxtapose inscriptions in Latin and Dutch, the former by the humanist Theodor Screvelius, the latter by Karel van Mander. Screvelius's verses are conventionally hyperbolic. In the print of 1598, for instance, he narrates the whale's struggle against the storm that drives it shoreward; the whale is termed "terror of the Atlantic" and is interpreted as a menacing portent against which the poet invokes the gods' protection. Concluding with a rhetorical flourish, Screvelius declares that he and Matham now commit the whale "to paper, to fame, and to the nation."[35] The Latin inscription of 1601 characterizes the whale as a "horrific monster" and "monstrous destroyer of the sea," implying that it deserves its sorry end.[36]

Van Mander's verses counter those of Screvelius, neutralizing his affective interpretation and asserting instead Matham's descriptive intention. By refusing to read the whale as a portent of political events, Van Mander distinguishes the prints from earlier broadsheets of strandings. The inscription on the print of 1598 explains simply that a fierce storm had forced the whale ashore near Katwijk on 3 February, that it measured fifty-six by thirty-six feet, and that it testified to the greatness of the Creator. The poem accompanying Matham's plate of 1601 is even more emphatically neutral; it again refuses to interpret the stranding as a political sign and harbinger of disaster in the Dutch war against Spain. Instead Van Mander insists that it gives evidence of God's artificing skill:

> Near Wijck on the Sea, towards the West, on December 19 in the year 1601, a sperm whale stranded on the beach, just as one may see in this print. 63 feet in length, each foot eleven inches long, 38 in width. Ocean briny in your foaming, what offspring have you delivered to us citizens? Is it a threat or a warning, the sort of thing which causes idle folk improperly to take fright? God warns us sufficiently in his holy word, to which we willingly and obediently submit. We praise his lofty name far and wide, whose wondrous works attest to his omnipotence.[37]

The inscription suppresses the conventional hyperbolic formulas used by Screvelius. It designates the animal a sperm whale, rather than using the more common *monstrum*. Van Mander's subtext is an attack on publications such as the booklet on the whale stranded at Berkheij in 1598, that take the whale for a portent demanding interpretation. He unfolds the print's purpose, which is to persuade the viewer that the image records a natural curiosity rather than depicting a divine sign. These plates, Van Mander argues energetically, are *not* political allegories. By contrast the anonymous booklet of 1598 that prompted Van Mander's disclaimers invites interpretation; this is evident even from the title, which reads:

"Whale of Berkheij: That is, a description of the great fish stranded at Berckhey in the year 1598 on the third of February, with an explanation of the things that followed upon it. . . . [38] These "things" include the Spanish invasion of the Duchy of Cleves and the depredations that ensued. The author's poem drives his point home: the whale is a portent of the Lord's decision to expose the Netherlands to a huge, cruel, and bloodthirsty animal—Spain—who seeks nothing less than the desolation of the Netherlands by fire and sword.

In conjunction with Van Mander's verses, Matham's prints illustrate the dual possibility of pictorial description and neutral beholding. The *Beached Whales* of 1598 and 1601 alert us to the distinction between observation and interpretation; they apply Goltzius's burin-hand in order to enrich description, making an enhanced appeal to the beholder's receptiveness to visual information. Their polemical purpose is the stripping away of what we might call the hermeneutical impulse, which they supplant with an epistemological one, providing unmediated optical access to the knowledge of nature. Moreover, as the inscriptions make clear, the images aim to cleanse memory; by inviting us to see what has been truly rendered *nae t'leven,* they encourage the reformation of memory, freeing it from interpretative distortions and delusive fears such as those in the anonymous booklet. They substitute wonder at God's artifice for the anxiety to divine his intents. These prints allow us to pursue cognition, freed from the assumption that nature is encoded with prior meanings.

Jan Saenredam's *Whale Stranded at Beverwijk* provides an elaborate commentary upon this cognitive project (fig. 7).[39] He reintroduces what Matham had stripped away, the figured allegories. However, they are segregated to a frame surrounding the most precisely detailed of all the scenes of a whale and its onlookers. The frame contains the personification of Time with his scythe and hourglass, who alludes to the eventual corruption of the carcass, shown at the left and right after the incoming tide has ripped it in two. Other metaphors invoke the momentous events signaled by the beaching: solar and lunar eclipses, and an earthquake emblematized ingeniously in a vignette inscribed *Terrae motus.* That the stranding has significance for the political future of the nation is signaled by the presence of the armed Belgian lion, vigilant within the enclosed garden of the Netherlands. Above, Saenredam inscribes the plate to Count Ernest of Nassau, dedicating to him "this monster newly imprinted in this wondrous time."[40] In Greek and Latin, this formulation refers both to the engraving,

Figure 7. Jan Saenredam, *The Whale Stranded at Beverwijk on 13 January 1601*, engraving, 1602, 407 × 596 mm. Atlas van Stolk, Rotterdam.

newly executed, and to the whale itself, newly imprinted upon the Netherlands as a sign of God's intentions. Banderoles at the left and right are inscribed "Ectypoma ceti adversi"—a neologism that describes both the whale and the print as "a portentous sea creature worked in high relief," again referring to the artificing powers of both God and the engraver.[41]Below, the long inscription, again supplied by Screvelius, takes up the theme of prophecy. Screvelius interprets the wonder as an evil omen and rehearses the military setbacks that followed the beaching of the whale at Katwijk in 1598.

    With the exception of the personification of Fame or Rumor flying eastward to spread word of the event, however, the allegories have been confined to the frame, clearly separated from the descriptive format and function of the scene of beaching. Everything within this scene revises the mode of the allegories in the frame. Count Ernest Casimir of Nassau-Dietz appears in the center foreground, observing the whale intently while shielding his nose from its stench; labeled *viva effigies* (living likeness), the figure of Count Ernest appears as an alert witness, rather than the illustrious knight and vigilant hero invoked in the inscription above, ready to

deliver the nation from the Spanish threat evoked by the stranding. Saenredam, who had inscribed the dedication, thus avowing his political concern for his country, also inscribes himself within the scene. He stands to
the left of his patron, shielded from the wind by a large cloak, so that he
may draw the whale *nae t'leven.* He has signed the large sheet propped up
before him, identifying himself as the source of both the drawn *modello*
and the engraving made after it in 1602. Saenredam presents himself here
as an onlooker who records what he sees, imprinting the memory of the
whale by drawing it after life. The beholders who attend to his drawing
suggest that viewing it is tantamount to viewing the whale at first hand. Just
below Count Ernest, an inscription framed by flourished shells inventories
the animal's dimensions and the circumstances of the beaching, providing
a factual alternative to the affective inscriptions of the frame. Although this
inscription opens by dubbing the whale one of "Neptune's extraordinary
monsters," it quickly sets about the task of familiarizing the extraordinary,
grounding the animal in mundane details. Its closing line declares the
faithfulness of Saenredam's image, which has been drawn and engraved
true to scale—*Geometricam exactiss. delineatio.*[42]

The terms that Saenredam has written on the sheet are *inve.,* short for
inventor—literally "inventor," but here the "source of the *modello*"—and
sculptor—"engraver." Within the frame, he attaches his name to a dedication that conflates the print and the whale as omens to be interpreted.
Below, he insists that drawing the whale involves viewing it and translating
from sight to the hand; he alleges in effect that the image is separate from
the thing itself. Viewing and recording are the cognitive processes that
intervene, and it is through them that the layers of interpretation can be
stripped away, revealing the difference between the whale and the beholding of the whale on which the production of its likeness is based. Saenredam builds a taxonomy in which nature, viewing, and drawing are categorically distinct; we perceive the whale by looking at it, and we come to
know the whale by representing it. Representation is therefore the in-
eluctable condition of knowing, representation that is, shorn of interpretation. It is seeing and knowing, processes mediated by representation, that
are the subject of the descriptive scene. While the frame narrates the tale
of the whale's ultimate demise and its rending by the sea, the scene below
takes cognition and image production for its main events. Saenredam
narrates in this descriptive scene the very conditions of its production.[43]

To do this, he has deflected attention from rendering, or rather

posited a very fine version of Goltzius's burin-hand as the complete absence
of self. Within the frame, the use of the terms *characteron* and *ectypoma*
signals the conflation of the portentous whale and the print recording it,
arguing that the whale is what we and the image make it—that to engrave
the whale is to embed it in a network of meanings which are indubitably
human and into which Saenredam himself is locked. The scene within the
frame disputes this reading. The same rendering we saw above, like the
whale interpreted above, makes description possible. It issues, Saenredam
seems to be saying, not from himself but from the contours of the thing
itself. Rendering, bound on the frame to meanings issuing from the self,
issues now from the hand, which enacts the cognitive process of beholding.
This is the logical outcome of Goltzius's protean strategy; however distinctive we may take the print's burin-hand to be, it resists, in Saenredam's
account, any insertion of self that might convert nature into our reading of
it and might translate natural history into emotively human history.

The print's clear separation of allegory and description argues that
interpretation, while possible, generates meanings extrinsic to the scene as
it occurred. Saenredam introduces yet another inscription to clarify this
point. Just to the right of the Batavian lion on top, a child displays an open
book in which are written some of the rhetorically based names Cicero
gave to history: *historia testis temporum, lux veritatis, vita memoriae,* and
magistra vitae nuntia vetustatis—history, the witness of time, light of truth,
life of memory, and guardian of the life of antiquity. These Latin terms
define history as a mnemonic process that organizes the past, shaping the
present by referring it to what is worthy of collective recollection. Cicero's
epithets, inscribed near the threshold between the frame and the scene
proper, identify allegory and description as two modes of historical construction. The image, Saenredam tells us, juxtaposes the allegorical interpretation of portents and the description of nature, political history, and
natural history. Saenredam gives new focus to Cicero's terms, suggesting
that history can consist of the enriched description of place—the beach,
dunes, ocean, and community at Beverwijk in its response to the whale.
This is finally where the examination of Goltzius's *handelingh*—the burin-
hand valorized in the drawing of his disfigured hand—has taken us. Rendering is the transparent means through which seeing becomes the representation of nature, unalloyed by what the mind makes of nature. By
looking attentively at Saenredam's print, we can come to know nature's
history of herself.

To posit the whale as history is to allege its memorability, and Goltzius, Matham, and Saenredam unfold mnemonic function as an act of social formation. The crowds who gather to view the whale, seeing it in order to imprint it as natural knowledge, articulate social hierarchies, arranging themselves into the representation of the Dutch polity—court, city, and country—enacting complex protocols, interacting as buyers and sellers, superiors and inferiors. Seeing, knowing, and remembering, the enterprises that bind this diverse community, mediate and are mediated by the process of social construction, which is also a mode of historical construction. In turn, the printed image—affordable, multipliable, portable—inverts the process it represents, bringing the whale to a far wider audience than first gathered to view it, and ensuring that pictorial representation continues to revise the cognitive habits of the society at large.

Malangan

Of the many non-Western art forms that continue to flourish in the Pacific region, the sculptures from Papua New Guinea known under the indigenous name of *Malangan* are among the most striking and best documented.[44] Western museums house more than five thousand Malangan, primarily carved and painted sculptures collected over the past 150 years from the north of New Ireland, Papua New Guinea.

Western artists and collectors were attracted by the art because of its visual and conceptual complexity (fig. 8). The sculptures can be vertical, horizontal, or figurative and are usually between one and three meters long. Carved in the round, the soft wood *(Alstonia scholaris)* is so richly incised that the sculptures appear to be perforated, held together visually by painted patterns that envelop the carved planes. The painted surface, coterminous with the engraved wood, belies the three-dimensionality of the carving. The sculptures are framed by thin parallel rods connected by short bridges; contained within this frame is an assemblage of carved motifs comprising different kinds of birds, insects, fish, and shells, but also mythical images, as well as musical instruments such as the panpipe. Each sculpture depicts between two and seven of the approximately twenty-seven motifs possible. These motifs are thematically independent of the main body of the sculpture and sometimes even carved from separate pieces of wood. Malangan sculptures can also be woven from fiber or

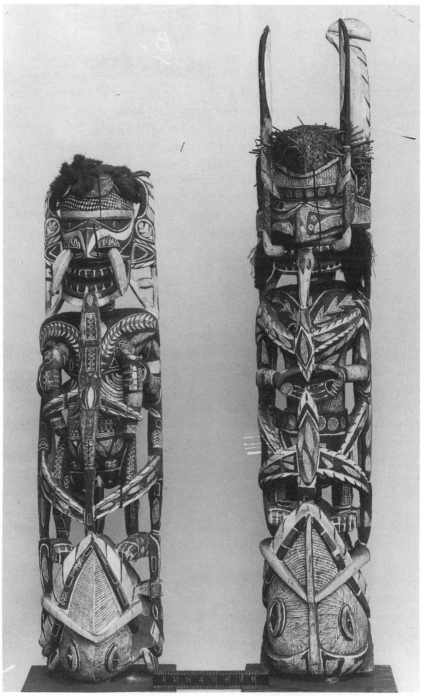

Figure 8. New Ireland, *Malangan*, sculpture, wood (Alstonia scholaris), ca. 1880. By permission of the Trustees of the British Museum.

molded from clay, but these have not reached museum collections, nor do they share the complexity of the wood carvings.

The richness of design seems to suggest that the sculpture has a heightened importance to the indigenous culture. Yet, though the process of production can last up to three months, the finished work is exhibited no longer than a few hours before it is left to the wind and the rain, which rapidly erase all trace of craftmanship. The sale of the carvings to Western collectors is a welcome alternative, as money has come to play a prominent part in the present-day economy of the indigenous culture. Nevertheless, sculptures continue to be produced primarily not for sale, but for the ritual climax of the Malangan mortuary ceremonies.

The long, drawn-out process of carving the Malangan "finishes the work for the dead" *(haisok ine mamat);* it is the final ceremony for the dead who have been buried in the local cemetery since the last Malangan was made. The process of sculpting is described in the indigenous language as *tetak,* literally "the making of skin." Sculptures are conceived as skins that replace the decomposed body of a deceased person and thus provide a container for his or her life force. The life force merges with the material, which is thought to come alive in the process of sculpting.

This art has been studied mainly in terms of its ostensible commemorative function. Attempts have been made to establish and decipher the visual code, which is believed to express the social status of a deceased person.[45] As only sculptures produced in the presence of the ethnographer could be thus contextualized, museum collections of Malangan art were never considered possible data for analysis.

There are many examples from the western funerary tradition in which it is pertinent to assume that a sculpture placed on the grave is a memorial or, at the very least, an *aide-memoire.* With respect to Malangan art, such an assumption is totally misplaced. The sculpture represents and is itself part of a process that could be better interpreted as a metaphor for the life force, considered to be renewed upon death. Rather than alluding to the uniqueness of an event or to the finality of a particular life, the engraved images posit their own biography by being depicted as an assemblage of independent motifs with their own history and their own future.

Thus far from being unique, the sculptures are considered to be the temporary embodiment of images that are conceived of, in analogy to the life process, as renewable and relocatable entities. The northern New

Irelanders differentiate six image types made up from approximately twenty-seven motifs that are circulated throughout the culture and recalled in the process of reproduction.

Collections of Malangan art document the distribution of the images across the culture. Each sculpture displays an image as an entity that is subject to a process of selection, combination, and arrangement of carved motifs. Images recognizable by the arrangement and combination of motifs are found in sculptures produced more than a century apart in many different places. Yet, despite this visual constancy, there is not one sculpture that could be defined as a copy of another.

In a preliterate culture, these images are what might be called the subject of social memory. They are remembered for themselves and are passed on to others as something to hold in memory.[46] The very manner of their transmission, involving both remembering and forgetting, fashions the intellectual field of the culture that in turn responds to the concerns arising from socially and historically relevant situations.

Paramount to the analysis of Malangan art, therefore, is the question of image transmission, which demands a very different kind of contextualization from that hitherto attempted. I want to argue in the following pages that Malangan sculptures, as documented in museum collections, are not remnants of an ancient and dying tradition, but a historical phenomenon. It is not that there was never any carving or sculpture in general associated with the final mortuary ceremony in the precolonial past, but rather that, during a time of major economic and social disruption, carving for mortuary ceremonies became the center of the political economy, and as a result the images began to attain the status of what might be called social memory. Carving then took on the role of creating new forms of consolidation through the fashioning of this social memory. Neither the carving nor the social relationships defined through their beholding remained unaffected by this development.

The Malangan material enables us to study the emergence of the political economy of memory, with its strategic remembering and deliberate forgetting of shared images, processes that alone articulate what is held in common by an otherwise divisive and fragmentary society. Far from being merely about an isolated and unusual art tradition, the analysis of the production of social memory through Malangan art has repercussions for our understanding of the role of image production and its relation to memory in the development of a kind of regional social organization not usually associated with small-scale non-Western societies.

The Malangan culture embraces six language areas in the north of New Ireland, mapped by the Dutch and Spanish in three successive campaigns of exploration between 1527 and 1761, and visited frequently by traders thereafter.[47] Indigenous warfare seems to have escalated sharply in the early years of the nineteenth century, its character having changed due to the introduction of iron weapons by traders, as recalled in oral tradition. Matrilineal clans that up to this time had been associated with certain places were broken up and scattered across the north, as many people were forced to flee and others were transported to new locations through marriage by capture. Due to this large-scale migration of clans, their classification into exogamous halves, which had provided a pattern for social integration, labor, and the distribution of land, became ineffective.

Around the time of the imposition of German colonial rule in 1885, foreign-owned cash-crop plantations were established in the north of the island. The resulting alienation of large stretches of land along the narrow coastline seriously restricted the use of land for agriculture. Land shortage became particularly acute after the resettlement of the mountain population on the coast in the early twentieth century. This coincided with the building of a road connecting the colonial administration centers in the north and south of the island. Additionally, the death toll continued to rise, while the birth rate decreased until the 1950s.

During this period of uprootedness and uncertainty, the carving of sculptures in mortuary ceremonies was the predominant cultural expression of the region. Judging from the large collections of sculptures gathered around the turn of the century, one or more sculptures must have been produced for every ceremony held in each village.

The production of carvings escalated to such an extent that anthropologists have suggested the sculptures were made directly for sale to Europeans and not for ritual usage. There are, however, a number of factors that can explain the apparent efflorescence, or at least heightened importance, of sculptural production. One obvious reason is the rising death toll around the turn of the century, and another is the impact of cash-crop production on the indigenous economy. Those who earned new securities through cash-cropping no longer relied on the indigenous shell currency of the elders; tapping resources outside the indigenous economy, they could themselves pay for the carver and the expenses incurred by the long and complex Malangan ceremony.

The indigenous political economy, moreover, had become inseparable from the Malangan. This factor, well known from ethnographic reports, has not yet been successfully linked with sculptural production. In spite of the ever-growing impact of Western monetary economy, the mortuary ceremonies remained the single most important setting for ceremonial gift exchange, which is the forum for social and material interchange in the Malangan culture, as elsewhere in Melanesia.

The medium of exchange is the sculpted image. It is not the sculpture itself that is transacted in the exchanges for money and indigenous currency, but the right to reproduce the image, which thus enters and defines networks of exchange across the region. The embeddedness of sculpting in gift exchange confers political and economic importance on image transmission.

The Malangan material is unusual in that the object made to serve as gift is also an anthropomorphic sculpture, which participates in an indigenous exchange economy situated exclusively within the mortuary context. Elsewhere in Melanesia exchange media are primarily bodies, bodily products, or body decorations, and their transaction is not exclusively confined to the mortuary context.

The distinctiveness of the Malangan case might be at least partly a result of the comparatively early and, for a long period, indirect Western influence on the island, which enabled the development of new forms of consolidation prior to direct colonial intervention. In the face of a dying economy and mounting threats to social continuity, interest in the dead flourished as the forum in which to deal with issues of labor and loyalty, which could no longer be appropriately addressed by the precolonial institutions of kinship and marriage.[48]

The manner in which such issues were dealt with, however, was not random, but was inspired by the conception of death as a process of the renewal of life. Because the sculpture was fashioned as an artificial container for the life force, it took on the status of an object of sacrifice.[49] The sculpture was not fashioned as a gift between men, but as a "Gift to God."[50]

The sculpture is displayed in the cemetery, where it dramatically fulfills its role as a sacrifice. The sculpture, which had come to life during carving, is symbolically killed through the transference of ownership of the engraved image from the deceased's family to the related kin in exchange for currency and indigenous shell money. After this transaction, the sculpted material is thought to have lost its life force and is disposed of like human remains. The image, on the other hand, visible in the sculpture in the form of motifs and painted patterns, is preserved in memory and is transmitted through regional networks of social relationships in the course of its continuing reproduction and repeated transference in subsequent Malangan ceremonies.

Image production for sacrificial exchange is reminiscent of the famous potlatch of North America, during which engraved copper plates were ritually destroyed and the pieces repeatedly reconstituted for renewed ritual transaction.[51] While one might argue that both institutions of sacrificial exchange are set against a similar historical background, their development had a different impact on their cultures and societies, due to their distinct modes of image transmission.[52]

The physical permanence of the copper plate and the limit placed by the material on the inscribing hand restricted its visual development. Even though constantly broken to be refashioned as gift, the copper served as the visible and accessible sign of rank within the ritual confederations that had formed around the networks of its circulation. As new patterns of differentiation evolved in the course of potlatch activities, the copper, with its limited scope for differentiation, ceased to serve as a convenient metaphor for networks of social exchange.

In contrast to copper, the material medium of Malangan exchanges is soft and ephemeral. Social processes can be visually articulated more fully in this medium; in turn, the resulting networks of relationships are inherently short-lived because of their subjection to memory, which allows for strategic acts of erasure and refashioning.

By attaining rights over the reproduction of an image carved into wood, "members of Malangan" *(raso)* frame a relationship. Members have access to each other's cash-crop plantations; they exercise rights to garden land in each other's villages and joint responsibilities to work for the dead. Such membership networks, defined in terms of a common stake in the transmission of an image, extend over the northern part of the island. There are numerous intersecting networks, as each image can be circulated within numerous localized relationships, while individuals can have a share in several images.

The relationships that comprise such ritual confederations are never fixed, but are constantly revised in the light of economic and political interests. This flexibility in patterns of social differentiation results from the definition of social relationships in terms of image ownership, which is not just transmitted from one generation to another, but is also subject to changes through either circumstantial or deliberate forgetting of how an image was acquired.

There are two main situations in which confederations are reformed

in the light of the history of image ownership: by the loss of images, or by
the forgetting of relationships tied to the ownership of images. On the one
hand, we have a situation in which a localized kin group, having lost their
own stock of images, is forced to acquire new images from other villages,
expanding the networks of exchange. Oral tradition recounts the loss of
many images due to a group's inability to stage Malangan ceremonies
during the Second World War, when agricultural production was disrupted. They are perceived to be lost, because an image that is not seen in
a sculpture during one generation can not be reproduced, just as the
relationships established through its past transference can no longer be
invoked.

On the other hand, the extinction of one of two localized clans
owning an image jointly leads to the forgetting of the relationship and the
appropriation of control over the reproduction of the image by the surviving clan. After a generation, the past pattern of ownership is no longer
remembered by anyone, and the image is reproduced for transaction in
different sets of relationships.

The most distinctive aspect of the ritual confederations is their expansive regional character. Confederations cut across villages and language
areas, integrating them into networks of social exchange through the transmission of images as tokens of social relationships. Still present as an object
of ownership after the decay of the material form, the remembered image
functions like a footprint in the tracing of "roads" (selen) connecting
people and places, along which produce and valuables move. The reciting
of what might be called the biography of an image, that is, the history of
its past transferences and their embeddedness in social relationships, is
important in defending a claim both to the image and to the networks it
defines.

The image as metaphor for spatial and temporal relationships implies
the conceptual separation of the invention from the remembered form. The
six named images circulated and repeatedly reproduced in carvings are
found throughout the Malangan culture, even though they are said to have
been invented mainly on the islands of Tabar northeast of the mainland.
The mythical origin or locus of invention of an image, what I would call
its template, is conceived of as fashioned through dreaming.

The dreaming of carved forms is still the only legitimate way to enter
the ceremonial exchanges in the absence of ownership rights over an
image. Like carving itself, the invention of new templates for wooden

sculptures has become a frequent occurrence following cash-crop production. This boom in invention, however, has not increased the mythical constitution of templates, because the invented image is assimilated into one of the six existing templates as soon as it is transferred in the ceremonial exchanges. Collections of wooden sculptures, constant in their arrangement and combination of motifs, give evidence of the persistence of templates.

The templates for wooden sculptures continue to be associated with the places of their mythical invention. From these places, named and memorized images are thought to have been scattered across the region and, in the course of their repeated reproduction and transference, shattered into numerous parts. A carving can be made only if the image is remembered and its position in the history of its circulation known. The image of the wooden sculpture, thus, is not just another version of its template, but is elicited as a response to its own transference; whenever an image is reproduced in a carving it is varied in certain ways in the light of the type of social relationships its transference will engender.[53]

The relation between the image and its locus of invention is described in the indigenous language by the term *wune,* which can be translated as "womb," "smoke," or "source." Corresponding verbal comparison is made between visual images associated with a template and children born from the same mother or mothers of the same matriline, clouds of smoke emerging from a fire, or waves on the surface of a river. The template is envisioned as the generative and connective agent that imposes on the sculpted image the potential to be at once "new" and yet recognizable.

This indigenous perspective on image production raises the question of what enables the identification of a template in a given sculpture. To answer, one must consider the question of the nature of the limitations placed on the transformation of an image in the course of its repeated production and transference. The answers to both questions are important for an understanding of how these images can function as subjects of social memory by both addressing and fashioning the intellectual field of the culture.

The visual analysis of the carvings is like a puzzle. Confronted with an abundance of carved motifs, even the untrained eye can easily discern a pattern; what one might describe as themes appear over and over again in many sculptures that can nevertheless be distinguished in terms of their shape and the number of motifs depicted. A predominant theme, for

Figure 9. New Ireland, *Malangan*, sculpture, wood (Alstonia scholaris), ca. 1930. Museum Für Völkerkunde Basel, Vb 10583 and 10584.

example, is depicted by a giant fish in whose mouth one can see a person (fig. 8). This theme can occur either in vertical or horizontal sculptures and with or without the bird that is usually depicted sitting on top of the fish as if about to catch it. Another prominent theme is actually given a name in the indigenous language; it is called "the eye of the fire" *(mataling)* and is represented as a raised, round, dotted area in whose center sits the "eye," the irislike suction pod of the shell *Turbo petholaurus*. This is characteristically used only in Malangan carvings (fig. 9). The presence of such themes allows one to distinguish the six named templates.

Each such theme consists of motifs that are combined in particular ways and are visually, if not physically, attached to the main body of the sculpture. The impression of assemblage has led some to suggest that the sculptures result from the operation of a visual grammar with rules for selection, combination, and arrangement of motifs. That a representational system can be likened to language is debatable and must be firmly rejected with respect to Malangan. Analysis in terms of grammar-type rules would ignore the role of memory in image transmission. It is remembering and deliberate forgetting, either individual or social, that influence the assemblage of motifs that give rise in turn to the visual properties of the sculptures.[54]

There are only three distinct ways to combine and arrange motifs and to integrate them into the main body of the sculpture: as entry, as containment, or as exit. These motif combinations metaphorize carving as a process of sacrifice whose thematic structure provides the framework within which the image can be transformed in the course of its reproduction and repeated recall from memory. Each of the three types of combination and arrangement refers to one of the three main stages of carving, which sees the absorption, containment, and release of the life force into the sculpture that takes the place of the sacrificial victim.[55]

The first mode of combination visualizes the gradual absorption of life force into the wood by depicting it as the process of ingestion. Motifs such as a bird, a fish, a snake, and sometimes a person, are represented as part of a food chain (fig. 10). What appear in this figure to be the feathers of the bird, visible as chevronlike incisions, are a representation of the palolowurm. This creature is a complex cultural symbol that refers both to the heat associated with life force and to differing modes of incorporation, most explicitly to eating and planting. The palolowurm mates during one night at the onset of the planting season in the lagoon and is caught and eaten as a main staple food for about a week; the "heat" that is absorbed by those who taste this food is transferred during planting to the crops. The process of reconstituting life force through incorporation is vividly represented in a Malangan sculpture that depicts the bird's head and the palolowurm in a stage of fusion (fig. 11). The variations in representation themselves allude to process by visualizing stages of absorption with decreasing differentiation of part/whole relationships.

The second manner of combination depicts the completed contain-

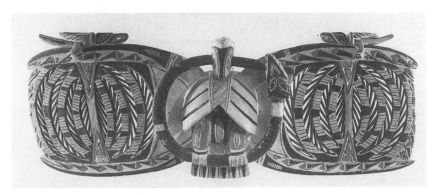

Figure 10. New Ireland, *Malangan*, sculpture, wood (Alstonia scholaris), ca. 1910. Museum Für Völkerkunde Basel, Vb 231.

Figure 11. New Ireland, *Malangan*, sculpture, wood (Alstonia scholaris), 1932. By permission of the Trustees of the British Museum.

ment of life force in the sculpture by attaching motifs not to each other but to the shaped figure. Motifs such as the rib cage, the flying fish, and the "eye of the fire" appear inseparable from the figure, as they are bound by it or even part of its anatomy (fig. 12).

The third manner of combination visualizes the death of the sculpture, opening the possibility for continued image reproduction. The motif combination alluding to this third and last stage of image production is a fish that ambiguously swallows or ejects a person (fig. 13). Another motif combination assembles water container, bottle stop, and figure.

The six templates that are recognized in sculptures and given distinct names are grouped into pairs, each pair featuring the same manner of motif combination and arrangement. There is always a certain ambiguity as to which template a sculpted image might belong, yet the choice is always narrowed to the template pair.

The division of wooden templates into pairs results from fashioning carvings as gifts. As gift, the object embodies the pattern of social relationships, which in precolonial times consisted of exogamous halves. Dual organization, which once served to govern relationships of labor and loyalty, is assimilated into sculptural production, where it serves as the classificatory principle that differentiates images.

The most important visual aspect of the carvings is their synthetic quality. The classification of engraved images alludes to digestion (absorption, containment, release) and duality (template pairs). This allusion to the embodiment of memory in image classification, however, is not a statement of fact but the result of the manner of image production—that is, of carving.

Malangan carvings are not just sculpted in the round but are truly three-dimensional, incised to such an extent that they appear fragile and challengingly complex. The perforation of the material posits the virtuosity of the skilled hand that mediates between the material and the image.

The carver is a specialist renowned for his skill. Each language area within the Malangan-producing culture has on the average two and in many cases only one man who carries the title of *retak,* "the maker of skin." His skill, like his tools, is handed down within the family from generation to generation, yet it is often only late in life that he begins to carve, after

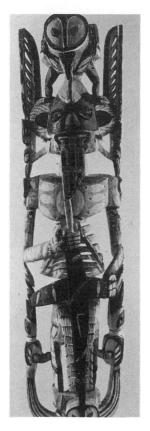

Figure 12. New Ireland, *Malangan,* sculpture, wood (Alstonia scholaris), 1932. Museum Für Völkerkunde Basel, Vb 10576.

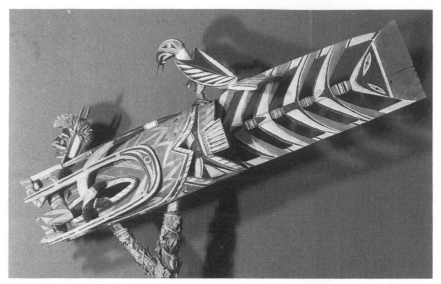

Figure 13. New Ireland, *Malangan*, sculpture, wood (Alstonia scholaris), 1932. Museum Für Völkerkunde Basel, Vb 10562.

having assimilated the ritual knowledge surrounding image production, which is the prerogative of the elders.

Rather than controlling the look of the sculpture, the carver is simply the means to its production. An elder, having last seen the sculpted image during its acquisition by his kin group, tells the sculptor what he is supposed to carve. In addition to receiving this verbal description, the carver views the sculpted image in a dream, induced by the ingestion of plant materials.

His role is not that of an artist, but that of a man making a sacrifice, who prepares his victim for the offering. The carver has to undergo a number of ritual preparations that make him enter a state in which he comes close to the force he is to channel into wood during carving. Indeed, the prescriptions for the carver are the same as those for one making a sacrifice: they strip him progressively of his temporal being and cause him to be reborn in an entirely new form.[56] He must live secluded inside the hut in which the carving takes place and may only emerge from it at night. He must also avoid stepping over rubbish or excrement, abstain sexually, and follow rules of fasting during the period of his work, which lasts from one to three months, depending on the size of the sculpture. His food is prepared by an older woman past childbearing, who must likewise fast and abstain.

That the sculptor is thought of as someone making a sacrifice has an impact on how he undertakes his work: he imbues the material with the force of which he has partaken during preparations. Heat *(malang)*, the metaphorizing life force, not the carver's tools, is taken to be the agent that perforates the material. The carver's hand, extended into the heated tool, literally burns itself into the material, thus impregnating it with the life force.

The heat ascribed to life force and recaptured in the sculpture at this stage is itself the residue of the long process of funerary rituals. Starting with the burial, these rituals trace bodily decomposition as a process of the freeing of the life force, which is metaphorized as the building up of a fire from glowing ashes to intense heat.

One can discern an analogy between carving and giving birth: the wood that is chipped away is thought of as life-giving and has to be discarded, like the placenta, for true life to begin. As the carving advances and the incised planes become interpretable as motifs, a mountain of wood chips rises, which is heaped at the back of the hut in which the work is undertaken. These chips are considered to be the potent "residue" *(rotap)* of the embodiment and coming to life of the sculpted image. Anyone entering the hut at any stage during the production and display of the sculpture has to participate in a ritual bath that is meant to cool the body after its contact with the "hot" *(malang)* woodchips.

Malangan, translatable both as "likeness" and "heat," refers not so much to the sculpture as to the process of carving and to the waste it entails. The amount of shell money and currency required for the ceremonial sacrifice of the sculpture is measured in terms of the amount of wood chipped away during carving, which is thought to correspond to the intensity of life force embodied in the sculpture.

The sacrifice of the sculpture metaphorizes the erasure of the image. As wind and rain wipe out the traces of the carver's hand, the image that was visible for a mere moment vanishes. Neither mentioned nor thought of for twenty years or longer, the image can be said to be at least temporarily forgotten; it reappears only if its remembrance helps to interpret the networks of social exchange that have formed around "the work for the dead." When the image is recalled through the mediation of the carver, the prior erasure and forgetting are essential to the status of the engraved image as social memory. The image thus posits a certain, and disputable, version of the history of social exchange.

Memory in the Malangan culture does not seem to be perceived as the place of stored information from which recollection ensues. Rather, it is envisioned as aiding, through the process of forgetting and rerembering, the reworking of what is thought to constitute cultural tradition.

The subject of social memory, Malangan sculpture is visual yet hovers on the edge of the sensible through its invention in dreaming. Malangan engages historical processes of image transmission that correspond to the emergence of "the political economy of death."

The Essays

In the case studies above on Goltzius and Malangan, we have tried to apply the premises basic to our interpretative enterprise, showing how Dutch commemorative prints and Papuan mortuary sculpture can be understood as constitutive of social memory. The beached whale prints, Saenredam's in particular, cast engraving as the locus of cognitive reform, discriminating between two modes of mnemonic processing: the act of recording, and the act of interpreting. By circulating these prints, Goltzius and his collaborators not only disseminated information about the strandings, but also posited them as natural history, liberating recollection from the process of allegorization. As these prints must be interpreted in terms of mnemonic function, so Malangan sculptures must be understood in terms of remembered images whose transaction engenders social coherence, enfolding the family of the deceased in the history of image production. The act of carving issues from, but also in, the act of remembering, which must be renewed to ensure the dynamic of social construction.

The seven essays that follow pursue the aims of the case studies above, expanding upon the assumptions and argument of this introduction. Each of the authors negotiates between the preoccupations of his or her own field—philosophy, anthropology, art history—and the premises outlined here. Mary Pardo opens the discussion by examining Leonardo's critique of the Aristotelian psychophysiology of sensation, cognition, and memory, in "Memory, Imagination, Figuration: Leonardo da Vinci and the Painter's Mind." Focusing on the place of memory in Italian artistic training and practice, she discerns its double function as the repository of nature and the thesaurus of style: the painter exercises memory to imitate nature precisely, but also to impose style upon it. Painting results from the combined action of *memoria* and *fantasia,* the mnemonic and imaginative faculties of mind, whose limitations Leonardo sought to define and offset. In his theoretical manuscripts, as Pardo shows, Leonardo observed that memory fails to retain human actions, while imagination fails to compose human actions into *istorie,* the narrative configurations that are the painter's primary concern. Two kinds of drawing invented by him—what Pardo calls "sketch-pad memory" and "sketch-pad fantasy"—redress these flaws, suggesting negotiations of eye, hand, and mind beyond the scope of Aristotle.

In "The Imaginative Basis of Meaning and Cognition," Mark Johnson complements Pardo's essay by offering a contemporary critique of Aristotle's psychology of the mind. To the Aristotelian model of discrete sensory and cognitive faculties, Johnson opposes an integrated model of structured imagination, through which he secures linguistic meaning to the organization of perceptual experience. Following Bartlett, he expounds the operation of "image-schemata," recurring cognitive patterns that order experience and its representation. Unlike Bartlett, however, he proposes that the schemata are grounded in the body; as the body contains and is contained or touches and is touched, so these processes are translated by image-schematic structures of containment and contact. These schemata, "metaphorically and metonymically elaborated," and "implicated in virtually every aspect of our experience," mediate processes of social formation, understanding, and memory. They constitute the public world as shared, both because they are rooted in the body and because they articulate symbolic meanings.

In "Visual Narratives, Memory, and the Medieval *Esprit du System,*" Wolfgang Kemp discerns the mnemotechnical operations embedded in the complex image structures of medieval stained-glass windows. Concentrating on thirteenth-century examples, he demonstrates that they involve memory systems different from the ancient technique of *loci* whose history Frances Yates has traced. Kemp explores medieval modes of visualization, describing the interactions between processes of mnemonic and pictorial organization. Through the dynamics of these interactions, new narrative techniques are established for both artists and spectators. Kemp shows that certain kinds of meaning can be generated only from images, just as new meanings can arise from new image systems. Examining stained glass, liturgical calendars, and calendrical forms of architecture, he argues that they do not function simply as *aides-memoires,* encoding memorable information extrinsic to the image; rather, they must be understood historically in light of the relation between image production and the production of memory.

Whereas Pardo and Kemp deal with the nexus of picturing and remembering central to the theory and practice of European art, Adrienne L. Kaeppler and Gillian Feeley-Harnik consider the ways in which memory is actively embodied in non-Western cultures. In the absence of a written system of notation, the relation between dance and memory is self-evident, yet it has been virtually ignored by anthropologists. Extrapolating from evidence collected during fieldwork in Tonga, Polynesia, Kaeppler in "Memory and Knowledge in the Production of Dance" defines dance as a "socially constructed movement system," governed by motifs that enable both visual and kinesthetic memory. These motifs, composed of kinemes and morphokines, smaller units of movement constitutive of motivic grammar, function as templates that are embodied, elaborated, and interpreted in performance. In the *lakalaka* dance genre, for example, which involves the dialogic encounter of poetry and choreography, the enactment of motifs generates networks of allusion, abstracting verbal metaphors that themselves allude to genealogies. Through the incorporation of motifs, dance engenders *heliaki,* the process of allusion that translates experience into metaphor. In Kaeppler's formulation, *lakalaka* secures social knowledge to the motivic functions of memory while embodying memory in socially and culturally specific events.

Feeley-Harnik discerns the complex place of memory among the Saklava, for whom remembering is bodied forth as the formation of ancestries, the performance of royal service, and the congress of the living and the dead. In "Finding Memories in Madagascar," her concern is with the ways memories are renewed through strategies of rooting the body that are exercised at royal tombs. Memory is constructed, not through images of bodily movement, as among the Tongans of Polynesia, but rather through images of reburying and regenerating the royal body, enacted by dismantling and rebuilding the royal tomb, the architectural embodiment of ancestral power. Feeley-Harnik relates this imagery to the theme of the underworld in epic poetry, as described in Ronald MacDonald's *The Burial-Places of Memory.* In the verse epic, the underworld is the place where the author may "effect historical reversals, question the order that chronological and narrative history dictates." From the Malagasy perspective, Feeley-Harnik asserts, the burial places of memory allow precisely this reversability of the temporal order that divides the living from the dead. The creation of ancestors through the rooting of bodies in the land secures social and cultural growth. As the Saklava see it, "tomb building recalls people to the struggle with outsiders to protect their ancestors from theft by regenerating them in the very bodies of those who remember them."

Arthur Miller and Richard Vinograd consider the ways in which memory can be withheld, both to resist the kinds of expropriation to which Feeley-Harnik alludes and to establish social and cultural identity. In "Transformations of Time and Space: Oaxaca, Mexico, circa 1500–1700," Miller explains how the Zapotec appropriated Spanish devices—alphabetic script and the Julian calendar—transposing the native calendrical system into writing in an effort to preserve it from foreign incursions. The pre-Hispanic calendar, controlled by a knowledgeable elite, had been performative, articulated through rituals in which social memory was reconstituted. By transliterating their calendar, the Zapotec believed that such rituals, and the mnemonic functions they engaged, would be safeguarded. However, complex and perhaps unforeseen adjustments ensued; in particular, the power of those who had wielded calendrical and territorial knowledge was undermined, just as native territories became increasingly subject to Spanish administrative and judicial authority. Miller's central topic is the intricate negotiations between different modes of control, a contest played out in the realm of mnemonic templates.

In "Private Art and Public Knowledge in Later Chinese Painting," Richard Vinograd considers the ways in which Chinese literati painting as it was practiced and appreciated from the late Song to the Qing dynasties resists the application of the two ruling metaphors through which European painting has been traditionally understood—painting as a window on the world and as a mirror of it. He shows that literati painting is metaphorical rather than veridical, that it is the residue of consensual events, renewed and recollected by the viewer who apprehends the image's mode of production and glosses the scroll with verses and seals. If the private response to painting is ultimately communal, Vinograd asks, what constitutes the public record of images? He argues that before the Qing dynasty, images circulated widely in literary form, but that woodblock manuals of painting had begun to displace the calligraphic record by the seventeenth century. This dissemination of standardized and appropriable images disrupted assumptions about the participatory nature of painting and viewing and spurred attempts by masters to privatize the process of painting and curtail its consensuality and open temporality. Virtuosic execution and literary assertions of originality personalize the process of recollection, declaring that memory is as exclusionary as painting is inimitable.

MARY PARDO

Memory, Imagination, Figuration: Leonardo da Vinci and the Painter's Mind

Painting has in itself a divine power not only to make—as is said of friendship—the absent present, but to make the dead remain almost alive after many centuries, such that they are recognized with much pleasure and much admiration for the artist. Plutarch tells that Cassandrus, one of Alexander's captains, trembled all over at the sight of a portrait of Alexander, his king. Agesilaus the Lacedaemonian never allowed himself to be painted or sculpted by anyone: he was so displeased by his own appearance, that he avoided being known to posterity. And so it is certain that through painting the face of one already dead lives a long life. Moreover, it has ever been a great gift to mortals that painting expresses the images of the gods such as they are adored by the nations, since painting thus contributes greatly to the piety that binds us to the gods, and keeps our spirits filled with religion. It is said that Phidias made in Elis an image of the god Jove whose beauty contributed not a little to the received religion. . . . The painter Zeuxis began to give away his own works, which, as he said, could not be bought; nor did he think any suitable reward could be found to satisfy one who, in modelling and painting living creatures, showed himself to be almost a god. . . .
Therefore, painting possesses this distinction, that any master painter will see his own works adored, and will hear himself judged, as it were, another god.

—L. B. Alberti, *Della pittura* (1436)

Preliminary Remarks

The essay that follows is concerned with memory as a definable constituent of visual expression in the Italian Renaissance.[1] Obviously the topic is large and daunting; I have chosen to limit it by focusing on the references to memory in several of Leonardo da Vinci's surviving notes on the training of painters, the nature of painting, and the processes of human perception. Leonardo's position at the vertex of Renaissance artistic practice and theory, and the extraordinary impact of his representational method, justify so selective an approach. However, before his contribution, with its marked technical component is addressed, it will be useful to examine some of the broader senses in which memory is integral to the public implications of Renaissance image making.

In the celebratory passage used as epigraph to this paper, Leon Battista Alberti embraces a view of painting as an "art of memory."[2] This view is backed by long-standing beliefs about the evidential force of images placed in the service of a written record, particularly one of doctrinal import.[3] By Alberti's day, the repertory of painted images was rapidly diversifying beyond the accustomed categories, and the means of representation were undergoing decisive changes—even approaching the possibility of painting for its own sake—but this only enriched the memorial significance of image making. A pictorial tradition long justified by the replication and variation of approved models (and consequently, by the reiteration of a kind of public memory of shared themes) began to address different aspects of memory deriving from the subjective experience of the artist and, by implication, the viewer.

By considering for a moment the sense in which medieval image making anticipated the mnemonic functions of Renaissance painting, we may better gauge the impact of the shift in representational approach that took place toward 1300. Michael Baxandall underscores the element of continuity in his discussion of the Renaissance "period eye," where he shows that most fifteenth-century painting continued to answer to a medieval formulation of the three principal functions of religious imagery.[4] These functions were: to serve as books for the illiterate; to impress on the memory the contents of the faith by keeping them present before the eyes; and to rouse the viewer to devotion, again by an appeal to the immediacy of sight. These are not properly separable tasks. They are connected by the assumption that images can convey "textual" arguments without requiring of the viewer a special training in the conventions of discourse, because unlike the word, the image achieves a direct psychological effect through its mimicry of appearances. To be sure, a source text is always implied, and as a rule the word retains absolute primacy as the custodian of the content to which the image refers. But the greater efficacy as a spur to devotion is granted to the image, with its direct sensory appeal and power to exemplify concretely actions worthy of imitation. And it is at the level of its reenactment (in the psyche and as behavior) that content becomes a living memory.

It will be noticed that in the politically consequential field of religious image making, memory effectively governs all three functions of painting—memory in its ordinary sense as the individual's psychological reservoir to be stocked and tapped for devotional ends and in the extended sense of embodied knowledge (books for the literate and the illiterate) transcending the individual life span.[5] It is personal memory that fuels the emotion triggered by the sight of the religious image, since each viewer's absorption, over time, of an illustrative repertoire, imparts to it as it is reexperienced the intensity of individual recollection. Because the image has a figurate "body" apprehensible in the concreteness of the present moment, it can mediate between its canonical source and the fluid particularity of experience. Thus, to recall the text through the image is to recall one's singular encounter with it as an incarnate presence. For this reason, every new picture literally enacts—but also necessarily limits—the religious text's claim to a universal accessibility.

The limitation is crucial to religious painting's significance, for if image and text are equally memories in their transmission of a historically certified message to posterity, the work of visual art, as a mere shadow to the text, is not locked into a fixed order of expression and keeps pace with changes in taste, circumstance, and psychological expectation. (In the case of the text, this adaptability would be reserved for the gloss and the commentary.) But the very license granted to the image on account of its derivative status is, simultaneously, an occasion for transgression. The same early churchmen who certified the image's usefulness recognized, on traditional philosophical grounds, the persistent (and often negative) connection between pictorial fiction and the displaced realities of oneiric and visionary experience, not to mention outright falsehood.[6] The persuasive qualities of visual representation (like the associative play, the transpositions of personal memory), ultimately eluded precise control.

It is commonly agreed that Renaissance images differ from medieval ones in their degree of visual persuasiveness—their display of a naturalism based on the attentive study of light and shadow and of relationships of measure in the actual world, as certified by the science of optics, or *perspectiva*. This is the realm of the quantitatively (measure, diminution) and qualitatively (light, color) verifiable image. It completes the mediation between history and the personal and momentary by proffering the fiction of a fully embodied subjective view on things. As Baxandall implies, the medieval doctrine of images did not undergo substantial adjustment because of the shift to a more acute and systematic naturalism in the illustration of the articles of the faith—the image had always been there to assist the worshiper's "eyewitness" recovery of the text.[7]

The new means of representation did affect the psychological conditions under which the image was absorbed and recalled, particularly because they magnified the artist's role as a fabricator of "memories" that might claim an authority of their own, based on the truthfulness of sense impressions. The pursuit of naturalistic styles led to a paradoxical valorization of deception, since the latter certified the artist's success in giving to images the sensory specificity of the actual—success, that is, in remaking the image by the light of the artist's own irreducible perceptual experience.[8] And this entailed a further paradox, since personal manner, stylistic individuality, assumed an unexpected prominence at the very heart of the imitation of appearances. Along with the rise of illusionistic art there emerged an audience of cognoscenti eager to discern and relish, in the image's deceptive "truth," the characteristic pattern of an individual's choices and manipulations. This very pattern suggested that, before it could be anything else, the painted image first had to be for its maker something like a fictional personal recollection.

The Albertian quotation with which we began encapsulates many of the points just made. It should be recalled that *Della pittura* (together with its somewhat earlier Latin version) was the first—and in many respects the best—modern treatise to justify methodically a perceptual and rhetorical foundation for painting. Its arguments were central to the articulation of a representational canon in the Renaissance. Alberti's comparison of painting to friendship proposes an empathetic give-and-take among artist, image, and viewer that (like the magnetism exerted by the traditional devotional image) goes beyond the mere registering of appearances; but there is no question that Alberti is fascinated by the photographic aspect of painting.[9] His choice of portrait images and a cult effigy to exemplify the "divine power" of painting acknowledges the paradoxical reach of pictorial memory. On the one hand, it seems to carry the present unaltered to some later age, through likenesses whose psychological authority derives from their authentic relation to a vanished original.[10] On the other hand, the example of the Phidian Zeus shifts the argument, from painting's commemoration of the individual person embedded in history to its shaping of the collective imagination, of future forms of belief.[11]

Already this inverts the priority of text over image implicit in the medieval functions of painting, but where Alberti truly reveals himself a modern is in the way he concludes by focusing on the painter, the source of so much magic: to be able to make the absent present and the dead live on is to have a unique power over time and oblivion. The writer's analogous power (Alberti uses the full force of the word when he calls the painter's greatest work an *istoria*) lacks the concreteness of reference. The image maker generating exact semblances of living things contributes a higher degree of sensate immediacy to the exercise of personal and collective remembrance. And while this is no more than illusion, it does place unprecedented demands on the artist's professional use of his own memory. To this, the painter's memory as a tool of art, we may now turn.

Memory and Making

The Renaissance view of the painter's memory—distinguishable from, but implicated in the type of memorializing assigned to the image—may be introduced by two texts separated by a span of nearly two hundred years. The first is an early art-critical statement from Filippo Villani's late-fourteenth-century enumeration of Florence's past glories. According to Villani:

> Giotto . . . restored painting to its former worth. . . . For images
> formed [*figurate*] by his brush agree so well with the lineaments of
> nature as to seem to the beholder to live and breathe; and his
> pictures appear to perform actions and movements so exactly as to
> seem from a little way off actually speaking, weeping, rejoicing . . .
> not without pleasure for him who beholds and praises the talent
> and skill [*ingenium manumque*] of the artist. Many people
> judge . . . that painters are of a talent no lower [*non inferioris*

ingenii] than those whom the liberal arts have rendered *magistros,* since these latter may learn by means of application and instruction [*studio atque doctrina*] written rules of their arts while the painters derive such rules as they find in their art only from a lofty natural perspicacity and a tenacious memory [*ab alto ingenio tenacique memoria*]. Yet Giotto was a man of great understanding even apart from the art of painting.[12]

The second text is an unusual illustration of historically mature artistic prowess cited in Vasari's 1568 edition of the *Lives*. In his "Life of Michelangelo" there is a passage about the artist's memory that puts a different emphasis on the topic of figure invention yet bears a curious affinity to Villani's insistence on Giotto's superior doctrine as an imitator of appearances. The first part is cribbed from Condivi's authorized Michelangelo biography of 1553, but Vasari supplements his theft with an anecdote whose source has not been identified:

> Michelangelo was endowed with a tenacious and profound memory, such that on seeing the works of others only once, he retained them so well, and used them in such a manner that practically no one was ever aware of it. Nor did he ever make among his own things one which was identical to another, because he could recall everything he had made. In his youth, he and his painter friends wagered a meal on who could best make a figure with no design whatsoever, inept-looking like those crude stick-figures made by artless people who deface walls. Here, Michelangelo relied on his memory; for, remembering having seen a clumsy scrawl of this sort on a wall, he made it as if it stood before him point for point, and surpassed all those other painters—a difficult thing to accomplish for a man so full of design, and trained on the choicest things.[13]

Vasari's magisterial *Lives* bracket the triumphant renewal of Italian *disegno* between Giotto (its single-handed rediscoverer) and Michelangelo (who brought it to an unsurpassable perfection). What did "tenacious memory" contribute to this development? Were Giotto's conquest of exact and lifelike representation and Michelangelo's uncanny mimicry of primitive art governed by the same sort of faculty, and did this amount to more than the mere power of accurate recall? In the pages that follow we shall see that Villani's straightforward praise and Vasari's paradoxical praise of their artist-heroes do indeed refer to similar properties of artistic *memoria*, which is bound up with the discrimination between good and bad forms and with the choices made in the actual shaping of an image. Indeed, memory's power to forget selectively, to edit out undesirable or inessential qualities, turns out to be one of the more important among its properties. This may be verified by turning to the evidence provided by Leonardo da Vinci.

While Leonardo does not quite propose what one might call a psychology of art, he engages crucial aspects of the relationship between human perceptual and evaluative abilities on the one hand and the production and reception of images on the other. The pedagogical tradition of which he was the beneficiary provided, beyond technical and stylistic preparation, explicit directives for the cultivation of the craftsman's psychological makeup. Leonardo investigated this makeup much as he probed the rules and principles of artistic production, with an obsessive attention to the structuring of unprecedentedly vital images—images straining at the limits of their own fictitiousness. In the process, he broadened the artist's exploration of the mind's internal senses (briefly, common sense, imagination, and memory), revolutionized the means by which mental discovery was translated into visible form, and made an influential contribution to the critical analysis of verbal versus visual understanding. Leonardo's reflections are of particular interest precisely because they do not rise to the level of philosophical generalities but remain tied to the practice of art. They inform us, above all, about memory as a productive faculty with a discrete realm of operation.

The remarks that follow draw on well-known aspects of Renaissance artistic training, but their purpose is to engage a type of Renaissance psychophysiological speculation that remains little explored by art historians—though some of its chief possibilities were adumbrated twenty-five years ago in Raymond Klibansky, Erwin Panofsky, and Fritz Saxl's great interdisciplinary collaboration, *Saturn and Melancholy*.[14] More recently, David Summers has brought together and interpreted an extensive series of ancient, medieval, and Renaissance sources on the psychology of sense perception and esthetic judgment.[15] In terms of method, Summers's investigations complement Baxandall's earlier analysis of the visual culture of Italian Renaissance artists and their public. Baxandall explores the concrete practices (church-going and private devotion, preaching, sacred and secular drama, dancing, accounting and gauging, surveying, moral instruction) marking the horizon of an average patron's perceptual training, but he deals only obliquely with the understanding of perception proper that was also a part of this acquired equipment.[16] His concept of the "period eye," which calls attention to the separate strands of experience that might account for distinctive features in the art made at a patron's bequest, is provided with a "period matrix" by Summers's analysis of the traditional yet constantly revised models of perceptual and mental activity common to Renaissance viewers and image makers.

My discussion of memory as a source of artistic judgment is especially indebted to Summers's work; however, the form of my inquiry is modeled after E. H. Gombrich's remarkable essay on Leonardo's compositional method, which established the connection between Leonardo's evaluation of another internal sense—the imagination—and his methods of image production, in particular through the revolutionary invention of the compositional sketch.[17] We shall see that Leonardo also formulated a novel category of memory sketch with a precise role in the planning of the finished painting. Gombrich's thesis will be examined at greater length, since it clarifies the scope of memory's artistic function.

The surviving manuscripts indicate that Leonardo wrote several series of notes on painting at various points in his career, beginning with his first Milanese period, around 1490, and continuing to the final years of his Italian residence, 1510–15; but the greatest concentration of material, with a decided emphasis on the painter's apprenticeship and on painting's cognitive function, belongs to 1490–92, a time close to Leonardo's first systematic anatomical investigations.[18] These earlier notes may be read as a gloss on Alberti's *Della pittura,* which is notably lacking in its treatment of workshop practice. Unlike Alberti, Leonardo faithfully surveys (albeit, with telling amplifications) the established pattern of quattrocento artistic training—a pattern already implicit in Cennino Cennini's *Libro dell'arte* of about 1400 and handed down, with gradual adjustments, through the seventeenth century.[19]

Cennini's treatise provides the fundamental schema for the post-Giottesque apprenticeship, opening with a sequence of exercises specifically tailored to the gradual mastery of illusionistic rendering—that is to say, the modeling of figures and their credible arrangement. Each variety of introductory drawing leads the apprentice to another facet of pictorial problem solving: for one year, he makes pure grisaille drawings from an *essempio*—a two-dimensional model that embodies the tricks of contouring and shading he must acquire. This patient discipline in turn prepares him for pen-and-wash drawing, which makes him *pratico*, skilled in drawing, as Cennini says, "inside your head" (it will be noticed that the swifter technique, which presumes a self-assured automatism of execution, is thought to stimulate the mental production of images). Finally, before being taught to mix colors, the student learns to copy (indeed, to trace) works by select masters, using variously tinted grounds (which introduce him to the value ranges possible for different hues). It is at this last stage, as Cennini indicates, that the development of a personal style—but also the enrichment of one's repertory by drawing from natural objects—takes place.[20]

Leonardo's apprentice also begins with a progression of careful copies from which the elements of style are learned, but in this case the express goal is to attain the freedom to work from the natural model, without having relied overmuch on the tracing of images recommended by Cennini. First one copies drawings by an artist of quality (made from life rather than done by rote—*di practica*); next, one portrays sculpture in the round ("assisted" by having on hand the example of a drawing made after the work being copied); and finally, one draws from a select natural model (Leonardo's *buono naturale*), which can then be added to a personal repertory for eventual use in painting.[21] The sequence is crucial, since the first objects of training are to provide the young artist with a technique—modeling to suggest roundness, and the ability accurately to transpose spatial intervals in contour-drawing—and simultaneously to form his power of judgment: the artist must learn to *select* from three-dimensional reality those features that can be successfully reembodied on a surface as a pattern of shading and contour marks. The exclusion of model-drawings made *di practica* is significant, since no matter how skillful, these are "traced" out of one's head (or with mechanical aids) and will not exhibit the characteristic mediation of three-dimensional forms that is the object of instruction. But before the three dimensional is even confronted, one must first be made at home with the artificial idiom of chiaroscuro illusion, with its peculiar cogency, which is why the first exercise is to copy master drawings.

By working from such drawings the apprentice learns about *maniera*, or style, at the very outset—his models for the rudiments of technique and representational strategy also possess a signature quality. In this sense, the development of the painter's judgment goes beyond learning to see three-dimensional entities in two-dimensional terms and embraces as well the production of expressive embellishments (effects of grace, vehemence, precision, richness, and the like) identifiable as the distinctive contribution of the artist's *fantasia,* to use Cennini's term. Thus copying opens onto imitation in the classical literary sense of stylistic apprenticeship—something already explicit in Cennini's manual.[22] In replicating a master's designs until they become second nature—that is, in stocking his memory with them—the apprentice acquires an internal criterion by which to select and embellish forms out of the flux of three-dimensional reality.

This critical aptitude, bound up with certain habits of execution, is the fundamental component of style. It becomes a personal possession as the young artist—after the transition of making "assisted" portrayals of static sculpture—puts it to the test by copying live natural models. In a contemporaneous version of his guidelines, Leonardo calls attention to the intellectual, judicial basis of visual selection by recommending before the copying of master-drawings a term of theoretical training in perspective and the proportions *(misure)* of things—which is to say in external, mathematically expressible criteria for the interpretation of appearances.[23] In the same passage, the copying of natural models that crowns the abbreviated sequence is followed by a period of examining (but not necessarily copying) works by a variety of masters. This last recommendation in effect encourages the young artist to gauge, against his own internal criteria, the implications of stylistic individuality. It may be taken as the subjective counterpart to the objectivity of theoretically apprehended rules such as perspective.

Memory in 1490 was as central to the training of the artist as it was in 1300—indeed because of the growing attention to memory as a stylistic thesaurus encoding sophisticated judgments about (and methods for negotiating) the appearances of things, an increasing demand was placed on its capacities. For Leonardo, the visual equivalent of word-for-word memorizing provided the painter with static or corrected images to serve as norms in the later elaboration of figures. This is apparent in the checking device he proposes to ascertain the success of the student's copying of master drawings—the technical and stylistic rudiments of apprenticeship:

> When you want to thoroughly learn by heart a thing that you
> have studied, proceed in this manner; that is, when you have
> drawn the same thing so often that you seem to have it

memorized, try drawing it without its exemplar or pattern; and trace the exemplar on a glass pane, and place it on the drawing . . . and note well where the tracing does not match up with the drawing. And where you find that you have erred, remember not to err again, but return to your exemplar in order to copy the mistaken part as often as will enable you to fix it in your *imaginativa*.[24]

The memory work in this case fixes the model's appearance so that it can be easily summoned in the image generating faculty of the mind, the *imaginativa* (Cennini's *fantasia*)—though Leonardo significantly elides the distinction between the offices of memory and imagination. This partnership between memorizing and visualizing is the subject of another precept two pages further on in the same manuscript, where the painter is advised to exercise his visual memory while lying in bed at night or before rising by tracing in the dark with his *imaginativa* the contours of things studied earlier.[25] The self-criticism (guided by the memory of correct form) that crowns the apprentice's copying after the natural model also takes place in a nocturnal setting:

> Winter evenings ought to be employed by the young in studying those things prepared during the summer, that is, it will be appropriate for you to gather together all the nudes you made over the summer, and elect the best limbs and bodies among them, and make use of these and commit them to memory.[26]

This procedure calls to mind the story of the ancient painter Zeuxis, who created a perfect exemplar of female beauty by imitating the most beautiful parts of the most beautiful maidens in the town of Croton.[27] In the Renaissance, the Zeuxian example was cited repeatedly to illustrate imitative strategy, but its most important restatement is at the beginning of Vasari's definition of the modern sixteenth-century style in the preface to Part Three of the *Lives*.

For Vasari, "election" was the key to inventing canonical (though personal) figures, and he made it virtually synonymous with *disegno,* the traditional basis of illusionistic painting. His words conveniently bring together the several points covered thus far:

> Design [*il disegno*] consisted in imitating the most beautiful aspects of nature in all figures, whether sculpted or painted, and this

comes from having a hand and *ingegno* that can translate onto a plane surface all that the eye sees . . . with the greatest accuracy and precision; the finest style [*la più bella maniera*] was then achieved, and this was done by frequently copying the most beautiful things, and from that which was most beautiful—be it hands or heads or bodies or legs—assembling a figure as beautiful as possible, and making use of it in all the figures in every work; and on this account is it called *bella maniera*.[28]

If we pause to consider Vasari's anecdote about Michelangelo's prodigious memory by the light of this passage on style, it becomes apparent that what enabled Michelangelo to replicate an untutored scrawl was an absolute mastery of style, *memoria* in the higher, critical sense. Vasari implies that it would have been easy for his hero to make a perfect figure, since he had a complete knowledge of art's chief rhetorical ornaments—its figural schemas.[29] But if he could transcend his training altogether and still achieve an authentic image (discern a style to imitate in a wholly styleless image), then surely there was no limit to his artistry.

Returning to Leonardo, we find out how the results of this analytical procedure to extract the elements of a fine style are reinvested with the fluency of living bodies:

In the following summer you should elect someone of fine carriage . . . and you shall make him strike graceful and gallant poses; and if his muscles do not stand out well within the contours of his limbs, it matters not at all—it is enough for you to have the good poses; and you may revise the limbs with those you studied in the wintertime.[30]

The memorized figures and figure parts embodying a sequence of choices by the apprentice are a stylistically perfected garment applied to the separately studied actions of figures. We may recall the distinction in Villani's passage between the realism of Giotto's figures (their correspondence to nature's lineaments) and their utterly lifelike behavior. *Memoria* is both the faculty that helps fix the "lineaments" of things, and the repository of artifice that guides the painter's hand as it retraces the contours of the visible.[31] But the equally essential artistic imitation of "movements and actions," as Leonardo discusses it, engages faculties of a different order from those that govern precise description and corrective selection. As a preliminary training for composition, the higher stage of pictorial endeavor (tellingly absent from the elementary training exercises), it points to an aspect of image making that exceeds the traditional capacities of memory.[32]

The figure in action was the chief compositional ornament in Alberti's syntax of painting. Leonardo is emphatic about movement's central importance to the successful painting's quality of purposeful animation. He also makes it clear that the painter cannot acquire and conserve dynamic figurative effects by the ordinary methods of copying; rather, these effects require the creation of a kind of auxiliary and stylistically uncensored memory in the form of portable sketch pads:

> When you will have learned perspective well, and have in memory all of the limbs and bodies of things, be pleased often, as you go about your recreation, to observe and consider the . . . actions of men as they speak, as they argue, or laugh or fight together—their actions and those of the bystanders . . . and note them down with brief marks in this manner [the accompanying drawing shows a small, jointed stick-figure] in a little book which you must always carry with you; and it should be of tinted paper, that you may not rub it out, but just replace the old one with a new one; for these things are not to be rubbed out, but rather preserved with the greatest care, because the forms and actions of things are so infinite that the memory is incapable of retaining them; wherefore you are to keep these as your authorities and masters.[33]

The last line grants these crude yet copious jottings from nature an exemplary status precisely analogous to that of the *maestri* whose drawings and prescriptions furnished the memory and judgment in the early stages of training. The rough action-notes in Leonardo's sketch-pad memory— undoubtedly resembling the vivacious jottings that crowd such sheets as Windsor 12644r (fig. 14)—are in precise contrast to the diligently accurate drawings produced out of the critically informed faculty of memory.[34] Instead, they are visually aligned and functionally bound up with Leonardo's concurrent invention of a sketch-pad fantasy, as embodied in the type of compositional sketch analyzed by Gombrich:

> O you who compose *istorie,* do not distinguish [*membrifficare*] with finished contours the members of those *istorie.* . . . For many are the times when the living being represented [*lo animale figurato*] does not have a movement of the limbs appropriate to its mental movements. . . . Now have you never considered how the

Figure 14. Leonardo da Vinci, *Studies of Men at Work*, pen and ink over black chalk, ca. 1506–8. Windsor Castle, Royal Library, 12644r. ©1988 Her Majesty Queen Elizabeth II.

poets composing their verses do not trouble themselves to write beautifully, and do not mind crossing out some of those verses, rewriting them better? Therefore, painter, compose roughly [*componi grossamente*] the members of your figures . . . for you will understand that if such an uncultivated composition [*componimento inculto*] is appropriate to its invention, so much the more will it satisfy when it is adorned with the perfection appropriate to its parts. I have seen in clouds and walls blots [*machie*] that have roused me to fine inventions of various things, which blots, though they were wholly lacking in the perfection of any one member, did not lack perfection in their movements or other actions.[35]

As Gombrich has shown, Leonardo's marvelous compositional sketches in pen and ink for the *Battle of Anghiari* (1503–5) faithfully embody this method of composing, even to the atmospheric turbulence, the patchy shading evoked by the cloud/wall analogy.[36] It is noteworthy that the sheet in Venice (Accademia, no. 215; fig. 15) exploring the dynamics of the *Battle*'s central cavalry group, also includes in its lower portion the briefest of jottings for a combat of foot soldiers. These jottings suggest (and could have originated as) the sorts of memoranda or *ricordi* in which Leonardo on his habitual walks captured the motions of men working or contending.[37] The reference to cloud images and their cognates recurs in at least two variants of the passage just cited, both of which identify the *ingegno* as the faculty thus stimulated to the invention of active forms.[38] Indeed, I suspect we have in Leonardo's writing the other mental power that is especially developed in Villani's ideal artist: *ingenium,* characterized in terms of a specific pictorial activity.

If *memoria* is a control, informing judgment and insuring the persuasive consistency of the artist's vision, *ingenium,* normally identified with innate intuition and problem-solving ability, is a natural ally of fantasy, a faculty endowed with a kind of excitability not present in either intellect or sensation.[39] Alberti admits as much in a crucial passage on the composition of gestures and actions, where, with characteristic moderation, he warns the painter against displaying a "too fervid and furious *ingegno*" by making wildly animated figures.[40] In medieval and Renaissance usage, the imagination in its higher functions was a visualizing and "permutational" faculty (the guise in which Cennini gives it a central importance); in it, sensation was recomposed into a kind of immaterial picture before it was

Figure 15. Leonardo da Vinci, *Studies for the Battle of Anghiari*, pen and ink, ca. 1503–5. Venice, Accademia. Photo Giacomelli.

passed on to the rest of the mind, and acts of will were translated into a pattern for action before they were implemented.[41] Imagination's inherent, fluid "pictorialism"—as demonstrated by its activity in dreams and day-dreams—made it receptive to forms of all kinds, precisely like the mobile clouds and spotted walls used by Leonardo as screens for imaginative compositional projection. It was this indeterminacy that specifically suited imagination to the registering and visualizing of movement.[42]

With the compositional sketch, Leonardo formalized a method of graphic conjuring that is the visible, external counterpart to the inner realm of the fantasy and imagination. Loose, indeterminate drawing gives a body to the very act of pictorial invention—which is to say, the movement of the painter's *ingegno* in quest of living or active figures. But by taking place in the light of day, on a material ground, this record of fleeting permutations differs radically from the mental activity it embodies, since it becomes fixed and open to a kind of direct critical revision like that of the image drawn for accuracy from a static model. The major difference between this sort of sketch and Leonardo's action-*ricordi*—which are meant to capture external occurrences at the source—is not so much in style as in purpose: the latter make up a thesaurus of single impressions, while the former is associative or combinatory, literally and metaphorically.[43]

Both kinds of drawing present us with an energized treatment of line. (In the case of the compositional sketch, line anatomizes the forces released around the action's focuses.) This suggests a connection between their evocation of flux and Leonardo's evolving concern—as expressed in this passage from about 1505–8—with the dynamic potentiality of the fundamental units of geometry, point and line:

> Line is made by the movement of a point. . . . Although time is numbered among the continuous quantities, because it is indivisible and without body, it is not wholly contained by the power of geometry, which would otherwise divide it into figures and bodies of infinite variety, as it can be seen to do in visible and corporeal things. But time only agrees with the first principles of geometry, that is, the point and the line. The point is to be compared with an instant in time, and line resembles a length of time.[44]

Since his special use of the conceptually related action memoranda arose from a critique of memory as a supplier of animate images for painting, it is worth asking whether Leonardo was not also concerned with the special limitations of natural imagination, and whether he sought to compensate for them—through art—with novel means of exterior visualization. The emphasis on externalization suggests that for Leonardo, the power of sight, artificially enhanced through *disegno* by the power of painting, gave access to a higher order of reality than the senses could normally convey to the mind. A rapid glance at his so-called *paragone* arguments on behalf of painting may show more concretely how a dissatisfaction with the uncertainty of inner visualization might lead him—paradoxically—to strengthen vastly the artist's hold on imaginative experience.

Painting and the Mind

Towards 1490, Leonardo wrote down a series of arguments in defense of painting as a cognitive endeavor. In part, these were based on the analysis of sensory knowledge that also informed his recent skull studies (fig. 16). Thus, as drawing became for him an instrument of scientific visualization, Leonardo placed an increasing value on the power of the image to open up for inspection the very structure of reality. In the skull studies, pen and ink are used with the delicacy and sureness of touch characteristic of Leonardo's silverpoint drawings of horses from the same period.[45] The degree of finish and the chiseled clarity with which the volumes are suggested belong under the discipline of the static study drawings from which the painter's repertory of "corrected" forms is drawn, but they also call to mind copper engravings and suggest that Leonardo was already considering a novel type of didactic publication.[46]

In a careful analysis of the skull drawings, Martin Kemp has shown that Leonardo's references to the soul, imagination, judgment, and the senses—and, one should add, memory—were based on late medieval faculty psychology, which remained normative in the Renaissance, though its physiological basis was undergoing constant revision.[47] This psychology, ultimately derived from Aristotle's *De anima* and its related treatises, posited a kind of image derived from sensory stimuli as the vehicle for all mental operations below the level of abstract reasoning. The prerational mental functions (the *faculties*) were localized in three linked ventricles or cavities within the brain: the three ovoid enclosures in the middle of Leonardo's schematic transverse section of the head, dated about 1485–89 (Windsor 12626r; fig. 17).[48]

In the traditional model of sense perception, the five external or "special" senses transmitted impressions to the common sense in the anterior ventricle, where the separate objects of special sensation (light and color for the eye, for example) were composed into a fleeting preliminary image of the thing perceived (including such "common sensibles" as magnitude, duration, movement).[49] The common sense, in turn, communicated

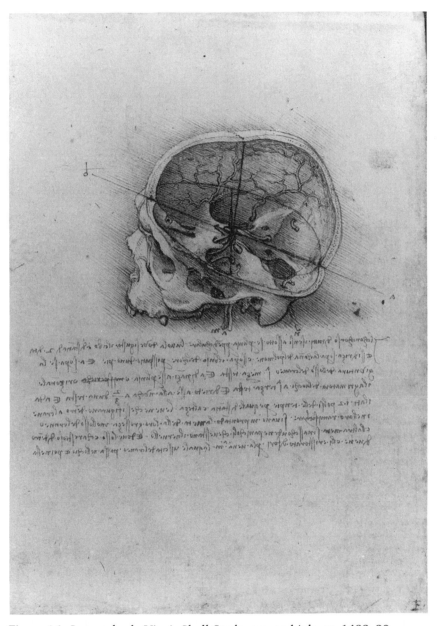

Figure 16. Leonardo da Vinci, *Skull Study*, pen and ink, ca. 1489–90.
Windsor Castle, Royal Library, 19058r. ©1988 Her Majesty Queen
Elizabeth II.

Figure 17. Leonardo da Vinci, *Section of a Skull*, silver point, ca. 1485–89. Windsor Castle, Royal Library, 12626r. ©1988 Her Majesty Queen Elizabeth II.

with the fantasy or imagination, which retained the image and made it accessible to preliminary faculties of judgment (the cogitative/estimative) in the middle, and to the memory in the posterior ventricle.[50] On this internally mediated world of concrete sensation, the immaterial rational soul performed its abstracting operations.

Leonardo's ventricular schema in Windsor 12626r is a personal adaptation of this system, which already showed a certain variability in the distribution (and number) of the front and middle faculties. It bears emphasizing that his mental ground plan is purely hypothetical, as he does not appear to have undertaken brain dissections until after 1500 (possibly not until 1505). The ventricles in Windsor 12626r are labeled in a fashion that suggests the powers of mind associated with them: from bottom to top they are the *imprensiva* (receptor of impressions), paired with *inteletto* (understanding); *senso commune* (common sense), paired with *volontà* (will); and *memoria,* which stands by itself. Only *memoria,* the sole faculty whose placement had always been nearly invariable, exhibits the traditional placement.[51] Leonardo's nomenclature for the first two ventricles is atypical. The *imprensiva* (a term exclusive to Leonardo) occupies the cavity and takes over the sense integrating functions usually assigned to the common sense. Moreover, it is given a special relation to the optic nerves, which merge at its anterior surface after issuing from the bulblike cavities of the eyes.[52] The lines representing the olfactory and auditory nerves go directly to the common sense in the middle, which serves unequivocally as the faculty of judgment.[53] As we shall see, this physical separation between sight and the other senses is related to Leonardo's arguments for the cognitive superiority of painting. However, the skull studies that come between Windsor 12626r and the writings of 1490–92 do not observe the separation, though they do provide a different sort of physiological grounding for the centrality of sight. We must envision Leonardo, in this short span of years, devising alternative ways of connecting his mature views on painting to a continuously evolving interpretation of nature's mechanisms.

As Kemp has shown, the skull studies of 1489 are a posteriori demonstrations supporting Leonardo's conviction that harmonic ratios, analogous to those that distinguish the superficial anatomy of well-built bodies, govern the internal disposition of the cranial structures, and that this disposition is in turn dependent on the arrangement of the organs of sense in relation to the central location of the *senso commune*. In Windsor 19058r, Leonardo notes that the meeting point for all of the sensation-bearing nerves (which can be seen emerging at the intersection of the coordinate axes passing through the dome of the skull), is at a rational distance from the skull's major divisions in depth and breadth, and vertically aligned with the heart (which is the source of the vital spirits).[54] An anatomical note from this same period makes it clear that Leonardo considers the *senso commune* the seat of the soul—the point from which the latter presides over the lower psychological and corporeal functions.[55] The drawing's coordinate system in effect marks the passageway between soul and body.

Leonardo's concern with the harmonic siting of the instruments of sensation corresponds to his understanding of sense-knowledge as the unified apprehension of a composite reality. The individual self is a composite entity (spirit and matter; diverse organ systems) for which the soul provides the principles of both unity and differentiation—as Leonardo puts it, the soul fashions, and loves, its particular body.[56] The separate senses, with their specialized perceptions fitted to the complexity of a world resolvable into constituent elements, are analogously "composed" in the common sense. And that composite knowledge is the basis for the soul's reflections on the nature (the harmonic integration) of what lies outside itself. It is not surprising that Leonardo viewed composition as painting's crucial stage, where the artist endowed the image's body with a principle of unity (a soul)—and hence a movement—adequate to its significance.

In the *paragone* arguments of 1490–92 the superiority of painting in conveying the composite unity of things is defended in terms of both painting's own powers and those of its special target, the sense of sight. Knowledge received through the eyes is more certain than other knowledge, because both light and the eye are geometrically structured; more important, it is received almost at once as a simultaneity of interrelated parts; painting's worthiest rivals, poetry and music (the better of the two, since it produces audible harmonies), are both apprehended over time, bit by bit.[57]

This amounts to ascribing a limitation to the organ of judgment proper, since the totality of a poetic or a musical composition is never taken in at first hand but must be constructed and evaluated in the *senso commune,* which apprehends the common-sensible of duration. The sense of hearing, which depends on duration for its full effectiveness, is thus more akin to the common sense. The sense of sight, on the other hand, is more akin to the soul itself, the principle of harmony informing the entire sentient organism; it can offer the soul a vision of harmony almost without mediation. What is more, the very fixity of the painted image imparts to the simultaneity of vision's perceptions a kind of artificial eternity, which Leonardo contrasts with the poignant evanescence of musical harmony (and living bodies, as well).[58] Painting as an art of memory (*replacing* memory) is justified here at the level of the soul's yearning for harmonic correspondences. One begins to see why Leonardo sought to separate sight from hearing in Windsor 12626r; indeed, by assigning to the eyes a medium (the *imprensiva*) upon which visual sensations are imprinted and grasped before they pass to the central cavity, he was diagrammatically anticipating his extraordinary claim for painting's superior intelligibility.

Kemp has indicated that Leonardo does not localize the *imaginativa* in any of his surviving diagrams, though it is as prominent as the *imprensiva* in the arguments on the superiority of painting; but he concludes (and the texts support this) that Leonardo envisioned it in the central ventricle, together with the *senso commune,* so that their activities are intertwined.[59] As Leonardo presents them, the *imprensiva* is closest to unmediated sensation, because the eyes directly imprint upon it the radiant panorama of the actual world. The seat of judgment or common sense relies instead on its companion middle faculty, the imagination, to help it assemble temporal perceptions. Though reality is naturally composite, common sense does not experience this as a given, but as the result of its own (assisted) act of recomposition. Memory, because it is in the brain cavity furthest from immediate sensation, is even more dependent on the additive perception reassembled by the judgment. This is what Leonardo implies in a note that may have been written as late as 1500–1505, though it summarizes some of the key arguments datable to about 1492:

> The imagination cannot see with the same excellence as the eye sees, because the eye receives the species or similitudes of objects and gives them to the *impressiva,* and gives that *impressiva* to the common sense and there it is judged; but imagination does not go outside the common sense except to go to the memory, where it stops and perishes if the thing imagined is not of great excellence. And this is the condition in which poetry is found in the mind or imagination of the poet, who feigns the same things as the painter. . . . Therefore, concerning these fictions, we may truthfully say that the proportion between the science of painting and poetry is as great as that between the body and the shadow that derives from it—and it is even greater, for that body's shadow at least enters the common sense through the eye, but the imagining of such a body does not enter that sense, but is born there in the [imagination's] tenebrous eye. O, what difference there is between imagining such light within the tenebrous eye, and seeing it in act outside the darkness![60]

With that closing interjection, Leonardo provides a graphic image of internal sensation deprived of reality's stimuli. It brings us back to the critique of imagination and memory implicit in Leonardo's drawing innovations. To the dark, if fertile, eye of the imagination, he juxtaposes the brightly visible yet malleable imaginative space of the compositional sketch; and he supplements the memory's finite and static thesaurus with the portable and inexhaustible thesauri of the action memoranda.

After 1505 Leonardo undertook brain dissections and discovered a method for making wax casts of the cerebral ventricles; this led to a series of remarkable drawings, of which number KK6287 at the Weimar Schlossmuseum (fig. 18, datable to about 1506–8) is a characteristic example. The sagittal section of the head in the upper half of the sheet shows that, while he preserved the nomenclature from his earlier diagrams, Leonardo found the *imprensiva* to be a double cavity extending backward and above the middle ventricle. Both the optic and olfactory nerves enter the brain in an area midway between these horns and the *senso commune*.[61] The ventricular casts undermined whatever physiological argument might have been made for sight's link to a special faculty of mind; they also muddled the neat architectonics of the earlier skull studies, where the higher sense nerves converged at a central location. As he observed more accurately the labyrinthine course of biological process, and grew more skilled at charting it, Leonardo cast off the straightforward geometries of his proportional studies. In the brain drawings the neural connections are not traced back to a definite locus. Leonardo acknowledges that he does not yet know how they are integrated, but it does not affect the boldness of his visualization.

The Weimar sheet exhibits an analytical complexity and a *terribilità* characteristic of the late phase of the artist's physiological researches.[62] Sectioned, transparent, and exploded views, enhanced with a variety of hatching techniques, elucidate for the soul's insatiable curiosity the three-dimensional composition of the microcosm. In the Weimar sheet the dominant image, a head of the Anghiari warrior type, has a psychic animation that exceeds its illustrative purpose—or rather, completes it, since the scowl, the set lips and jaw, even the piercing stare of the lidless eyes translate into outward expression the pattern of facial innervation exposed beneath the flesh.

The Weimar drawing, matching outward appearance to an internal mechanism for psychic expression, can also be viewed as an apologia for the biases of Leonardo's own style. It may not be a coincidence that in his notes on painting of around 1508–10 Leonardo returned with fuller argumentation to the style-regulating activity of the *senso commune* and, by implication, to the vulnerabilities of the artist's stylistic memory:

> How figures often resemble their masters. This happens because our judgment is that which moves the hand to create the lineaments of those figures from a variety of aspects, until it is satisfied. And because that judgment is one of the powers of our soul, with which it shapes, according to its will, the form of the body it inhabits, it happens that—having to remake a human body with the hands—it willingly remakes that body which it first

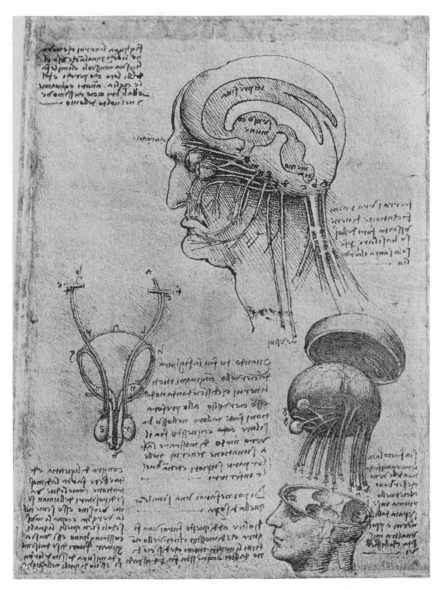

Figure 18. Leonardo da Vinci, *Anatomical Studies*, pen and ink, ca. 1506–8. Weimar, Schlossmuseum, KK6287. By permission of the Kunstsammlungen zu Weimar.

Figure 19. Leonardo da Vinci, *St. John the Baptist*, oil on panel, ca. 1509. Paris, Louvre. Photo Alinari.

invented. And from this it follows that those who fall in love, willingly fall in love with things that resemble them.[63]

Kemp has shown that Leonardo's starting point was a proverbial expression—"Every painter paints himself"—current in the Florence of his youth.[64] In his early notes on painting the artist already warned against the unconscious tendency to replicate one's features, but it does not seem that he provided a full psychological explanation until the later period, when the mainsprings of inner sensation had become more difficult to track. (Even the *imprensiva* bore a less direct relation to the acuity of sight than he had previously assumed, since its large size meant that it was relatively difficult to illuminate.)[65] At this time, in an outstanding series of embryological and urogenital anatomies, Leonardo was also investigating at length the other, naturally ordained, means by which the soul replicates itself. (The diagram of the male urogenital system on the Weimar sheet corresponds to a series of studies on the reverse, accompanied by notes on the different sorts of children produced by variations in the desire informing the sexual act.)[66] Perhaps he grew more conscious of the sheer necessity impelling the soul to make bodies in the mold of its own particular harmonies.

In his later years, then, Leonardo may have become more skeptical of the deep mechanisms governing the young painter's stylistic development.

Only the greatest vigilance could protect the image maker's soul from Narcissus-like infatuations. But what of Leonardo's own art? Reading his advice, one imagines he would have preferred a fully objective method of representation (if corrective of nature's flaws), a transparent style. This is manifestly not how he painted, since his oeuvre (especially in the later years) is dominated by the distilled figure-types that Vasari identified with the display of *bella maniera* (fig. 19). No doubt Leonardo felt that his own artistic judgment had met the test of a higher knowledge; still, in view of the obsessiveness with which he dwelt on the evocative force of certain configurations, one is tempted to view his endless interrogation of appearances as a lifelong escape from the prison of the *senso commune*.[67]

MARK JOHNSON

The Imaginative Basis of Meaning and Cognition

The papers in this volume are the result of a symposium described officially as an "interdisciplinary discussion of the distinction between visual and linguistic constructions through which experience is constituted as knowledge." Obviously, there are major differences between vision and language processing, but I want to focus on at least one important way in which both of these aspects of cognition are united by shared structures of imagination. A growing number of empirical studies in linguistics and the cognitive sciences reveal the existence of patterns of imagination common to visual perception, sensory-motor activity, and linguistic (syntactic and semantic) structure alike. The research program that has come to be known as cognitive semantics investigates the way in which patterns in perception, bodily (spatio-temporal) orientation, object manipulation, and other bodily movements provide the structural basis for linguistic meaning, our conceptual system, and the ways we reason.[1]

My hypothesis is that the central linkage among our bodily experience, perceptual processes, and these linguistic and more abstractive cognitive constructions is provided by structures of imagination that emerge in our bodily interactions and are metaphorically extended to form our understanding of abstract concepts and patterns of thought. Other papers in this volume discuss visual imagery, icons, visual memory, dance, language, and knowledge. I am claiming that all of these varied activities are fundamentally matters of imagination. So my chief task will be to elaborate this notion of imagination in such a way as to explain how our visual and other perceptual modalities are connected to concepts and abstractive rational operations via shared patterns of imaginative activity. I shall also make some more speculative remarks concerning the implications of this view for our understanding of how memory works.

Talk of imagination is likely to be regarded within the community of cognitive scientists as a remnant of an outdated faculty psychology. But I suggest that the term *imagination* is still quite useful as a way of identifying nonsentential and nonpropositional dimensions of cognition that are now being recognized as important to meaning and reasoning. My view of imagination does not focus on static images, but rather on dynamic patterns of processes or activities that are basic to our inhabiting a shared, meaningful world. This attention to the *active* side of visual representation and memory challenges the empiricist view of images and memory that has characterized much of modern philosophy. I am thus rejecting the classic empiricist picture of cognition, as it is most clearly articulated by Thomas Hobbes. He regarded perceiving subjects as *passive* recipients of sense impressions that arise in their minds when external objects impinge upon their sense organs, since "there is no conception in a man's mind, which hath not at first, totally, or by parts, been begotten upon the organs of sense."[2] An external object thus imparts an "inward motion" that has sufficient force to carry over into the mind as a representation in the form of an image. Then, "after the object is removed, or the eye shut, we still retain an image of the thing seen, though more obscure than when we see it. And this is it, the Latins call *imagination*."[3] Hobbes uses the metaphor of "decaying" sense impressions as a way of explaining how images, ideas, and memories are all traces of original sense impressions whose initial forcefulness is diminishing: "This *decaying sense,* when we would express the thing itself, I mean *fancy* itself, we call *imagination,* as I said before: but when we would express the decay, and signify that the sense is fading, old, and past, it is called *memory.*"[4] This same underlying notion of the forceful impression of objects upon passively receptive subjects, giving rise to images that decay into ideas and memories, is found in similar versions in Locke and Hume, and it became the basis for the mainstream associationist psychology of the eighteenth and nineteenth centuries.

While it is almost universally recognized today that memory is a much more active and selective function, the apparatus of the empiricist model is still widely retained. In his survey of models of memory in cognitive psychology, Henry Roediger has traced the recurrence of a dominant spatial metaphor that underlies our folk conception of the mind as well as many theoretical accounts: the mind is a spatially extended container-object; ideas and memories are metaphorical objects stored in a mind space; and we search for and retrieve these idea-objects via procedures analogous to physical search and retrieval.[5] In the vast majority of these models, images, concepts, and other representations are treated as metaphorically discrete objects with a fixed character. Roediger observes that only within the last two decades have we started moving toward constructivist models of the sort anticipated decades earlier by F. C. Bartlett when he asserted, "Remembering is not the re-excitation of innumerable fixed, lifeless and fragmentary traces. It is an imaginative reconstruction, or construction."[6]

The account of images and memory I will sketch emphasizes this active, selective, constructive dimension of cognition. My focus is on structures of imagination that are recurring patterns of active cognitive processes by which we constitute our meaningful experience through perception, action, and communication. They are not private, idiosyncratic acts, but rather structures of shared processes of understanding that make it possible for us to inhabit a *common* world.

The key to articulating a sufficiently rich and comprehensive notion of imagination is to recognize its bodily character. Cognitive semantics starts from the obvious but important truth that we human beings have bodies in and through which we inhabit a shared world. In order to survive and to flourish as functioning organisms, we have had to develop perceptual and motor skills that permit us to interact more or less successfully with our environment and to modify our environment, where possible, to accommodate our needs.

All of this necessary, life-sustaining activity depends on the human organism's ability to recognize and respond in suitable ways to patterns in the environment. If we did not perceive recognizable, constantly recurring patterns and learn to move our bodies in appropriately structured ways, our lives would be utterly chaotic and completely beyond our control. Consequently, we *do* learn to comprehend our world via common gestalt structures, that is, we experience meaningfully unified wholes within our experience that constitute an ecologically appropriate level of organization for the kind of beings we are. We learn, for example, to recognize various forms of containment: we experience our bodies as containers for vital fluids, organs, and gases; we are contained within rooms, walls, fences, and clearings; and we learn to perceive other physical objects as containing one another. All of this sensory-motor activity, most of which is carried on unconsciously, gives rise to a recurrent pattern or schema of *containment:* in each case some space or object is circumscribed or enclosed by a spatial expanse or volume. Although each particular instance of containment will have its own distinctive features, it is crucial for an organism's maintenance that there be a repeatable generic structure that permits us to characterize all of these as instances of a containment schema.

So far, we have considered only *physical* containment; but, of course, the containment schema pervades our understanding of all domains of our experience, physical and nonphysical alike. We understand our bodies as containers for our emotions.[7] Our minds are containers for our ideas.[8] Our linguistic expressions (and their sentential formulations) are containers for our thoughts.[9] And we come to understand all sorts of abstract objects (institutions, political parties, societies, mathematical sets, logical categories, and so on) as abstract containers for both concrete and abstract objects.[10]

Once we begin to think about it, we realize that the container schema is present in our understanding of virtually every aspect of our experience. In some cases containment is meant to be understood metaphorically, as when we understand one abstract object (for example, a scientific theory) as containing another abstract object (for example, an argument). Nevertheless, the same containment schema prefigured in our bodily experience structures our understanding of abstract containment.

Here we have one important basis for the connection between visual (and other perceptual) experience and so-called higher linguistic meaning, with its attendant forms of knowledge. The primary evidence for this connection comes from cognitive linguistics. There now exists an impressive body of empirical research regarding the syntax and semantics of natural languages, which explores the way in which schematic structures, for example the containment schema, structure and relate semantic domains of many different kinds.[11] For instance, extensive work has been done on the semantics of various prepositions to show that they depend upon what George Lakoff and I call *image-schematic* structure (here called merely *schematic* structure).

To cite just one example, Susan Lindner's work on the semantics of *in-out* reveals three basic image schemas underlying virtually all of the enormous number of related senses of *out.*[12] Consider what she refers to as the OUT_1 schema:

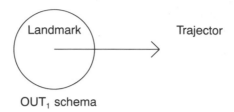

OUT$_1$ schema

Notice that OUT$_1$ involves the container schema (represented by the circle circumscribing a bounded space, or, in three dimensions, an enclosed volume). In simple cases of OUT$_1$ orientation the basic interpretation of the schema is very straightforward, as in:

1a. Sarah toddled out of the kitchen.
1b. Sandi drove us out of the county.
1c. Tear out that Larson cartoon and save it.
1d. Pick out the bad apples.

In 1a we understand the room as a bounded container, with Sarah tracing a path out of it. Notice that even in such a simple case as this the path is not an actual object in space, but is imaginatively projected by us in our perceptual grasp of the scene. The container need not be three dimensional, as seen in 1b, where it demarcates only a bounded two-dimensional space. In 1c we understand the newspaper as a container out of which the cartoon comes as it is cut and removed. And in 1d the pile of apples constitutes the relevant bounded space.

So far, all of this is rather pedestrian. It looks as though the image schema is really nothing more than the structure of an image or other perceptual representation. However, such cases constitute only a small portion of the vast range of instances of *out* orientation. In the majority of cases our understanding of the meaning of *out* depends upon metaphorical elaborations of the OUT$_1$ schema, as in:

2a. Max was forced out of office.
2b. I'm getting out of the race.
2c. The debutante came out.

In each of these cases the container schema is understood metaphorically: political office as abstract container, race-event as container, and private versus public as contained "spaces." In 2a, since physical movement out of a bounded space frees one from the forces acting there, it follows that movement "out of" a metaphorical container (political office) likewise frees one from both the privileges and responsibilities that impinge on anyone within that office-container. Similarly, in 2c the debutante "comes out" into a *public* space, a space of high profile and availability, and she leaves the private space she has heretofore inhabited, both literally and metaphorically understood.

There are three important points I want to emphasize about this brief analysis of an image-schematic structure.

While image schemata will typically have what is apparently a universal bodily (biological) basis, there may be considerable variation and selection possible in the ways a cultural group might imaginatively elaborate and extend a particular schema. For example, while one would expect every embodied creature to experience bodily containment, we would not expect, nor do we find, universality in the various metaphorical uses of the container schema within different cultures and groups.

Second, what these examples suggest is the way in which *linguistic* meaning is connected to visual (and other) modes of imagery. I am claiming that *the same* image schemata so crucial to our sensory-motor activity are equally crucial to our more abstractive modes of understanding that involve language proper. Patterns of significance and symbolic import are thus prefigured in the imaginative patternings of our bodily experience. And such patterns are often the basis for memory.

Third, the image schema is always a flexible pattern of imaginative activity. It is never merely a static template, a frozen structure of a visual image (even though we may diagrammatically represent it this way). According to the view I am espousing, we must understand imaginative activity as including all sensory modalities, motor programs, and even abstract acts of cognition such as the drawing of inferences. In this very broad sense, imaginative activity is the means by which an organism constructs an ordering of its perceptions, motor skills, and reflective acts, as it seeks to accommodate itself to its environment. Imagination, so understood, thus includes the full range of organizing activities, from the forming of images (in different sensory modalities), to the execution of motor programs, to the manipulation of abstract representations, and even to the creation of novel orderings.

This requires that an image schema be flexible and malleable. An image schema is the structure of a dynamic imaginative *process* that we bring to experience by way of anticipating recognizable forms, but that is itself modified in and through its instantiation in a particular context.[13] Seen in this way, imaginative creativity can be said to be in even the most mundane and unconscious sensory-motor activities of an organism. We much creatively and imaginatively engage our environment every second of our lives, for no situation is ever exactly the same, and we cannot extricate ourselves from temporal and spatial *process*. What we regard as our prototypical examples of imaginative creativity in art and science differ only in degree and importance from the mundane modification and modulation that is our everyday experience.

It should now be clearer why Lakoff and I have named these patternings *image* schemata—in order to highlight their nature as structures of *imaginative* processes that emerge in our bodily experience. As an illustration of this, consider another omnipresent image schema, the *source-path-goal* schema. From the moment infants become mobile they perceive visually, and instantiate in their bodily actions, movement along a path from a starting point to an endpoint.

The schema consists of a starting point A, an endpoint B, and a series of contiguous intermediate points forming a path from A to B. A large part of our day is spent instantiating the source-path-goal schema in the mundane actions that make up the fabric of our lives, for example, stumbling into the kitchen from the bedroom, moving from the sink to the cupboard, reaching from the chair to the toaster, and so on. In this way, our understanding of action becomes inextricably linked to the source-path-goal schema.

The schema provides the crucial relevant structure that comes to define action, in contrast to mere movement. Action is purposive. It is directed toward goals. And as soon as we turn away from exclusive focus on actions that involve physical movements only, we see that the source-path-goal schema gives us the means for understanding and experiencing nonphysical, or "mental," actions, such as the solving of a quadratic equation. We understand the mental *process* metaphorically as movement along an abstract path. There are *steps* to be taken in solving the equation. We can thus make, or fail to make, *progress toward* the solution. We can *encounter obstacles* in our proof procedure. But, as we *move closer to* the correct solution, we can *see more clearly where we are going*.

Processes in general, not just mental processes, are schematized in the same way. We spatialize time in our understanding by plotting a *path* of movement through time from initial state to final state. In this way, any process over time (for example, a chemical reaction, constructing a logical proof, suffering through an illness, or preparing for a test) can be structured via the source-path-goal schema.

These brief examples indicate that image-schematic structure is common to, and connects, our perception, motor activity, conceptualization, and the language with which we communicate our experience. Image schema and metaphor are not primarily, therefore, merely matters of language. Rather, they have linguistic manifestations, and they structure our syntactic and semantic systems as a result of their being underlying structures of cognition and experience.

A satisfactory theory of imaginative activity would require investigation of large numbers of image schemata and the ways in which they are metaphorically and metonymically elaborated across various domains of understanding. Among the more prominent image schemata would be the following: *object, container, part-whole, center-periphery, figure-ground, source-path-goal, link, scalarity, compulsion, attraction-resistance, potentiality, contact, cycle, matching, iteration,* and so forth. Other image schemata would be specifications of, or superimpositions upon, these more basic schemata, such as the superimposition onto the *center-periphery* schema of *near-far, here-there, subject-object, toward-away,* and so on. The nature and metaphorical projection of several of these schemata have already been investigated in some detail within cognitive linguistics.[14] This general orientation provides us with a means for exploring the connections among perception, language, and acts of reasoning. It gives us a way of explaining how it is that our bodily experience comes to structure abstract acts of cognition and the symbol systems they generate.

The hypothesis of image-schematic structure is thus a possible starting place for our attempt to understand the incredibly complex relations among visual perception, imagery, memory, and language. The physical instantiation of these processes in the organism is even more perplexing, although very recent work on parallel distributed processing models of cognition has generated accounts of topographic maps in neural networks that seem compatible with the positing of image-schematic processing.[15]

I would like to end on a more modest and chiefly illustrative note by reflecting on the role of image schemata in the data discussed by Adrienne

Kaeppler in her contribution to the present volume, "Memory and Knowledge in the Production of Dance," and in her other work. Kaeppler's treatment of dance is especially interesting because dance can be both *visually perceived* and *kinesthetically felt* in bodily movements. The basic "images" in dance are movement structures that are imaginatively patterned and flexible, both in terms of their physical instantiation and their symbolic interpretation. In dance, the embodied structures of imagination are what Kaeppler calls *motifs,* that is, "culturally structured pieces of movement tied to a specific dance tradition or genre." The kinship to language here is obvious:

> Movements acquired visually . . . and physically . . . can be
> validated when they are reproduced either with the body itself or
> through movement notation. . . . Movement systems are structured
> in ways similar to language systems—so much so, that we speak of
> them as having grammar, syntax, and rules. Indeed, it is difficult
> to sort out just what part language plays in movement acquisition
> or memory.

The key notion here is that of a grammatically structured movement sequence as a basic semantic unit that is influenced by its syntactic placement and whose character exists relative to a symbolic and purposive activity (that is, a dance that serves a definite set of purposes for a community). One cannot help but think of ritual action in this context as exactly paralleling this description of dance. In both cases there are image-schematic structures or patterns that are connected to our everyday activities and that take on a symbolic importance, in the broad sense of that term as employed by Clifford Geertz,[16] for whom all sorts of bodily processes and organizations of physical elements have symbolic significance.

Kaeppler claims that such motifs are "carried in memory as templates for reproduction to be used spontaneously or in a well-thought-out choreography." This is surely correct, but we must be careful not to regard such schemata as *mere* templates, for that would make them overly rigid, fixed, and static. Thus, Kaeppler is careful to show how a given motif can be recognizable across many very different Tongan dances, and yet in each instance the motif takes on its own special meaning and symbolic import.

Kaeppler focuses on the *lakalaka* genre of Tongan dance, which is a type of choreographed movement (incorporating poetry) performed typically in formal ceremonies celebrating important events for the village or nation. What interests me in the *lakalaka* is the role of image-schematic structure that comes to be metaphorically elaborated via the procedure of *heliaki*. In general, *heliaki* is an esthetic principle of saying or doing one thing while meaning another. This metaphoric movement can reside either in the poetry itself, in the movement structure of the dance, or in the tension between what is said and what is done.

Let us look more closely at what is involved in such a movement of understanding. The dance itself involves the source-path-goal schema in a most basic way:

> *Lakalaka* literally means to keep on walking or to "step it out" and figuratively means to advance or make progress. Foot and leg movements are basically a continuous walking by stepping to one side, bringing the other foot to touch next to it ("place"), stepping to the opposite side, and touching the opposite foot to place.[17]

The *lakalaka* gives us a visual instantiation of the source-path-goal schema in its very movement structure (walking or "stepping it out") and it calls up the metaphorical interpretation of that structure as making progress toward some concrete or abstract goal.

Heliaki, then, is understood and experienced in relation to walking straight or stepping it out, for *heliaki* is literally "not going straight"—it is a deviation or swerving from the straight, proper, or normal path. So it, too, presupposes the source-path-goal schema in relation to which it gets its definition as a kind of deviation or a turning away from the path. Now, this not-going-straight schematic action can be accomplished by physical movements as well as by what is said. In both cases we have the metaphoric act of doing or saying one thing in order to mean another thing. We have a schema of diversion or swerving from the path that is manifested visually (in the movements of feet, legs, head, and hands) and verbally (in the poetry of the *lakalaka*). Kaeppler explains the various possibilities for *heliaki*:

> The most important movements in a *lakalaka* are the movements of the arms and hands. These movements form motifs, which are strung together in such a way that they can be said to "comment" on a word or concept of the verse of poetry that they accompany. In effect, they make visual some aspect of the text by alluding to it—another form of *heliaki*. The arm movements form a secondary abstraction, alluding to selected words of the text that themselves

allude to a deeper meaning. Or the arm movements, instead of alluding to the poetry, may allude to the deeper meaning, giving the superficial appearance that they have little if anything to do with the text. That is, the arm movements say one thing, but mean another. In short, the arm movements are the *heliaki* of the poetry while the poetry is the *heliaki* of the text.[18]

Kaeppler's account of the *lakalaka* and of *heliaki* illustrates the way in which patterns of movement (not just visual patterns) are structured by basic image schemata that are themselves source domains for metaphorical elaborations. The source-path-goal schema and the structure of "walking or stepping it out" apply first to actual bodily movements and then metaphorically to temporal processes of specified sorts. Likewise, the related image schema of not-going-straight is manifest both physically and metaphorically in terms of mental swerving or deviation of various kinds.

In sum, we have here imaginative, bodily-based schematic structures that connect up perception, bodily movement, mental acts, and language. Image-schematic structure is surely not the *only* means for connecting and relating these experiential realms, but it is so basic and pervasive that it tends to be implicated in virtually every aspect of our experience.

Finally, the example of Tongan dance is important because it highlights the shared, social, communal character of image-schematic structures. We have been exploring a level of imaginative activity that is the very means by which we inhabit and understand a *shared, public world.* Image schemata and their metaphorical extensions are shared and communally constituted in at least two senses. First, they depend heavily on our bodily makeup, on the limits provided by our biological nature. Second, they are matters of socially validated, transmitted, and preserved symbolic meanings. They provide a relatively stable, and yet modifiable, structural basis for functioning within, and seeking understanding of, our world.

By way of summary, it might be useful to relate my account of image-schematic structure to the central themes that loosely unite the essays in this volume. First, we have a growing body of evidence from cognitive psychology that there exists a general image-schematic level of cognitive processing.[19] Such structures of dynamic processes of perception, conceptualization, and reasoning have what appears to be a universal basis in our biological makeup. In particular, they are the chief means by which we have an ordered, meaningful bodily experience, through perception, image formation, manipulation of objects, and bodily movements.

Second, recent empirical studies in cognitive semantics have also demonstrated the indispensable role of image schemata in the development of complex networks of meaning.[20] Image schemata that are grounded in our bodily experience are the basis for metaphorical and metonymic mappings by which we understand various nonphysical, abstract domains, such as those of mental processes and epistemic relations.

Third, these are shared structures of imagination, which in this capacity is neither private nor idiosyncratic. On the contrary, it is the very means by which we communally inhabit a shared world and are able to communicate about our experience of it. Our conceptual systems are connected into a unified network in part via imaginative extensions and transformations of image schemata. There is no reason whatsoever to think of this form of imaginative activity as individualistic. Our capacity to share meaning and to reason is imaginative through and through, starting from our most mundane, unreflective bodily interactions and working up to our most impressive activities of hypothesis formation, problem solving, and reasoning. How these image-schematic patterns are elaborated and developed will depend upon the contingencies of our historical situation, with all its economic, political, religious, mythic, and ritualistic influences; so there will indeed be culturally varying selection and elaboration of the universal conceptual resources of imagination.

Finally, the evidence concerning memory is less clear, and I have been mostly speculative in suggesting that image-schematic structures are one of the principal forms of cognitive organization, and thus of memory. In cognitive psychology, schema theory has played a major role in constructivist views of memory—the schema provides the structure or skeleton around or upon which memories are (re)constructed. And, more recently, connectionist models of memory (which involve strengths of activation patterns of neural nets) find a place for something akin to image-schematic structure.[21]

However preliminary and exploratory the research on memory is at this time, the evidence for image-schematic bases for image formation, perception, concept formation, linguistic communication, and rational inference is strong indeed. And this should not surprise us at all, since we are embodied animals whose capacities developed to satisfy our needs for bodily activity within our physical environment (in the form of various sensory-motor capacities), to permit us to dwell socially within cultural communities with historical traditions (in the form of ritualistic, mythic, and linguistic representation and activity), and to allow us to reason abstractly about our ever-changing problematic physicosociocultural environment (in the form of imaginative patterns and processes of conceptualization, model formation, and inference). All of this life-sustaining and life-enhancing activity draws on the same general cognitive capacities that become specific to various tasks. So it is to be expected that image schemata are also the basis for our shared, constructive, historically situated, and culturally articulated memories, which are the crucial means whereby we are able to inhabit a shared, meaningful world.

Visual Narratives, Memory, and the Medieval *Esprit du System*

I

Aristotle, known to the Middle Ages as *the* philosopher *(philosophus dixit)*, created the enduring categories that are my subject: the difference between *mneme/memoria* and *anamnesis/reminiscentia*, between the ability "to remember by chance something previously experienced, allowing it to resurface in the soul," and the power "to concentrate oneself fully on something," recapturing from memory that which was forgotten.[1] It is not difficult to recognize in this formulation the origin of later conceptual pairings, such as *Gedächtnis* and *Erinnerung*, Proust's *mémoire involontaire* and *mémoire volontaire*, Warburg's *Mnemosyne* and *Sosphrosyne*, Halbwachs's *mémoire* and *histoire*, and Benjamin's *Eingedenken* and *Andenken*. Finally, along the same lines, there is Roland Barthes's argument, based less on psychological operations than on substantiality, assigning to historical material two essentially different qualities of attraction, which he terms *punctum* and *studium*. *Punctum* is the detail that radiates from the historical material, catching my eye and taking me by surprise; *studium* is something that has only an "average effect," but one which I can nonetheless put to good use for my own purposes through diligence and knowledge.[2] The specific characteristics of *mneme* and *anamnesis* may also be encountered in the basic structures of institutionalized memory-labor: this applies to places and works of objectified memory and also to their evocation in the historical sciences.

When we consider art history and its relation to the problems of memory and tradition, two approaches prevail as models. The "normal" approach involves conscious recourse to the remembered fact, which possesses the character of a quotation; it is removed from its older context and reinserted into a new one, which it legitimizes and authorizes, satisfying the need of history. The palace chapel of Charlemagne is a case in point: the columns of the octagon actually derive from Ravenna, as does the use of grated arches; they evoke the ancient world, Rome, and Byzantium, embodying the project of restoring the imperial idea and the *translatio imperii*. Not all examples are so programmatically packed. It is enough for an older formulation to be present: a woman sitting on a bed with her back to the viewer, a figure rushing out toward the picture plane, or a man extracting a thorn from his foot—all such borrowings facilitate artistic labor and have done so for centuries, making works of art that much more secure.

The second approach is essentially bound to the life work of Aby Warburg. For Warburg and his followers, recollection must pass a test: each recollection must be stored in the collective memory, where it is rooted in the primal experiences of sorrow, ecstasy, and passion that have left their indestructible *"engrammes"* on the psyche of humankind. When a memory arises from these depths, it must work in a "polarizing" way, as an "explosive," as a formula of liberation and activation. Warburg's notion of recollection originated in his response to the images of nymphs who, trailing their hair and garments, seemed to burst into the city dwellings of Florentine merchants; in themselves and as they functioned in his intellectual biography, they seemed to him comparable to Proust's *madeleine*, something that, in Barthes's sense, befalls one and does not allow itself to be controlled or bound, and that sets free unsuspected energies. These residues, this whole approach, stand under the sign of *Memoria*, just as the theory of quotations, borrowings, influences, and assimilations, understood as functions of the conscious labor of memory, may be gathered under the headword *Anamnesis*.[3]

The treatment of our subject sketched above, in its traditional form, is unsatisfying for three reasons. First, the relation of the remembered and remembering positions is comprehended in a completely undialectical manner, a posteriori. Neither approach evinces an understanding of, nor even an interest in, how an era inscribes itself in memory, what strategies it employs to recommend itself to posterity. Second—and this criticism is practically the flip side of the first—both approaches stand helpless in the face of the dual aspect of forgetfulness: the era that produces (for) forgetfulness is also the era that forgetfully receives. This deficiency has long been acknowledged;[4] its consequences, however, have not yet been considered, at least not in the field of art history. Third, there is the observation that prompted this essay: both approaches operate atomistically, driven by their basic rationale. This criticism addresses an incontrovertible fact. Both approaches conceive of an exchange between two epochs that proceeds without consequences or results for either of the participating systems, or, expressed differently, an exchange that does not take place between system and system. In neither case—quotation or pathos formula—does anything obviously accompany the transposition.

Warburg laid great stress on the guerrilla nature of his pictorial *"Urworte";* only as foreign bodies could they become liberators of sudden remembrance and as epiphanies assist Western expressive culture to break through the layers of decorum. And the theoreticians of quotation have repeatedly made it clear that it is precisely upon the historical material that assimilation works, transforming reminiscences and adapting them to the new context in such a way that their origins are no longer recognizable.[5] This means on the one hand that the *giving* formation does not have an aftereffect as a context, and on the other that the *receiving* context likewise remains untouched by the work of memory (leaving out of consideration for the moment the fact that the volcanic pathos formula can create an internal field of tension). This brings us to the counterquestion: Does transmission between eras always operate like the retail trade in commodities? Are systems also remembered and transmitted?[6] Or is it not rather than remembrance and transmission take place within, and with the help of, systems?

Other disciplines have long since addressed these questions. Literary criticism can claim that, insofar as it has occupied itself with the oral transmission of tradition, it has overcome atomistic conceptions, if it ever harbored them. Superficially considered, its concern with formulas and themes functions like the petty trade in motifs mentioned above. More is actually at stake, however, and this *more* can be understood as a systematic, interworking whole. Thus Franz Baeuml claims that spoken poetry

> is limited to two modes of existence: its utterance and its remembrance. Its utterance being ephemeral, its remembrance is critical and is served in the oral narrative tradition by the mnemonic functions of the means of oral epic composition:

> formulae and narrative themes are traditional and therefore
> quantitatively organized; themes are units of narrative composed
> primarily of an imagery of action, which, like the act of delivery
> itself, are practically arranged in temporal sequence; and
> abstractions, if not personified, rendered in visual imagery, or
> cast in the form of proverbial expressions, are absent.[7]

Thus here we have an applied art of memory, a multilayered system of transmission and realization correlated at various levels, not all elements of which have been named. One misses, for example, the technique of rhyme, and the large and small divisions into sections, episodes, days, and so on.

Until now, no one has attempted to apply the whole apparatus of this oral delivery school to the contemporaneous pictorial production of the early and high Middle Ages, nor has anyone tried to reformulate this apparatus to suit the considerable demands of image production. What then, in the language of images, would be the formulas, themes, rhythms, rhymes, or patterns capable of being remembered? And how would a whole constituted of transmission look? I think that these are legitimate questions, since the conditions for the transmission of oral and pictorial information are completely comparable in the epochs of which we speak. Just as the bard or *jongleur* could not depend on written notes, the painter or sculptor did not have at his disposal drawings or standard formulas that could function as a practical storehouse for whole compositions. The stock small-format drawing (what Oertel calls *Vorratzeichnung*) and the preparatory sketch are relatively late phenomena in the history of artistic method. Without such means of support and repetition the professional demands placed on mnemonic ability would be enormous; useful mnemonic techniques take on in themselves an existential necessity, and the artistic realization becomes also a function of memory work. Thus we can observe with Susanne Küchler that "the question . . . is not why and how imagery continues, but what difference its mode of transmission creates in the appearance of the art."[8]

II

Let us now consider two pictorial cycles that treat the story of the Prodigal Son. Separated by two hundred years, both are monumental works, meant for the public space of a church.[9] The earlier cycle is an example of French stained glass, produced around 1220 to decorate an aisle window in the choir of the Cathedral of Bourges; its position ensured its visibility (fig. 20). Aside from the first three sections (fig. 21, 1–3), the so-called signature panels dedicated to the donor's occupation—in this case that of a tanner— the cycle consists of seventeen episodes narrating the parable. In contrast to the biblical text, the stations of the Prodigal's worldly encounters are painted with great gusto. He is shown as a chivalrous, overconfident youth departing from his father's house with an ample inheritance, visiting the brothel and carousing there, being expelled from the brothel after having been robbed, attempting to change his luck by playing at cards in the tavern, failing and being ejected once again, working as a swineherd, repenting, and finally returning to the welcoming feast at his father's house, where he is reconciled with his two brothers (figs. 22, 23). These scenes are strung together in a way that underscores the story's unity, its expository and sequential logic, and extracts fully the narrative possibilities of basic situations. This important window, along with closely related examples in other churches, is among the first depictions of the subject. Lacking an iconographic tradition, the Prodigal Son theme became increasingly popular in the thirteenth century and was treated not only in monumental painting but also in dramatic and epic recitation, often in free and lively variations.

Two hundred years later, on a tapestry now at the Marburg University Museum, little had changed in this regard (fig. 24). Whoever can read the stained-glass window can also understand the much shorter narrative program of the tapestry. Here only eight of the window's scenes are depicted: the Prodigal with his inheritance departing from his father's house, the journey, the arrival at the brothel, the merrymaking, the ejection from the brothel, the herding of swine, the return to the paternal abode, and the ensuing feast (figs. 25–27).

The figures populating these scenes have been modified, as has the mode of dress, which is contemporary. The tapestry medium also brings about certain changes: the narrator, taking advantage of the tapestry's size and function—it is larger and positioned more accessibly than the window—allows us to follow the progress of the overfull purse from the hand of the father to the money belt of the brothel keeper, details that would have been lost in the window. The same holds true for the Prodigal's elaborate coiffure, which is displayed prominently. By contrast, the window operates like a form of colored shadow-theater; its scenes are more concise and intense, relying on striking expressive gestures (figs. 22, 23, 26, 27).

Figure 20. Cathedral of Bourges,
Window of the Prodigal Son,
stained glass, ca. 1210–15. Photo
after Cahier and Martin.

Figure 21. Cathedral of Bourges,
Window of the Prodigal Son,
diagram.

Figure 22. Cathedral of Bourges, *The Prodigal Son Sets Out for the World*. Foto Caviness.

These superficial variations cannot, however, alter the fact that an identical set of narrative units articulates the story in both cycles. The figures on the window and on the tapestry correspond to the concrete and contemporaneous *parole,* which is nourished by the unchanging repertory of *langue,* by the lexicon and grammar of narrative language. What has been written about the *chansons de geste* also applies to the *image de geste:* "the *langue* in which the *chansons de geste* are codified systematically limits its repertories, thereby producing very repetitive texts in which small effects of variation stand out in high relief."[10] This statement characterizes the level at which we are operating; beyond merely formulaic linguistic units, we are dealing with themes or motifs that generate fundamental narrative situations, and do so as stereotypically as does formulaic narration. Parting, journey, arrival, and hospitality are motifs to be found in the cycles under discussion. Other narrative units that belong to the standard repertory are the contest, the tournament, and the love scene.

It is important to note that these units are not simply building blocks, but function rather like links in a chain, connecting and leading in a definite

Figure 23. Cathedral of Bourges,
The Prodigal Son Herding Pigs.
Foto Caviness.

direction. As in the case of formulas, aids to memory are built into these
units; whoever employs them knows not only what to say at the moment,
but also what follows next within the probable frame of the narrative
parcours. That we must take note of this suggests that we have not accepted
the possibilities of a *langue* of narration, of a grammar outside a repertory.
I quote again from a text that sees in Middle English romances formulaic
structures at work as hypostases, from the largest down to the smallest
linguistic units:

> The basic double patterns of the two major linking structures
> *(separation-restoration, love-marriage)* provide the foundation for
> the story, with required (and to some degree ordered) episodic
> slots that may be filled by some scenes but not by others. These
> scene-patterns, in turn, possess a formulaic slot structure which
> may be filled by certain motif-patterns. Finally, the motifs are
> made up of structured sequences of syntagms, or formulaic

language structures, which constitute the stylistic texture of the work.[11]

One cannot of course transfer this structural model in its entirety. What is important for our purposes is that, by moving from above downward, the model poses a question that seems to me decisive: Do the elements, whatever level they occupy, possess "only" a certain connectional logic? Does the story-syntagm surrender itself to a directional principle, conforming to definite transformational and iterational rules when it changes positions? In other words, must "departure" necessarily follow "arrival"? Must the struggle with evil elements be developed in three episodes before it can progress further? Or is there a larger, regulatory structure? And if so, is this structure necessarily identical to that "immanent level" or "grammar of depths," in which narratology claims—or hopes—to see forged a "kind of common structural pedigree in which the narrativity is placed and ordered prior to its manifestation?"[12]

Susan Wittig, whom we quoted on Middle English romances, uses the term "major linking structures" to designate precisely this abstract level of depth structures—*"separation-restoration, love-marriage"*—a level that French narratology has tried to articulate in a series of alternative models such as Greimas's sequence of "functions": *"Concentration of misfortune—loss—removal of the element of error—reward of the hero,"* a chain of functions other researchers have reduced even further to formulas such as Dundes's *"lack—lack liquidated."*[13]

Figure 24. Marburg University Museum, *Tapestry of the Prodigal Son*, ca. 1425. Bildarchiv Foto Marburg.

There can be no doubt that our pictorial stories hold their own when compared to the narrative elements of such schemata, for, like these, the pictorial stories are built upon separation and reunification (along with the series of adventures that lies in between). The pictorial cycles replace the *love-marriage* schema with the schema of youthful rebellion against the patriarchal figure to whom, by story's end, the youth is again subjugated. In this family tale starting with rebellion against and ending in subjugation to the father, we can recognize a double codification especially character-istic of medieval storytelling,[14] a classical syntagm of *separation-return,* which is, ultimately, cosmologically based.

The only problem with such schemata is that they play a calculably small role in the actual execution, realization, and transmission of the narrative work. The researcher, having erected the generic narrative for-mula "A versus non-A, non-A versus A" (for example Oedipus: seeing yet blind, blind yet seeing), must then admit that "narrative texts have at their disposal . . . almost unlimited possibilities of differentiation and distinction of opposite concepts."[15] This is precisely the problem. Although these contradictory terms present the large perspective, they do not assist at all in unfolding the stations of the story, nor venture in beyond the story's outermost perimeters. To address this crux, one might develop a hypo-stasic model, as Wittig has done; or one might probe further and ask whether or not a continuous regulating structure, a generative pattern, is at work, existing at the level of syntax, above the depth structure (which is occupied with content).

Our two pictorial stories are not simply divided into the same se-quence of thematic units; they simultaneously organize the sequence on the basis of a shared matrix, doing so despite the fact that they are articulated in two quite different structural forms and media. At Bourges the window utilizes an elaborate geometrical pattern, expressed in five-part quatrefoils and three-part rows (fig. 21). At Marburg on the other hand we have a bilateral division into two parallel rows of quadratic pictorial sections (fig. 25). Nevertheless, the typological order that governs the sequence of both cycles and groups them into a recognizable unity is identical.

Whether one calls it narration through oppositions or internal typol-ogy, the key to the structure lies in each scene's having a double (with the exception of the donor representations and the reunification scene at the apex of the window). Each scene is mirrored on either side of an axis that divides different orders of being and worth: Good and Evil, the Familiar and the Foreign, Above and Below, Before and After, the Serious and the

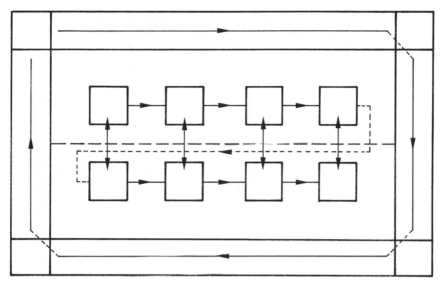

Figure 25. Marburg, *Tapestry of the Prodigal Son*, diagram.

Comic. One can see this principle at work most clearly in the Marburg tapestry, where the connectional logic of the thematic units coincides with the overall logic of a systematic narration. The narrator, responding to the horizontal progression of the design, adheres to the rule of rows, exercising it with textbook strictness. In both rows a complete set of interrelated actions is played out through mirror images: the hero departs; he journeys and is in a transitional situation, a foreign place; he is received; and then, after this three-part sequence, sufficient and complete in itself, there follows, as if after a colon, a fourth position—the feast—which constitutes the end, the closing point of the row. Fulfilling its primary function, the parallelism of rows enables a vertical reading, producing four contrasting pairs: cheerful parting from the family versus ejection from the brothel; in a foreign place, accompanied, versus in a foreign place, alone and bereft; reception by prostitutes versus reception by the father; feast in the brothel versus feast in the familial abode. These oppositions produce the following sequence: $++--/--++$. This is as symmetrical as the order of logical succession, further proof that the pictorial narrative is both sequence and system.

Moreover, just as the negative-positive notation contains an enjambment, so the circularity of events negotiates the change of rows. Three

Figure 26. Marburg, *The Prodigal Son Sets Out for the World*. Bildarchiv Foto Marburg.

sections are devoted to the paternal abode, and therefore three to the brothel. The events relating to the brothel encompass the end and the beginning of a row, while the scenes in the father's house occupy the beginning and the end of the whole story, emphasizing the cyclical structure of the parable, and associating it with the encircling inscriptions and the enframing borders. We have thus not one but three semantic axes or directional senses: the horizontal of the pictorial sequence; the vertical of the antithetical pairs; and the enclosing circuit of the lettering, the borders, and the parable.

The Marburg narrator operates with eight pictorial sections, the narrator at Bourges with sixteen. At Marburg we have a single and relatively simple configuration of two parallel rows. At Bourges we have two alternating geometric configurations, the rows and the quatrefoils, which each have up to five pictorial sections. The correspondences of scenes do not involve alternation between flip sides, as at Marburg. The law of neighborhood plays no role here. Rather, one must either work upward, reviewing two to three sections in order to find the counterpiece, or one must have first understood the law of the configuration—this is the novel message of the window at Bourges.

Naturally, eight pairs cannot rhyme as ideally as four, and ultimately this configuration, as well as the thematic argument it engenders, is super-imposed upon a truly animated and exciting story. In this configuration, antitheses cannot always be read as moral constructions, and the narrator sometimes relies on simple analogies of form, which have no status as argument. We can clarify this point by comparing two three-part rows, for instance numbers 9,10,11 and 17,18,19 in figure 21. In contrast to the five-part complexes (such as 12,13,14,15,16) they fulfill the expectations of unity of action. Divided like chapters, they focus on feasts—the banquet in the brothel and the banquet celebrating the Prodigal's return to the father's house. The round centerpieces (10,18) are related to each other by analogies of form *and* content; the narrative context, in conjunction with details of the story, allows us to identify the roundels as versions of the same event, differentiated as good and evil. These analogies, normative for the window, are contravened by the pictorial sections at right; the ejection of the Prodigal (11) and the return of the older son from the field (19) have nothing in common as events. The artist uses relations of form to establish a common denominator. In both scenes we have a man standing at the

Figure 27. Marburg, *The Prodigal Son Herding Pigs*. Bildarchiv Foto Marburg.

threshold, garbed as a farmer with a knee-length green garment and red breeches. A third variation is offered by the pictorial sections at left (9,17), which share neither analogies of form nor, except weakly, of content. Above and below are preparations for the feast: the greeting and crowning of the guest, the slaughter of a calf. Here the analogy involves humorous metaphorical play, rather than positive-negative ordering: prostitutes decorate the Prodigal as if he were an animal being readied for slaughter.

In fact, this would be a contemporaneous, not an anachronistic reading. In his sermon *Ad virgines et puellas,* Gilbert of Tournais (d. 1270) said about prostitutes and the whorelike behavior of women: "It is clear that when they are luxuriously and indecently bejeweled they capture young men. . . . I compare the young man who encounters and follows such a woman on the street—a woman who in whore-like costume is out to hunt and capture souls—to a bull that is being led to the slaughterhouse."[16]

Having examined these rather problematic pairs, we may return to the five-part clusters (4,5,6,7,8 and 12,13,14,15,16), reading them as antitheses: in one the wrongheaded son demands his inheritance; in the other he loses a card game (4,12). In both scenes money, its acquisition and loss, is central. In the first scene the future looks bright, but not so in the second. The next two scenes take up the motif of parting: the father sees his enriched son off with words of good advice; later the Prodigal, robbed of all means of support, stands expelled from the brothel by the prostitutes (5,13). The center quatrefoils build upon the contrast of the two sons and their labor in the fields (6,4). The older son, his own master, works his acreage, employing noble animals. The younger son, by contrast, must dutifully submit himself to strangers, working as an inferior who guards unclean animals. The next section gives us two versions of life in foreign environs: the cheerful entry of the Prodigal as master and lord over his animals and his squire, and, at the lowest point of his journey, the Prodigal at the end of his tether, reduced to servitude, a servant even to beasts. Finally, the last and uppermost sectors of the quatrefoil (8,16) display the by now familiar scenic reversal: the Prodigal Son is received twice, at the brothel and at his father's house.

III

We propose that the Middle Ages transmitted their popular pictorial stories not only in sets of standardized episodes but also in the form of a narrative matrix. Comparison of the works at Bourges and Marburg suggests the deliberate implementation of two mnemonic strategies: that of theme and of schema. It is difficult to believe that the material simply fell into place. The transformation of material, its reorganization into another format, a quite different configuration of argument, and another medium, presupposes the existence of known structures independent of the motifs. These structures were, we suppose, cultivated and maintained—insofar as the matrix is concerned—somewhat differently from the mnemonic practices of the *jongleurs* and bards, being positioned rather in the domain of rhetoric, where since antiquity mnemonic technique had been established as a disciplinary aid. This assumption is supported by the fact that this art of disposition was first applied to the highly structured window cycles of French cathedral naves. What is more, we are dealing with a time that, besides experiencing structural reforms in music, book layout, and architecture, saw a major epochal change in sermonizing.[17] This change occurred as much in the quantitative as in the qualitative dimension. For the first time in Christendom, preaching became a regular function of religious life, a medium through which to address the masses, with its own specialists, schools, and techniques. More importantly, however, the sermon was given in a completely new form.[18] The homily, the recounting of a liturgically engaged biblical text, was succeeded by the highly artificial structures of the so-called thematic sermon.

The relation of window and sermon involves neither reproduction nor direct translation, however, for the new sermon form was not narrative and cited short biblical passages, sometimes only four or five words in length: by contrast the homily consisted of the rigorous structuring of the text. The thirteenth-century teacher of preaching evinced a "subdividing mentality"[19] when he defined his object as the "interpretation of the Holy Word through division and subdivision."[20] After choosing the theme, the next crucially important task was *divisio,* the division of the biblical passages and of the sermon according to words and to arguments. A compositional scaffolding was erected and enumerated ("preaching by numbers"), with the aim of arriving at a balanced presentation of all essential points of view, and with the further aim of achieving concord among the parts *(Stimmigkeit).* One of the favorite means of attaining this goal was the *parallelismus membrorum,* the analogical ordering of the arguments or parts in assonance or perfect rhymes. Here the mnemonic dimension of this procedure becomes especially evident: the thematic sermons were memorized with the help of these divisions and frequently transmitted only as a compositional frame which could be written down and passed on by a listener. Although this frame was in Latin, the sermon itself was frequently given in the vernacular, its text made even more accessible by several devices: enumeration, rhyming of cue words at the beginning and end of lines, and parallelisms or oppositions of content. The best arguments, according to one teacher of preaching, would sometimes have to be forfeited when no apt rhyme word could be found. Does this not finally establish the primacy of *divisio* and compositional scaffolding over *partes,* that is, of arguments and thoughts over narrative motives and themes? And had not this transformed *ars praedicandi,* under the pressure of practical necessities, long since exceeded what ancient mnemonic techniques could offer?

Renate Lachmann has recently given a concise summary of the historical reception of the ancient art of memory, based on the theory and practice of rhetoric which survived almost intact into the Middle Ages:

> The fundamental operation of devising places, *loci,* into which the images of remembrance, *imagines,* are layed down; the technique of transposing the object of memory into its pictorial representation; the creation of spatial sequences, *collocatio,* passage through which restores the thing to be recalled—these operations obey special rules. These rules regulate the semantic relations between the thing to be remembered (the signification) and the image (the signifier), give modes their characteristic features and their power to impress, and direct the choice of the memory space itself, which can be an imagined architecture with many rooms (a house, a temple), a garden, or a labyrinth.[21]

An example is perhaps required. Inspired by our story of inheritance, let us choose the criminal theme of legacy-hunting, figured by Cicero in a characteristic image later adopted by Albertus Magnus, among others. "When a prosecutor says of the accused that he poisoned a person for his inheritance and this with the knowledge of many witnesses," we can place this in our memory thus:

> A sick person in bed (the image of the dead one), the accused next to his bed, in his left hand a cup and in his right a document, and next to him a doctor holding the testicles of a ram. The cup reminds us of the poison, the document of the conferral of the bequest, the testicles of the witnesses [*testiculi—testis*], and the ram of the legal process against the accused.[22]

Everything here is developed according to the rules of art. The objects have become images, positioned in space and carefully ordered; precisely because of this, the characterizing image has become monstrous, its very monstrosity ensuring memorability. The problem was surely aggravated by the fact that Albertus translated *medicus,* the index finger, as doctor, thus introducing a third person into the scene. All this raises the sobering question posed by Frances Yates: "But might it not have been easier to remember all this through the actual facts *(propria)* rather than through these metaphors *(metaphorica)*?"[23] This question only confirms our impasse, so long, that is, as we continue to believe in the possibility and necessity of an art of memory.

The authoritative medieval treatments of the *ars memoriae*—the writings, above all, of Albertus Magnus and Thomas Aquinas—present by turns a disappointing and a moving picture.[24] Disappointing, because they become creative at the wrong place and with the wrong material; they are at pains to bring the capacities of *Memoria* and *Reminiscentia* within the province of scholastic-Christian psychology, in order better to understand the operation of mental processes. They submit the ancient psychology of temperament to an act of *interpretatio christiana.* Thomas Aquinas strives above all to free the whole problem of memory from the domain of rhetoric, reserving it for Christian ethics. There would be nothing to find fault with here were it not for the fact that our authors, revering the ancient models, assimilate them in detail, even while pursuing their own aims, aims alien to the tangible, practical functions fulfilled by the ancient art of memory. The prescriptions cited above are transmitted, glossed, and sanctioned. The scholastics do not concern themselves with alternative examples; neither as teachers nor as preachers do Albertus and Thomas acknowledge the demands of the new age.

Yet this deference toward the models, moving in its insistence, accommodates new structures, which fulfill the very task assigned to the ancient mnemonic techniques. I refer to the scholastic *modus argumentativus* with its three stages: "division into many parts," "rhythmical consonances," and "forced harmonizations."[25] These are the terms of Roger Bacon, who wished to apply the three stages both to textual interpretation and to sermons, enterprises closely connected within the scholastic regime. So too, the new representational and conceptual forms of theology and philosophy required preservation through oral transmission—as secure support for the teachers and as comprehensible schema for the students. While the thematic sermon is different from the scholastic treatise, com-

mentary, or pedagogical lecture, the latter three, especially as described by
Panofsky, can be compared in essential structure to sermons:

> (1) totality (sufficient enumeration), (2) arrangement according to
> a system of homologous parts and parts of parts (sufficient
> articulation), and (3) distinctness and deductive cogency (sufficient
> interrelation)—all this enhanced by the literary equivalent of
> Thomas Aquinas' *similitudines:* suggestive terminology,
> *parallelismus membrorum,* and rhyme.[26]

What the pedagogical lecture and the sermon share above all is the "will to
wholeness," the primacy of the overall plan, the conceptual organization in
terms of hierarchical structure, and the a priori possibility of representing
this unity in comprehensive schemata or diagrams. So the scholastic treatise
proceeds, following the order diagrammed in the outline with which it
begins; so the preacher constructs the framework of his text, using cue
words, rhymes, and *figures;* so the *dispositor* designs the church window,
accommodating his narrative material to the structural armature of iron
and lead.

In short, the memorability of these works and their power to impress
upon the mind are functions of *divisio* rather than of the ancient mnemonic
techniques, which would require their translation into images and their
positioning in a spatial sequence. With all due respect to Yates, the following passage from the *Art of Memory* seems eccentric and ultimately
misleading: "The extraordinary thought now arises that if Thomas Aquinas
memorized his own *Summa* through corporeal similitudes disposed on
places following the order of its parts, the abstract *Summa* might be cor-
porealized in memory into something like a Gothic cathedral full of images
on its ordered places."[27]

The medieval theoreticians would have been able to infer from their
models only that order can be a crucial aid to memory. The ancients
considered memory in terms of criteria such as perspicuity, similarity,
substitutability, and continuation; the potential of a stored structure, of a
diagrammatic compartmentalization of memorabilia, remained foreign to
them. Even Thomas Aquinas identifies order with an organized chain of
association, contradicting his own mnemonic practice by anchoring the
second rule of his art of memory to the principle of continuity:

> Secondly it is necessary that a man should place in a considered
> order those things he wishes to remember, so that from one

remembered point progress can easily be made to the next. Whence the Philosopher says in the book *De memoria:* "some men can be seen to remember from places. The cause of which is that they pass rapidly from one step to the next."[28]

This passage from Aristotle is among Aquinas's most successful propositions, but the process he articulates always breaks off at the same point. One reads further: "Thus one arrives at the color white through milk, to air from the color white, to dampness from air and on to Autumn from there—and this would be the season which someone sought in their memory."[29] It seems possible to doubt whether this passage concerns the doctrine of the places of memory *(loci),* as defined by Cicero; more to the point, the context makes clear that what occupied the philosophers and their disciples was not an ordering in the sense of a prior structure and program, but rather a theory of association relating to a serial ordering of ideas.

The second passage often cited from Aristotle does little to adjust the first: "It is easier to remember things which possess some order, such as, for example, the objects of mathematics."[30] All the same, it was this very passage that stimulated Thomas Aquinas to resolve his reflections on memory and remembrance:

> To achieve good memory and remembrance we can extract from the Premises the following four useful recommendations: 1. One must strive to bring that which one would remember into a specific order. 2. One must anchor the object deeply and consciously in the mind. 3. One must frequently reflect upon it according to the chosen order. 4. One must begin at the correct point when one wishes to remember it.[31]

It is beyond our scope to ask whether these recommendations derive simply from the premises, and how they resolve other trains of thought, answering in surprising ways to personal, improved, long interiorized, and practiced insights.[32] Self-reflection and a revised course of action did not result from Aquinas's recommendations. It should therefore come as no surprise that ancient mnemonic techniques, as transmitted by medieval exponents, were marginal to medieval mnemonic praxis. In the *artes praedicandi,* made necessary by the thirteenth-century reform of sermons, one finds few references to the great authorities, although these were well known to the learned authors of the handbooks who maintained ties to scholastic philosophy.[33]

Our critique can also serve to revise what Yates, inclined to favor text above praxis, writes in *The Art of Memory:* that for the Middle Ages on the whole ancient mnemonics remained the model—an inference that contravenes the practice of medieval rhetoric[34]—and that "Christian didactic art . . . may owe more than we know to classical rules which have never been thought of in this context."[35] In adjusting Yates's formulation, we must substitute for the classical *ars memoriae* the quite different, seminal practices that can articulate circumstances specific to the age: the mnemonic techniques of the sermon, of scholasticism, of oral poetry, and of the oral transmission of images. As regards the last, our examples suggest the following thesis: the transition from what Lachmann calls the "image deposit" to "systematics," far from occurring for the first time in the late Middle Ages and the Renaissance, had already taken place in the thirteenth century.[36] This is a thesis that implies, and even argues, that from then on these two forms, "image deposit" and "systematics," image and diagram, would coexist.[37]

IV

It would be a mistake to evaluate the new mnemonic technique solely for its functions. Intellectual techniques, besides complying with purely technical criteria—set styles and forms of thought—tend as a rule to accomplish more than their established tasks. This suggests that intellectual techniques answer to exigencies that are more than simply practical. With this in mind I shall address in closing three related aspects of the new, unified conception of memory.

Why the story of the Prodigal Son is, I believe, among the first to be placed in the tensional space *(Spannungsraum)* of the *modus argumentativus,* can be clearly explained. The narrative windows of the first half of the thirteenth century belong to three parties with thoroughly divergent interests: civic patrons, clergy, and the stained-glass painters. Of particular importance were the civic patrons, who were as a rule members of corporate bodies, and preferred long and lively narrative material, such as the lives of the saints, legends and miracles, parables and, occasionally, tales of chivalric adventure. (See for example the window at Chartres with the story of Julianus, or rather of Charlemagne.) The manner in which these subjects are presented reveals the style of the occupational storyteller, the *jongleur:* the window at Bourges, along with its pendants, consists without a doubt of *matière jongleuresque*. The churchmen were responsible for advising the stained-glass painters on religious matters and had the task, too, of distributing the material contained by the geometric formal skeleton. For them, the first step toward grasping the pictorial form and content, elements which were often not theirs to choose, was the strict application of the process of systematic narrative. Even when the cleric determined neither the themes nor their moral-didactic character, he controlled their articulation as figural geometry. As in a sermon, he could anchor the message to a prevailing structure, proving his authoritative command of resources. He demonstrated an art that circumscribed, that restrained dangerous license, that imposed a high degree of structure in order to foreclose any threat to order.

The parallels with rhetoric obviate the effort to differentiate between technical, persuasive, and aesthetic components. As a new study of thematic preaching correctly states: "The tendency to conceive *distinctiones* and *divisiones* in a form which seems to approximate rhymed verse is the externalization of an aesthetic element inherent to the sermon."[38] The structure does not simply encompass the author's mode of address and narrative construction, making them surveyable, memorizable and portable. The compositional frame also makes itself recognizable as a system, shaping the public's expectations and receptive attitudes; it is an aesthetic factor, as well, which attests that the material has been fully grasped and adapted. All in all, the compositional frame is a rhetorical medium, which makes it possible to apply rhetorical figures, and ultimately to classify statements, pruning and developing them according to the standard of an argumentative figure.

To my earlier assertion that artistic realization is a function of susceptivity to memorization, I would now add, speaking in addition for the Middle Ages, that artistic quality and effect are also functions of such susceptivity. "This (mnemonic) technique is central to the capacity to reproduce works that are convincing in their visual appearance."[39] Here we have a Darwinian motif: only that which impresses itself in presentation, allowing itself to be fully memorized, has a chance of surviving in the cultural memory. Harald Weinrich has expressed this observation in a concise formula: "Beyond the special historical character of aesthetics, style can also be termed the embodiment of all that is good for memory."[40]

In the highly structured enterprises we have considered, hubris and servility are closely bound. Whoever could construct his story or sermon perfectly, using argument and counterargument, sequence and system, could appoint himself the erudite *rhetor Augustinus,* applying his notion of a world structured according to rhetorical ideas. That God had "embellished the world like a splendid poem with antitheses," could be read in St. Augustine's *City of God.* And furthermore:

> The so-called antitheses are indeed the most beautiful of the embellishments of speech, one could call them in Latin *opposita* or better yet *contraposita.* . . . And just as such a confrontation of opposites makes the beauty of the style, so the beauty of the universe is fashioned through confrontations of opposites, in a style which does not deal in words but in things. This thought is clearly expressed in *Ecclesiastes:* "As evil is confronted by good, death by life, so are the pious by the sinful. And so should you consider the works of the Almighty in pairs, the one confronting the other."[41]

ADRIENNE L. KAEPPLER

Memory and Knowledge in the Production of Dance

Dance: A Socially Constructed Movement System

Socially constructed movement systems occur in all known human societies. In some, such as our own, one or more movement systems may be
considered a "visual art." Such an art form, which involves both process
and product, may be terminologically distinguished from other movement
systems used by that society and conceptualized in a manner similar to the
way in which our society conceptualizes *dance*. Not all societies, however,
consider dance or the movement dimension of certain activities to be an
art—even though such movement systems have esthetic characteristics.
Indeed, if performed in the dark, a dance might not even be seen—except
perhaps by the gods. But for the purposes of this paper, dance will be
considered a visual art and therefore appropriate for the focus of this
symposium on memory, cognition, and imagery in the visual arts. Dance,
of course, is also a kinesthetic art concerned with movement memory, but
this complex element will not be examined here.

Dance is a cultural form resulting from creative processes that manipulate (that is, handle with skill) human bodies in time and space in such
a way that the formalization of movement is intensified much as poetry
intensifies the formalization of language. The cultural form produced—a
dance in this case—though transient, has structured content, is a visual
manifestation of social relations, and may be the subject of an elaborate
esthetic system.

Dance and Memory

As a dimension of various activities, structured movement may be the main element of ritual—stately, processional, or cathartic. Or dance may be ceremonial, as are the formal Polynesian dances in which the praises of the chiefs are sung. Or it may be entertainment, in forms varying from watching a ballet to taking part in a disco. The movement dimensions of these various activities, or dances if I may so call them, may be participatory, such as taking part in a Greek line dance, or presentational, such as the formal performance of a Hawaiian hula. The physical movements of a dance may simply be memorized by a performer but never understood, or they may be cognitively understood by a specific individual who may never perform them. Simple memorization of movement is usually tied to language, rhythm, or pantomime. For example, when learning a Greek line dance, one might be told to do a certain four-count step three times, then a second four-count step three times, and to alternate these throughout a given piece of music. Or one might be taught a Hawaiian hula with pantomimic movements that would be recognizable to the student. Without knowing the structure of the movement system, however, the memorizer will not know how to use these pieces of movement in another context.

Alternatively, a person who has never performed in a ballet may cognitively understand not only the structure of the movement system but how Russian ballet differs from French ballet, and may be able to tell the differences between the choreography of Diaghilev, Ashton, and Bournonville. Such an individual, without ever having memorized a movement sequence bodily, may yet be able to call up mentally fifth position for the lower body and the arms and may be able to visualize a complex series of movements that make up a named motif. Or in yet a different manifestation of movement, a dancer of the fox-trot or waltz can move his partner through complex maneuvers on a large or small dance floor, all the while talking about subjects of interest.

Is the body remembering something separately from the brain as Cartesians might claim? Is the body "thinking"? Is the body imaging on its own? Is imaging visual, physical, or both? And how is imaging related to language? Movements acquired visually out of focal awareness and physically through habit can be validated when they are reproduced either with the body itself or through movement notation. More important than specific movements or their combination into a specific dance, however, is knowledge of the movement system. Movement systems are structured in ways similar to language systems—so much so, that we speak of them as having grammar, syntax, and rules. Indeed, it is difficult to sort out just what part language plays in movement acquisition or memory. Williams argues that dance is "linguistically tied" and "a form of semantic anthropology."[1] In my view, although mind and body are not separable, the mind has such powerful organizing abilities that its categorizing and structuring work is manifested in vocal language, visual language, and physical (body) language. Although these are really not separable, habit and long training might make it "feel like" the body is remembering on its own. In many ways it seems that body language is more closely related to visual language than it is to spoken language—but all of these languages are tied to the structuring mind, which is culturally influenced.

Memory and Motifs

What is it in dance that is remembered? While a dance exists in space and time, after it is performed what images are remembered and recalled? I believe that what can be called up visually and also what is remembered by the body are what I have termed motifs. The way the motifs are remembered in simultaneous and chronological order is assisted by a linguistic type of recall much like memorizing a poem—which is often assisted by rhythm. Beyond a specific performance or a rendition of the movements of a particular sequence of motifs is the structure of a dance and the system in which it is socially and culturally constructed. Through a specific choreography—a surface manifestation of the movement system—a sequence of motifs is given meaning. Although meaning might be linguistically tied, the motifs themselves—which can be visually and physically recalled—are structurally based.

Let me now elaborate on what I mean by motifs and then give an empirical example of how they are used in establishing meaning. On the way we may learn how the motifs become visual and/or physical and how or why they are held in memory.

Movement Motifs

Motifs are culturally structured pieces of movement tied to a specific dance tradition or genre. They are not interchangeable from one dance tradition to another. Although motifs taken from a traditional sequence may be used in the choreography of a dance drama for a Western audience, for example, the motifs themselves would be recognizable as Hawaiian or Korean or Javanese. In the Chinese ballet *Red Detachment of Women,* for instance, the choreography is Chinese, but the movement motifs are recognizable as Western ballet motifs. Motifs are held in memory by the choreographer, usually by the performer, and often by the audience; we will examine the memory and imaging power of choreographer, performer, and audience later in this paper.

Motifs are culturally grammatical sequences of movement made up of smaller pieces of movement, which I have characterized elsewhere as kinemes and morphokines (the terms represent movement analogues of phonemes and morphemes).[2] Kinemes, like phonemes, have no meaning in themselves and are the basic units from which the dance of a given tradition is built. Morphokines are the smallest units that have meaning as movement in the structure of a specific movement system. (*Meaning* here does not refer to narrative or pictorial meaning.) Only certain combinations of kinemes are meaningful as movement in a specific dance tradition. Morphokines may be found in more than one dance tradition, but it is the way they recur in a consistent manner in the next larger piece of movement— the motif—that is culture specific.

Out of the spectrum of all possible bodily movement, each dance or movement tradition selects and uses only a small part and combines these movements in culturally specific ways. These combinations or motifs are choreographed (that is, ordered simultaneously and chronologically) into culturally or generically grammatical sequences. These motifs are carried in memory as templates for reproduction to be used spontaneously or in a well-thought-out choreography. The Hawaiian dancer uses recalled motifs when called upon to perform during a *lū'au,* perhaps to a piece of music to which she has never before performed, just as Balanchine used known ballet motifs to choreograph a pas de deux for *Swan Lake.* Motifs can also be reworked—usually by adding or substituting morphokines or kinemes from the same tradition—or transferred from genre to genre within an overall dance tradition. Some genres, such as Western modern dance, are more maleable and open than others to the incorporation of motifs from other traditions. The choreographies of Ted Shawn and La Meri, for example, incorporated motifs from such cultures as India and Indonesia, and some of these motifs have persisted within modern dance traditions, but they are recognized as being "ethnic."

Motifs are frequently occurring combinations of morphokines that form short entities in themselves, similar to motifs in other visual arts and in folklore. They are recalled and reembodied in dances, and through this embodiment they acquire meaning and thus become images that take on cognitive status. When a new dance is produced, it is not only the motifs and their sequencing into a choreographed form that are of interest. In addition, who performs the motifs, how many performers there are, how the performers interact with each other and the audience (if there is one), and how they use vertical and horizontal space can tell us a great deal about the social and cultural context—and the culture itself.

In a new choreography of *Swan Lake*, for example, besides thinking of the movement motifs that will be used, the choreographer must image the stage size and layout, how many swans there will be, how one swan will perform differently from the corps de ballet, for which two bodies the pas de deux will be designed, and so on. Here the choreographer will bring to memory all the versions of *Swan Lake* seen earlier including those that he or she has choreographed in the past. These may be reproduced accurately, consciously rejected, reorganized or reworked, or reproduced according to the choreographer's memory. If the performers are not technically proficient, the reproduction will not be the same as the choreographer's image of the product. And the next time *Swan Lake* is recalled, this version will be added to all other versions.

In a Tongan dance called *ula* the structure requires that every second motif be the same, and this motif must alternate with a series of different motifs. This recurring "dividing motif" or *vahe ula* has traditionally been a sequence of movements based on a particular motif paradigm,[3] but I once saw a performance in which the dividing motif was based on the *si sia* motif,[4] which is usually used as one of the alternating motifs. The choreographer may not have been knowledgeable about the traditional choreography—which is associated with only certain villages or lineages attached to those villages, or the motif may have been willfully changed because the performer was not of the proper lineage or village. Nevertheless, this new product may become part of the remembered versions of Tongan *ula* and may be reembodied at a later time.

Thus, there are two kinds of things that need to be remembered in the art of dance: the culturally grammatical pieces of movement or motifs that the body, through long years of practice and habit, seems almost able to remember on its own; and the choreographed sequences of motifs for a specific dance, which seem to be memorized cognitively much like memorizing a poem. For those of us who deal with dance on a regular basis, remembering transient phenomena and the imagery they project into visual form is an everyday affair. It is difficult for us to get excited over statements such as those by Dan Sperber, Susanne Küchler, or others who ask such questions as, "How is it possible that the imagery embodied in the art has a continuity irrespective of the temporary existence of particular works?"[5] Dance must be the quintessential visual art in which embodied imagery continues without even the possibility of being permanent (until recently with the rise of film, video, and dance notation). Even so, although a particular performance is transient, the structure is not, and even if a specific choreography is forgotten, knowledge of the structure of the system and the inventory of motifs will be remembered.

Having dealt so far with memory and cognition, let me move on to the equally interesting aspect of the production of imagery in dance. As an example I will use the *lakalaka* dance genre of the Tongans of Polynesia. I will examine the motifs themselves, how they are put together (that is, choreographed), if the motifs have any imagery of their own, and how their relationship to each other and the cultural environment in which they operate gives social meaning to a performance. Social and cultural reproduction are two sides of the same coin, and though they may not necessarily be coterminous they are dialectical, each influencing and serving as a model for the other over time.

Tongan *Lakalaka* Motifs

Motifs form a stock of cultural knowledge that the Tongan choreographer uses to make a social statement. They are part of the collective visual and bodily memory that Tongans draw upon to learn and remember the half-hour *lakalaka* that the choreographer will teach them. The relationship between the motifs and the poetry to which they abstractly allude is part of the integral association of verbal and visual modes of expression so characteristic of Polynesians. To a non-Tongan, after sitting through three or four hours of a succession of village-based *lakalaka*, the next one will be just another *lakalaka*. To the Tongan, however, it is another challenge to understand the relationship of the dancers to each other; the relationship of the village and its chief to the king and the overall lineage and moiety structure; how the designs of the individual verses build on each other to form the overall design; and how the individual motifs either make hidden meanings visual, thus enhancing meaning, or allude to surface meanings, thereby hiding meaning from all but the most informed.

Motifs used in *lakalaka* are primarily those that allude to—and thereby interpret—poetry, in contrast to motifs used in the Tongan genre *ula*, which chiefly create beauty. Tongan dance movements are based primarily on three parts of the body—legs, head, and arms—but most important are arm-movements, known as *haka*. The most significant and often recurring motif in Tongan dance is a lower-arm movement that can occur in a number of spatial environments, depending on the placement of the upper arm. This specific motif is also called *"haka"* and will be enclosed in quotation marks to separate it from Tongan arm movements in general. The *"haka"* lower-arm movement is made up of a rotation or turn of the lower arm in conjunction with the curling of fingers and thumb to meet (or almost meet) and then extend with a slight accent. The "environments" consist of the placement of the upper arm and the palm facings created by the rotation/turn of the lower arm. This can be called the *"haka"* paradigm, in that a specific morphokine made up of the kinemes of lower arm rotation—curling and extension of the fingers, and flexion and extension of the wrist—occurs at the same time as a series of morphokines composed of arm placements and palm facings. Such a paradigm consists of a small set of related forms in which there is one morphokine common to the set and all the morphokines with which it can occur simultaneously.

Although *"haka"* is often used as a fill-in movement in some Tongan dance genres (that is, between narrative movements or to complete a phrase after the narrative section has been completed), in *lakalaka*, *"haka"* motifs are often used narratively to help tell the story. For example, *"haka"* can be used to indicate an ear ornament, *tekiteki*. In this case one hand performs the *"haka"* near the ear and the head is turned away from the hand. Another example of narrative interpretation uses *"haka"* to mean *kalauni*, crown, and refer to the sovereign. Here the right upper arm is placed and moved in such a way that the right hand is moved from the left side of the head to the right while performing the *"haka"* morphokine. In another narrative use, two *"haka"* that follow each other in different positions may indicate "from place to place." For example, in a sitting dance, *"haka"* in front of the body followed by *"haka"* at the side of the body interprets "from the sea to the beach."

A second paradigm uses the lower-arm-rotation kineme in conjunction with the flexion of the wrist but without the curling of the fingers in a variety of arm positions and palm facings. For example, the *luva* motif consists of starting with both hands near the shoulders with palms facing back, then performing the essence of the motif while stretching the arms forward. This often has the narrative meaning "to give." To convey the narrative meaning of "sweeping," the essence of the motif is performed by both hands while moving them from one shoulder to the opposite hip.

Other important motifs used in *lakalaka* are movements that can be brought to mind by the following terms: *ha'otā, kako, vete, milolua, toli, tui, tapa, ki'i pasi'i, teuteu,* and *pāpāuma* (although these are not really names for motifs, as will be explained).[6] *Ha'otā* consists of circling the right hand around the left (by a rotation of the right lower arm) and opening the arms slightly to the sides. It is usually performed two or three times in succession in different arm positions. *Vete* means to "unwind, unravel, scatter, or disperse," and the movement of this motif could be described as unwinding or similar movements. *Vete* can be conveyed by performing the circling-of-the-hands-around-each-other morphokine (also the essence of *ha'otā*) in different arm positions. *Toli* means to pick (flowers or fruit) and can be conveyed by following a *"haka"* with an accented curling of the fingers to form a C while extending the wrist.

Although certain movement motifs are associated with certain words, concepts, or ideas, this is not a one-to-one relationship, as one motif can be used to convey many concepts, and one concept can be conveyed by many motifs. As allusion is the essence of Tongan poetry, and dance movements are a secondary abstraction, it follows that motifs do not interpret in a realistic manner. One would not allude to a flower by holding the hands to look like a flower or to a bird by moving the arms to look like wings (as might be done in Hawaiian dance). Instead, the movement would suggest a flower or bird in an indirect way.

To illustrate the double abstraction that dance creates, one stanza of a *lakalaka* known as *Kalauni,* from the village of Lapaha, will be used. The stanza of poetry and its literal translation are as follows:

Kulukona 'o tavake fai'ana	Kulukona, flower of the tropic, bird created,
Na'e toli he matangi mafana	Plucked by the warm breeze,
Kohai 'e Ofo he 'ene ngangatu	Who is surprised at his fragrance?
Fakatoukatea 'i Monotapu	Double canoe of Monotapu,
He 'oiaue fakatoukatea 'i Monotapu.	Oh yes, double canoe of Monotapu.

This stanza of poetry describes Prince Tungi (now King Taufa'ahau Tupou IV), telling us that he was born of the highest male and female chiefs in the land. Tungi is referred to as the *Kulukona* flower (a variety of flowering tree), who was created by the tropic bird, *Tavake*, which symbolizes the highest male chief in the land, in this case Tungi Mailefihi, Tungi's father. He was the highest direct descendant of the Tu'i Ha'a Takalaua—which is a higher bloodline than that of the present line of kings, the Tu'i Kanokupolu (from whom Tungi descends through his mother). The nature symbolism continues in the second line with Tungi being plucked by the warm breeze, which is sometimes equated with Tonga. This line of poetry refers to Tonga, the land of warm breezes, which has picked Tungi for its next king. Fragrance is considered desirable and good, and the next line says that no one is surprised at Tungi's greatness (that is, fragrance, since he is a *kulukona* flower), because he is of double chiefly parentage. *Fakatoukatea* is a double canoe with both sides equal, and this poetically refers to his chiefly descent on both sides. Tungi is also sacred, which is suggested by the place name Monotapu, since *tapu* means "sacred."

The allusions, phrased in terms of nature symbolism, refer to Tungi and his genealogy, though neither of these concepts is mentioned in words. The dance motifs, in turn, allude to the nature allusions, and not to Tungi or his ancestry. The use of motifs is as follows: *Kulukona* is choreographed with the essence of the second paradigm (above) performed with both hands while moving them from shoulders to thighs. *Tavake fai'ana* is choreographed by *vete*—here interpreting "create." *Tavake* (tropic bird) is interpreted by adding a quick side head-tilt to convey the head movement of a bird. *Toli* is choreographed by *toli*, in this case meaning "to pick." *Matangi mafana* is choreographed by *vete; kohai* (who), by *"haka"* with the right hand at eye level and eyes focussed upon it; *ngangatu* (fragrance), by *vete*. *Fakatoukatea* (double canoe) is choreographed by a movement in which one hand extends to the side. On the repetition of the line of poetry, the opposite hand extends to the opposite side.

In this example *vete* interprets "create," "breeze," and "fragrance," all concepts that can be conveyed by the agitation of air which *vete* re-creates. *Toli* is the most obviously narrative movement in this group, with its depiction of picking. *Kulukona* conveys "beautiful flower" with the beautiful *luva* movement of the second paradigm, and is often associated with giving such things as a flower necklace. *Kohai* is conveyed by a *"haka,"* which, because the eyes are focussed upon it, one could say looks as if it asks a question. Two-sidedness is conveyed in two ways in this stanza. First, it is conveyed by arm movements to the right and then to the left. Second, it is conveyed by a change in formation of the dancers. In a *lakalaka,* the men and women are usually ranged in two or more rows facing the audience, the women on the left (from the observer's point of view), the men on the right. During the performance of this stanza, the men and women walk toward each other and the two lines become four. The men move to the front of the women, and then all go back to their original two lines. This intermingles men and women and then reemphasizes the two distinct groups in an additional reference to ancestry and Tungi's equal chiefly descent on both male and female sides.

There is a cultural preference for interpretation by allusion rather than by direct statement, and this may be the explanation for the lack of names of motifs. Naming a motif is too obvious; a name might limit motif use to one concept. Or the movement, if associated with a name, might convey that concept when no meaning is wanted. Movements, then, in Tongan dance, are not named, but they can be brought to mind by words. Motifs used in *lakalaka* create visual imagery that alludes to poetry. They present an abstraction through which the choreographer challenges his audience to understand the deeper meaning of the poetry indirectly by means of *heliaki,* or "not going straight," that is, saying one thing but meaning another. Tongan dance is a physical, mental, and esthetic activity to be enjoyed at one or more levels simultaneously. Some dance genres aim primarily at one or another of these possible levels. But even those that begin as an intellectual activity often create an intense emotional atmosphere and can become an esthetic experience for both dancer and spectator. When verbalizing this emotional aspect of dance, the Tongans say that they feel *māfana,* meaning "inwardly warm or exhilarated." Spectators also feel *māfana,* especially during the performance of their favorite motifs, which they say they can feel kinesthetically. It is common to see spectators move their heads along with the dance, and occasionally one or more will get up and join the performers, even though they do not know the dance, inspired by the inner feeling of *māfana.*

Structure, Imagery, and Meaning in *Lakalaka*

The structure of a *lakalaka* is based on formal speech-making, and has three sections: (1) an introductory *fakatapu,* which acknowledges the important chiefly lines relevant to the occasion; (2) the main *lakalaka* section that conveys information about the occasion, genealogies of relevant people, history or mythology of the village performing, and other relevant information; and (3) the *tatau* closing counterpart of the introductory *fakatapu*, in which the performers say good-bye and again defer to the chiefs. One stanza may be a *tau*, a verse that expresses the essence of the performance or work of art, during which the performers do their very best and compel the audience to pay strict attention. This formal structure forms the outline of the composition. The overall design, and thus the meaning of any specific composition, need not be apparent until the end of a performance. The meaning is revealed as each verse—through verbal and visual allusions and metaphors—builds on those that went before, mediated through the esthetic principle of *heliaki*. Two examples of this were given in my 1985 article "Structured Movement Systems in Tonga." In the *lakalaka* example which is the property of the village of Kolovai (whose lineage traditionally mixes *kava* [an infusion of the root of *Piper methesticum*] for the king), the dance was ostensibly about mixing *kava*, and two stanzas recreated in a realistic manner the mixing and wringing of this ceremonial drink. The meaning of the performance, however, had to do with the relationship of the village to the king, and through *heliaki* honored the thirteenth birthday of the (now) king, for which it was composed.

The second *lakalaka* example was performed during the 1975 centennial celebration of the Tongan constitution by the king's village of Kanokupolu and was ostensibly about the aristocratic sport of snaring migrating pigeons. The *heliaki*, however, was about the king's daughter (who on that occasion was the central female performer) and her relationships to the important Tongan lineages. The performance illustrated verbally and visually that she was the highest prestige-bearing person in the nation and that even Baron Vaea (the central male performer on that occasion), who but for an accident of history would have been king, paid honor to her dignity.

The imagery projected into visual form in these two *lakalaka* used a variety of stock Tongan movement motifs. They were put together in such a way that during certain stanzas movements made *kava* mixing and pigeon snaring visual, thereby enhancing the surface allusions but hiding the deeper meaning, while in other stanzas the movements alluded to hidden meanings, thereby enhancing meaning. As one image followed another, the relationships between the stanzas were clarified, as were the social relationships of performers to each other and to the hierarchical system visually laid out in the performance space. The next time either of these *lakalaka* are performed, the construction will be essentially the same—the motifs, however, will probably vary. A *luva* motif may be substituted for a *"haka"* motif, or the exact placement of the motifs that conveyed pigeon-snaring or *kava*-mixing may differ. But the combination of motifs will, by *heliaki*, convey the same meaning and a similar set of relationships. The art of *lakalaka* embodies social relationships by ordering culturally grammatical pieces of movement. Generated from visually and bodily remembered motifs that are known to most Tongans, the imagery projected each time the motifs are embodied in performance varies yet remains the same.

The interpretation of a *lakalaka* is based on cultural and social knowledge of history and mythology as well as on how motifs can be used to convey meaning. The preservation and production of knowledge of social and political importance has been intimately associated with the preservation and production of *lakalaka*. Some of the most important *punake* (composers) have been chiefs, nobles, aristocrats, and monarchs who have the knowledge of how to combine pleasurable activities and political acumen into works of art. The village dancer feels *māfana* or inwardly exhilarated by the process of performing, especially if the central performers are of high rank or prestige. The spectators pride themselves on metaphorical knowledge and the ability to recognize and understand the *heliaki* of the motifs and the essence of the overall design. The king or other important individual who accepts the artistic product realizes its importance as a political action. Although it will exist only in memory, the imagery conveyed by a successful *lakalaka* takes on the cognitive reality of a basic social icon in Tonga for the production, maintenance, and separation of power and prestige.

GILLIAN FEELEY-HARNIK

Finding Memories in Madagascar

There is a history in all men's lives,
Figuring the natures of the times deceas'd,
The which observ'd, a man may prophesy,
With a near aim, of the main chance of things
As yet not come to life, which in their seeds
And weak beginnings lie intreasured.
Such things become the hatch and brood of time.
—Shakespeare, 2 *Henry IV*, III.i. 80–86

Memories of People in Times and Places

Frances Yates in *The Art of Memory* has shown us how closely western ideas of memory are tied to linear conceptions of time, creating puzzles we still conceive in Aristotelian terms about how to differentiate memories of the past from perceptions of our surroundings and from fantasies of the past, present, future, or some temporal never-neverland.[1] Some current scholars, for example Mary Warnock in *Memory*, argue that the pastness and yet re-presentativeness of memory enable us simultaneously to know separate things and also to conceive of ourselves as integrated, multidimensional wholes rather than strings unraveling at both ends. Westerners have a long history of representing the integrative powers of memory spatially as houses, temples, theaters, and more recently storehouses that can be emptied and restocked. Underlying these architectural images seem to be—at least in literature and the visual arts—more visceral images of eating and vomiting out that come closer to the ways we feel memories become part of our very flesh.

Places are critical to memories in a variety of non-Western contexts as well. For example, James Fox, in "'Standing' in Time and Place," and Joel C. Kuipers in "Place, Names, and Authority in Weyéwa Ritual Speech," examine the role of place names in establishing ancestral authority in different parts of Southeast Asia. Keith Hamilton in "Stalking with Stories" and "Speaking with Names," shows how the western Apache use their place names to evoke images of landscapes attached to stories about past misbehavior in order to return people to proper ancestral custom. Susanne Küchler's work on the *Malangan* sculptures of New Ireland shows how memories of images, embodied in forms exchanged during lengthy funerals, are critical in resolving disputes concerning land and other resources among regionally dispersed groups.

In Madagascar, people are identified by their locations as commonly as by their genealogical or other relationships to one another. Toponymy is thus a subject of considerable interest throughout the island, as outsiders have recurrently noted.[2] The locations of reliquaries and tombs of Sakalava rulers in western Madagascar exemplify the association of places with memories of people (see fig. 28). Along with praise names given at death, these places are the most important structural elements in Sakalava oral and written histories commemorating Sakalava "rulers" *(ampanjaka),* "leaders of government" *(mpitondra fanjakana),* and their "followers" *(mpanaraka).* The praise names are mnemonic devices in themselves, summarizing the main achievements of a royal ancestor's reign as living ruler, which are associated with the expansion of the monarchy as a whole. The places do the same thing. They are not simply rooms or groups of rooms to be filled or emptied of this or that memory of the dead who are gone. They are filled with bodies rooted in the ground. In Madagascar, the importance of places in memorializing people seems to develop from ideas and practices tied to the ground, bodies, and the growth of bodies rooted in the ground. Royal ancestors in the highland monarchy of Imerina were commemorated during the nineteenth century by bags of earth from their tombs, which served as their *solo* or substitutes in royal processions.[3] Twentieth-century pilgrims to the tomb of the early King Andriamanelo of Imerina eat the "sacred ground" taken from his tomb to cure certain ills.[4] The restorative powers of Sakalava ancestral rulers in western Madagascar are embodied in relics carried on the backs of special porters.[5] Trees and people also serve as "sitting places" for Sakalava royal ancestors, who lodge in the bodies of their mediums when the mediums are wrapped in

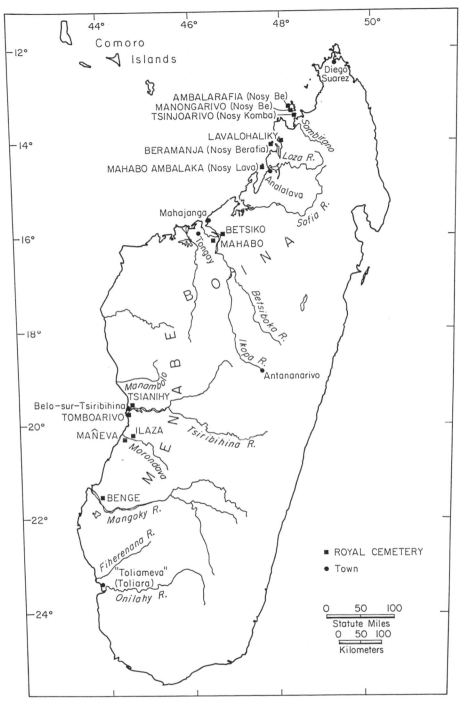

Figure 28. Map of Madagascar showing Sakalava Royal Cemeteries. Drawn by Dean L. Pendleton.

mantles that are simultaneously shrouds.[6] In this paper, I will focus on Sakalava royal tombs in northwestern Madagascar, places where royal followers collect the widest range of materials from which memories are thought to grow, including earth, rocks, trees, and bodies living and dead.[7]

The Living and the Dead

The Sakalava are one of the largest of the twenty officially recognized ethnic groups in Madagascar. They identify themselves and are identified by others in the Analalava region of northwestern Madagascar as descendants of original settlers, or "masters of the land," and as "servants of royalty." In fact, they are a diverse lot, associated only by their common respect for the monarchy founded by the Zafinímena dynasty in southwestern Madagascar in the late sixteenth century. Even as Sakalava continue to marry people who identify themselves with other ethnic groups, so the Sakalava monarchy continues to incorporate outsiders regardless of their origins. Sakalava domains, founded all along the west coast of Madagascar, include different groups of people in different habitats speaking different dialects. The Southern Bemihisatra branch of the monarchy in the Analalava region, founded in 1849, was the last to be established before the French conquest at the turn of the century.

The Southern Bemihisatra are ruled by living and ancestral members of the Zafinímena dynasty. The current living ruler, head of an extensive administrative network, rules from a capital *(doany)* on the mainland, overlooking the water, surrounded by "pens" or groups of guardian-slaves. The royal ancestors are her immediate ascendants and, except for an older brother, her predecessors in office. They are represented at the *doany* by relics and at the *mahabo,* the royal cemetery on the island of Nosy Lava, by the royal tomb surrounded by "pens" of guardians descended from former slaves, and by spirit mediums.

Scholars have often commented on the absence of eschatology in Malagasy thought.[8] A local Sakalava woman who was raised as a Muslim after her mother married a Comorian echoed a common assumption of many residents in the Analalava region when she explained differences between Sakalava and Muslim beliefs in terms of literacy:

> God watches over everything—over what's here and now
> [*doniàny*] and what's beyond [*kiàma*]. Fire [*Motro*] is where the
> bad people go and burn—murderers, sorcerers—they burn, burn

[*may, may*]! Heaven *(Pepòny)* is the beautiful place, like a beautiful house with cool breezes. Everything is clear, sweet-smelling. This is Muslim [*Silamo*] belief. The Sakalava say the Comorians lie. They say, "A dead thing has no life in it" [*Raha naty, tsisy velona*]. But it is the Sakalava who are lying. The Silamo have books [*boky*], histories [*tantara*]. The Sakalava have no books. The *mpanjaka* is their book. They pray to her. They have nothing written down like the Silamo. They don't know how to pray. They don't know how to read. Comorians like myself, we have books. They don't have anything like that.[9]

In fact, the Sakalava in the Analalava region do write and keep books. These are not treatises on the afterlife, but histories *(tantara)* of the royal ancestors during the times they were alive, instruction manuals for royal services, and descriptions of important events such as the birth of the local ruler's first child. Likewise, in ordinary conversations people do not speak about lives after death, but they are very precise about the activities of ancestors among the living. There is no separate land of the ancestors. The ancestors exist among the living. Or rather, it would be more accurate to say that people live among ancestors—their own if they are "masters of the land," living in their own "ancestral land" *(tanindrazaña)*, or the ancestors of others if they are "strangers" *(vahiny)*. To be is to live with ancestors. To live elsewhere is to be "lost" *(very)*, cut off from one's kin, tantamount to being enslaved.

The Creation of Ancestors

As in Africa and Asia, so in Madagascar, death by itself does not confer ancestorhood.[10] On the contrary, living people separate themselves from the dead through burial rituals. In northwestern Madagascar, ancestors emerge out of reciprocal relations with their descendants. This reciprocity is expressed especially in speaking and serving. People "call" their ancestors to "plead" for their blessings in rites of passage and other major changes in their lives, as well as at regular intervals, such as in the annual services honoring the royal ancestors at the *doany* and the *mahabo*. The responses of commoners' ancestors are often expressed through names. Reciprocity between ancestors and descendants contributes to their mutual growth. In recognizing their ancestors, the living "make them great" *(ma-*

habe azy); the ancestors reciprocate by blessing their descendants with fertility and prosperity. The growth of living people is a clear sign of the greatness of ancestors who are hidden from ordinary view.

Thus living rulers are described in praise songs as growing fat, not from buying or trading, but from ancestors, like a mango tree spreading up and out from its roots in the ground. Mango trees, which grow to immense size in western Madagascar, are an important image of ancestral and living royalty in praise songs. The dark, leathery, green body of the tree is crowned with the bright red leaves of young shoots with which the tree continually renews itself. The dense foliage of the tree provides shade in the dry and wet seasons alike. The tree produces large quantities of fruit, two and, in some species, three times a year, which can be eaten raw or in relishes, as well as cooked.

Royalty are thought to be *masina* or powerfully efficacious, for good or ill, in the way that *togny,* trees associated with certain earth spirits, are *masina.* As *togny* protect villages, so royalty protect their domains. Royal praise songs suggest that hard-working people will recognize and respect the benefits of monarchy. The indolent who go their own ways—imagining that prosperity and fertility come from buying and trading—will go hungry. In practice, respect for ancestors is expressed by serving royalty. Royal service ranges from working the royal rice fields to purifying relics and regalia.

Of all these forms of recognizing and nurturing ties between ancestors and descendants, none is more important in the Analalava region than the royal burial and the reconstruction of the royal tomb that follows, exemplified here by the funeral services for the *ampanjaka* Tondroko, who died in 1925, and was reburied in the reconstruction service of 1972–76.[11]

Tondroko's Burial

Tondroko, remembered as Ndramamahaña or "Noble Who Nurtured Thousands," governed the Sakalava in the Analalava region from about 1892 until his death in 1925. His funeral, curtailed by French authorities from the customary full year to the last three months of 1925, is described in the contemporary report of an *inspecteur des provinces,* C. Poirier, who thought to document therein the "Fin de règne et de légende" of the Sakalava monarchy.[12] Poirier outlined the customary procedures: taking the corpse by outrigger canoe from the mainland to the island of Nosy Lava where it would be buried; reducing it to a skeleton; wrapping the bones in precious silks; enclosing them in a coffin made from a tree trunk hollowed out like a canoe; putting the tree-boat coffin in a grave on a bed of charcoal and silver five-franc pieces; and covering it with stones, gravel, and sand that Sakalava followers describe as kinds of "waves" *(riaka)*. Like André Dandouau, the first head of the Ecole Régionale in Analalava, who published a general account of Sakalava burial customs in 1911, Poirier alludes to the obligatory sexual license, including the texts of several funeral songs exemplifying what he considered the salaciousness of Sakalava royal burials.[13] Contemporary followers of the monarchy are prohibited by taboos *(fady)* from discussing royal funerals, which require them to break many taboos on ordinary behavior. Nevertheless, the idea of sexual songs accords with what we know about the strong emphasis on sexuality and fertility in funerals elsewhere in Madagascar.[14]

Owing to Poirier's intervention in their legal battle over the succession with local French authorities, the Southern Bemihisatra were able to retrieve the royal regalia and install Ndramamahaña's successor, a posthumously born baby girl. However they were not allowed to resettle guardians at the royal cemetery on Nosy Lava or to carry out the reconstruction of the fence known as the *menaty* immediately surrounding the royal tomb. While the first obligation of a Sakalava ruler to the royal ancestors is to carry out the funeral of his or her predecessor, the second major duty is to repair the *menaty* or innermost fence around the royal tomb. The *menaty* is broken when the royal spirit suddenly compels the coffin bearers circulating the burial compound to crash through the fence to bury the corpse in the tomb within. The *menaty* service takes its name from the reconstruction of the *menaty* fence, but the work actually involves the refurbishment of the whole tomb as well.

Dandouau and Poirier both state that the fence around the tomb is repaired at the time of the burial. Mellis, a long-time *colonist* and student of local custom in northwestern Madagascar, provides an alternative view, stating that the reconstruction of the *menaty* coincides—or should—with the reemergence of the ancestor's voice through a publicly recognized spirit medium.[15] Contemporary followers of the monarchy confirm Mellis's view. But it is clear from their own comments, as well as archival sources, that this recognition was denied to all forms of Sakalava royal service during the colonial and immediate postcolonial periods.[16] By the time of the national uprising in spring 1972 and the following elections, when one of the candidates promised to grant the Sakalava permission to carry out the *menaty* service, Ndramamahaña possessed at least ten different mediums who had been legitimated at the royal cemetery, and numerous others in the surrounding countryside who had yet to undergo that process.

Once the candidate favoring "Malgachization" had won, granting Sakalava royal followers permission to carry out their own local version of this mandate, the Sakalava had to choose where the timber would be cut and whom to enlist as workers. In contrast to the timing of the service, which depended on Sakalava relations with outside authorities, these choices were made on the basis of relations among different factions within the monarchy.

The *menaty* service begins and ends at the *doany*, but the work of cutting the trees is carried out at a remote camp, while the work of taking down the old fence and putting up the new one is carried out at the *mahabo*. In principle, the longest portion of the service at the camp is held *anatiala* or "in the forest," that is, a place conceptually opposed to and usually physically distant from settled habitation. In practice, royal officials had to choose a location close enough to existing settlements that it would attract the largest number of workers who could not otherwise be forced to participate. The living ruler wanted a location east of her compound at the *doany*, where she was likely to get the most followers. The royal ancestors wanted a location on the mainland north of the royal cemetery, where the last *menaty* service had been held and not far from the village where leaders of the guardians at the *mahabo* still farmed. The disagreement was finally resolved when a woman, married into the area and thus a "stranger," dreamed of a location in the south, about equidistant from both the *doany* and *mahabo*, with some advantages for the living ruler, spirit-mediums, their officials, guardians, and followers alike.

The work camp was located on the site of an existing village, which was reoriented along the lines of a royal center. A platform called the "royal sitting place" *(fitambesaña)*, was built immediately south of the village to protect the cut timbers from contact with the ground. A "royal house" *(zomba)* was constructed northeast of the platform to house the equipment. The two structures were surrounded by a fence called a *tsirangôty* like the fence around the royal compound at the *doany*. A large tamarind tree in the village (possibly a *togny*, commemorating the ancestral "masters of the land" of that place) was designated as the "royal meeting house" *(fantsina)*. Workers were housed in the northern or southern halves of the village according to the location of their father's ancestral land north or south of the midline marked by living and ancestral royalty at the *doany* and *mahabo.*

Royal workers had to replicate the social organization of the domain. Leaders among the People of the Living *(Olo ny Manoro)*, the guardians who surround the royal compound at the *doany*, selected people to represent the living ruler, the members of her administration (officials known as the *manantany* and the *fahatelo*), the *Razan'olo* or "Ancestor People" in charge of royal burials, and followers from villages throughout the region. Likewise, the leaders among the People of the Dead *(Olo ny Mihilaña)* at the *mahabo* selected the mediums who would embody the royal spirits, and representatives from among the spirits' guardians who would call the spirits into the bodies of their mediums, clothe them, and cook for them. Two royal ancestors from alternate generations were selected to represent the four generations buried in the *mahabo.* Together with a young man from a nonruling branch of the royal dynasty who represented the living ruler, they formed a paired union of ancestral and living royalty. The other groups of participants were also organized in pairs consisting of a "head" and the head's "friends" or "partners," reckoned in terms of seniority, age, gender, and location. Selecting people to make up these pairs inevitably involved considerable controversy concerning people's abilities to lead and their willingness to follow. People's reluctance to serve in the *menaty* service dominated stories about how workers were enlisted from the general population.

A *menaty* service begins with the assembly of workers and equipment at the *doany* and continues with the assembly of workers and equipment at the *mahabo,* before moving to the work camp in the forest. This takes several weeks. Workers are expected to remain at the work camp cutting trees for several years, reckoned in pairs. They are said to have stayed six to eight years in the past. (In the case of Ndramamahaña's *menaty,* the service took six years.) The trees may be debarked at the work camp or at the place below the *mahabo* known as *Antsandrarafa* ("At the Drying Bed"), where the royal corpse is reduced to a skeleton. Once the trees have been debarked, they are brought up to the *mahabo.* The tomb is cleaned; the old fence is cleared away; the new fence is put up; and the door in the fence is sealed with the blood of a sacrificed ox. The third stage of the service at the *mahabo* takes several weeks, but the actual reconstruction of the fence around the tomb should be completed in a single day. Once the door in the *menaty* is closed, the service is considered to have "grown" *(tombo)* to its full size. Participants inform the royal ancestors at the *mahabo* that the service has been successfully completed; then they inform the royalty at the *doany;* then they are free to return home.

The organization of Ndramamahaña's service reproduced the body of royalty—every group, every object, every sequence in time and space having its head as well as its paired limbs, its leader and followers. It began at the *doany* or capital of the living ruler. The people of the living bought the equipment and assembled the workers. They offered the "service" (workers and equipment) to the royal ancestors at the *doany* when they announced the *menaty*'s beginning. They carried the "service" to the *mahabo* in a *laka jilo,* an outrigger canoe named for its clearly marked prow. They offered it to the royal ancestors at the *mahabo,* then stored the equipment in the ancestors' house inside the burial compound. The workers stayed at the *mahabo* for the pair of months (separated by an intervening "dead" month). Then they went on to the work camp by canoe and dhow. Repeatedly, participants emphasized that the equipment from the *doany,* to which had been added "the ancestors' contribution"—dancing costumes, drums, kaolin, and other required items—must be taken from the royal storehouse at the *mahabo* down to the shore and into the canoes in the proper order: that is, the head or royal offering dish first, and its friends following last.

Once they arrived at the timber camp, the workers stored the equipment in the royal house there and waited for the first "good day" (the Friday, Saturday, or Monday on which royal services are permitted, in contrast to the "bad days" of the rest of the week which are associated with the death of Sakalava rulers). Workers began by cutting the corner posts, then the rest. At the end of two years, they had cut—according to the official numbers that also conformed to the demand for pairs—two thousand tree trunks, each four meters long. The tree trunks were stored on the raised structure known as the "royal sitting place" so that they would not come in contact with the ground or any other source of moisture—associated with living things—or filth—associated with death.

Guided by the Ancestor People, participants debarked the trees in the village called *Antoby* ("At the Camp") and *Antsandrarafa* ("At the Drying Bed") on the coast of the island of Nosy Lava, below the royal cemetery, where royal corpses are prepared for burial. The timbers could not be taken up to the royal cemetery until the debarking had been completed. Here, too, participants emphasized that the "service," that is, the timbers and the equipment, had to be carried up to the *mahabo* in the proper order, meaning now that the timbers had to come first, followed by the equipment making up the rest of the paired whole.

Leaders of the service exhorted workers to be extremely careful when they "served inside," that is, on and around the royal tomb inside the old *menaty*. They "opened" the "red blood door" (*varavara menalio;* two adjacent posts in the middle of the western side of the *menaty*) by offering money and mead to royal ancestors through the Ancestor People. The living ruler's substitute, who sat on the top or "head" of the tomb to guard it from would-be sorcerers, and the Ancestor People, who cleaned the top, sides, and perimeter of the tomb from dead leaves and branches and washed the head stones on the east side with mead, were the only people who were allowed inside. The guardians from the royal cemetery simply brought things to the "door," where the official "supplicator" (*ampanga-taka),* who served as their leader, handed them in. The Ancestor People and the People of the Dead worked together to take down the posts of the old *menaty* and put them in the forested area east of the tomb, being very careful once again to begin at the "Head" (*Ankaheso),* or east side of the tomb, and end at its "Foot" (*Ampandia).*

The new *menaty* is supposed to be put up in a single day, like the *togny* trees recognized or planted to commemorate ancestors in rural villages. Owing to the widely felt "difficulty" of royal services, entailed by observing numerous taboos, especially concerning ancestral royalty, in this case it took two. The new fence had to be extended south of the old one to make room for the next burial, which would have been an act of rampant sorcery were it not required by royal service. The red-blood door (the two adjacent posts in the middle of the west side) that was opened with honey was closed with blood. Two cows were killed: the "head" *(lohany)* from the royal herd, which served as the ruler's sacrifice to her ancestors, and a second behind it, donated by a commoner, which served as its "mat" *(lafiny).* The red-blood door was then sealed by annointing the posts with blood brushed upward on their sharpened "heads." After the door was closed, participants drank mead and ate meat together. After staying until the end of the second month inaugurating the new year, they informed the royal ancestors that the service was done. The Ancestor People and other participants from the *doany* and surrounding villages then returned to a mainland village just north of the *doany,* where they stayed for a year to ensure that the total number of years of the service would be paired. In the month beginning the new year, corresponding to the time they had left the *doany* six years ago, they returned to the *doany,* paid their respects to the royal ancestors embodied in the regalia there, and informed them and the living ruler of the completion of the service. After they had returned to their farming villages, the spirit-mediums and their guardians also came to the *doany* to pay their respects and formally announce the completion of their service.

Planting Ancestors

Sakalava royal followers often describe themselves as "soft" or "simple" people who do not know how to make fancy speeches; they just know the customs. Such disclaimers of special knowledge are essential to good etiquette. People are too aware of the power of words to use them loosely. Furthermore, as one man put it, "masters of the land are people who know local custom." That knowledge of local practices, which is not written in books but embodied in the actions that come from living in a place, is what "makes people masters of the land" *(mahatompontany azy).* The *menaty* service is one kind of customary practice. Participants do not speculate on what the work is "about"; they focus on doing it right, that is, in accordance with ancestral practice. These practices are recalled from the "Customs of Royal Service Concerning the *Menaty*" *(Fomba Fanompoana Momba Ny Menaty),* dictated by a former royal official at the *mahabo* to his descendants, who wrote them down on paper sewed together to form a "book" *(boky).* They are also recalled from the "knowledge" *(fahaizana)* of past practice retained in the memories *(fahatsiarovana)* of these descendants and other elderly men who succeeded to positions of leadership at the *doany* and *mahabo,* and who have since their deaths in the late seventies and early eighties been succeeded by their sons. As all of these elderly men emphasized, the service must be done because the old fence is *mirôtso,* a term meaning "fallen down" in referring to things, but "asleep" or "dead" in speaking of royalty. Rebuilding the fence involves cleaning and enlarging the capacity of the tomb, but the tomb is almost never mentioned as the object of the service.

As long as the fence is down, the "powerfully efficacious place" *(tany masina)* could be destroyed by "dirty things" *(raha maloto)*. The tomb is also vulnerable to theft, especially given the presence of prisoners from a national penitentiary also located on the island, who leave their "dark house" *(trano maizina)* to farm during the day. Prisoners have tried to steal money and other valuables from the royal storehouse in the burial compound and from guardians' houses in the past. Far more dangerous is the rarely mentioned possibility that a sorcerer would attempt to steal parts of the "difficult things" themselves to use them in making "medicines" that would kill people.

Royal followers do speculate about the meaning of fences in the abstract, noting in particular that fences were forbidden to royal followers in the past, even while they were required to protect royalty and contain, metaphorically, the "pens" of royal slaves surrounding royal compounds and tombs. The service itself "fences" participants in by requiring them to leave their houses, granaries, and fields for weeks and months, even years in the case of the original group inscribed on the official list of royal workers. In removing the workers from their own livelihoods and requiring them to complete royal work according to highly specific rules before finally permitting them to return home, the service conforms to the pattern of a rite of passage given in Van Gennep's *Rites of Passage,* encompassing the entire region identified with Southern Bemihisatra rule. Participants are separated from the rest of the population and isolated in the forest for several years, during which they must work together harmoniously toward the single goal of reconstructing the royal tomb; only then can they be reincorporated into the populace that has had to support them in the meantime.

Participants explained the length of the service in terms of its "difficulty," the countless special restrictions that distinguish royal service from what would otherwise be ordinary work. They could only use certain kinds of wood; they could only work on the "good days" during the three weeks of the lunar month when the moon is "living," not "dead"; they had to do things in pairs, including pairs of years. The procedures for recruiting workers suggest that the *menaty* service is a rite of passage incorporating participants into a "total" or "complete and austere institution" to use the terms that Goffman and Foucault adopt, if not a kind of prison in its own right. In Goffman's terms:

> A total institution may be defined as a place of residence and work where a large number of like-situated individuals, cut off from the wider society for an appreciable period of time, together lead an enclosed, formally administered round of life.[17]

Goffman distinguishes several kinds of total institutions, including "institutions purportedly established to pursue some worklike task and justifying themselves only on these instrumental grounds," for example, work camps, colonial compounds, retreats, and the like, which Foucault would include in the "carceral archipelago."[18] Certainly common to both is the formation of "docile bodies" through spatial and temporal strategies: "enclosure," "partitioning," and the creation of "functional sites" in space; and further controls of inmates' actions through timetables defining not only new times when acts must be accomplished but also new rhythms for their bodily performance.[19]

Participants are trimmed of their particular origins in the surrounding region and reoriented to the agent the total institution represents, be it the state, the police, a corporation. Yet as Goffman notes, but neither he nor Foucault explores, "the formation of households provides a structural guarantee that total institutions will not be without resistance."[20] Whereas people are represented in the monarchy as members of lineages, they are recruited into the *menaty* service as individuals, not as members of kin groups. Indeed, the service entails the separation of people as kin and their reassociation solely as royal followers, that is, in terms of their common subordination to the royal ancestors.

Yet here "in the forest," perhaps far more so than in royal burials, participants have the opportunity to redefine those terms for themselves. After exhaustively detailing the "taboos" *(fady)* associated with every feature of royal service, one of the guardians at the *mahabo* finally concluded:

> You know why it takes so long to cut down those trees? Because nobody does any work! They just sit around and drink. We used to bring up those barrels of alcohol from Ambañoro. Friday would come. We still wouldn't have left [to cut wood]. Eating, singing, drinking! Friday, we just drank, we didn't go and serve. There were months we went only once into the forest! People just wanted to have a good time.

Goffman and Foucault focus on generic practices that may be common to total institutions cross culturally. They do not explore their social-cultural differences. Perhaps they do not need to explore these differences because of the pervasiveness of the mechanical metaphors for society that underlie their own analyses as well as their examples, all drawn from Western contexts. Indeed, it is essential to their analyses that participants themselves interpret these institutions "only on these instrumental grounds," or in terms of their "efficiency" and "normalcy."[21]

The Sakalava interpret the *menaty* service in productive terms when they emphasize that it is simply "work," albeit far more difficult and dangerous, since it is royal work. But the underlying social metaphor is completely different. The royal order that governs the work camp is conveyed nonverbally through the structure of the place and the organization of the work around the royal body. In *working*—moving about the camp, carrying out their allotted tasks according to the pervasive requirements of heads and pairs, leaders and followers—the Sakalava are incorporated into the body of royalty, specifically ancestral royalty. Conversely, the royal ancestors are regenerated through their incorporation into the bodies of the living.

The key factor in their interaction is the *teza* or cores of trees used to make the palisade in which the royal tomb is rewrapped. There are guidelines for the kinds and colors of woods that are permitted and prohibited; the ways in which they are cut, trimmed, and debarked; the places in which these procedures are done and the posts stored; and the agents involved in the work. In sum, the *teza* are handled like royal bodies. The transformation of the trees into posts put back in the ground around the tomb exactly parallels the transformation of the fleshy corpse into a skeleton enclosed in a tree trunk and buried in the tomb itself.

Rebuilding and Reburying

Workers serve the royal ancestors in the *menaty* service by taking down the old fence and rewrapping the tomb in a new fence. The form of the service is very like a reburial as practiced among the highland Merina and Betsileo. But it is not the same thing being reburied. In taking on the form of the posts the royal corpse has multiplied, and in multiplying it has become identified with the commoners stripped of their associations with kin in the process of reorganizing as individuals around the body of royalty.

Ancestors and descendants together are regenerated in the process of cleaning the tomb—removing the old leaves and branches from the top, washing off the stones with mead, weeding around the perimeter, laying down fresh sand, and putting up a new fence—all of which clarifies the form of the tomb within the dense thicket of trees that surrounds it. The *menaty* service regenerates the ancestors by forming new ties among participants drawn together on the basis of their common ties to royalty, by drawing workers into the center of the tomb, by incorporating living people into its very structure.

But it would be closer to the Sakalava perspective to say that the ancestors *are* this combination of dead and living beings, taking the form of an enormous tree-person rooted in this place. In reconstructing the *menaty,* royal followers have cleared the ground and replanted a giant dead-living tree. Taken all together, the tomb surrounded by its several fences forms one enormous tree-person composed of stones and trees, trunks and living branches, bones and flesh, dead and living persons, including royalty, commoners, and slaves.

As a body, the royal tomb is identified with the bodies within it. The east side, "At the royal head(s)" *(Ankabeso)* is the head of the body, associated with royalty; the west side, "At the feet" *(Ampandia)* is the feet of the body, associated with commoners and slaves. As a tree, the tomb includes the *menaty,* or innermost fence, formed from the strong trunks of dead trees, and the *fiaroaomby,* or outermost fence, made of quickset branches, especially branches of shrubs known as *matambelo,* literally "dead-living." The royal ancestors, buried at the center, are by implication the fertile roots from which it springs. As trees/persons, the *menaty* provides the dead trunks of the bodies, made of ancestral royalty and living commoners alike. The *fiaroaomby,* made of quickset branches, forms the arms (the terms for branches and arms are the same). Again the royal ancestors buried at the center of the tomb are, by implication, the fertile roots or genitals *(fototra;* the term is once more the same) from which they grow.

The whole service is saturated during the cleaning process with a material akin to blood: a fermented mixture of cooked honey and water. Honey, conceived as the sap or blood of trees *(lio,* the term is the same), is renowned for its purifying powers. As the chief ingredient in many Sakalava medicines, it is used to make children grow and to restore people to health. In its cooked form—*tô mainty* ("blackness"), or *tamberoño* to commoners—it is prescribed to drink in all cases where there is considerable blood loss, "so as to replenish the blood" *(biaka mimpodipody ley rahaben'azy, lion'azy).* And the door of the fence is sealed, completing the service, with the blood of a pair of sacrificed cattle, one for the royal ancestors and one for all their followers, including commoners and guardian-slaves alike.

Burial Grounds of Memory

In thinking about how Sakalava followers recall ancestral royal leaders by reconstructing their tombs in the form of immense tree-persons, I am reminded of Ronald MacDonald's analysis of the epic underworlds of Virgil, Dante, and Milton as "burial places of memory" in his book of that name. By invoking the dead in an underworld where "all the pasts are equally present," these poets were able to give them a simultaneity with the living that allowed them to rework their own relations with their predecessors in the epic tradition.

MacDonald does not consider how literary burial places of memory might have been related to broader sociocultural patterns in the poets' worlds. On the contrary, he sees them as limited even within literature to the epic genre. In his view, the epic ended with Milton's *Paradise Lost,* its foundations eroded by the growth of capitalist forms of political, economic, and social expansion. Approaching the questions from a later time, a distant place, and a different people, I have wondered how these epic forms have still been incorporated into the work of scholars such as Marx, Frazer, and Freud who explored the innermost regions of the "rational mind," its netherworldly "unconscious," and, possibly, new conceptions of "memory" that might have developed together with capitalist forms of social relationships and new ideas about time and space. Marx's allusions to Dante in *Das Kapital* and Frazer's allusions to Virgil in *The Golden Bough* are explicit. Through Frazer's work, and more recently through that of Marx, anthropologists have incorporated these epic forms into commemorative ethnographies of non-Western peoples. They began to write about these "disappearing worlds," as they are now popularly known, in the late nineteenth and early twentieth centuries, when Europeans saw their non-Western forebears as dying out or perhaps going underground, as indeed—at least in Madagascar—colonized peoples often saw themselves.[22]

Memory is associated with places, often burial places, in many parts of the world. In contemporary Madagascar, these places are the fertile, rocky ground where the living join with the dead to form ancestries, lest they die out together. In the words of one royal funeral song, "Ndramandisoarivo [the founding ruler of the Northern Sakalava monarchies] doesn't rule if he doesn't bring in his grandchildren." One woman who served as a spirit medium explained this line by saying:

> Ndramandisoarivo doesn't rule if he doesn't bring his grandchildren into the monarchy. When a ruler gets old, the children and grandchildren bring the monarchy up, they make it great, they raise it, they grow it. There is no monarchy if the children and grandchildren don't take the elder's place.

Others pointed out the way in which mediums are often possessed by royal spirits who are related as grandparent and grandchild because of the affinity between them. Such connections were said to be similar to those among living people, older and younger.

Rebuilding royal tombs provides Sakalava followers with many different opportunities to "effect historical reversals, question the order that chronological and narrative history dictates,"[23] concerning their own leaders as well as their colonial and contemporary successors. While epic poets may contend over authorial originality, the Sakalava see the burial places of their memories as vital to their very existence, not merely documenting but achieving the renewal of reigns and the revitalization of legends. People with ancestors thrive; people who lose or become lost to their ancestors dwindle and die. Sakalava precolonial and colonial history from a European perspective commemorates forgotten glory: dead kings, stolen relics, and lost followers. As Sakalava followers see it, tomb building recalls people to the struggle with outsiders to protect their ancestors from theft by regenerating them in the very bodies of those who remember them.

The Hatch and Brood of Time

Although this brief summary does not do justice to the complexity of Malagasy ideas and practices concerning remembering, a few general points might be made in conclusion.

Remembering in northwestern Madagascar is indeed socioculturally and historically "constructed," as Küchler and Melion suggest in their introduction. In fact, remembering is here a form of work, more exactly "service," inseparable from the re-creation of social hierarchies in practice.

Spaces are salient features of this process here as elsewhere. Malagasy might well agree with the Western Apache that land provides a more enduring reminder of proper ancestral behavior than living people who die.[24] As people in northwestern Madagascar express it proverbially: "It's not land that comes and goes, but living people" *(Tsy tany miherinkerigny, fa olom-beloño)*. Nevertheless, they do not see ancestral land (there is no other kind) as a static receptacle for the dead, but as a creation of recurrent human effort. In the reconstruction of the "powerfully efficacious land" *(tany masina)* of the royal tomb, spatialization appears to be the foundation of this process, creating proprioceptive memories lodged throughout the body, into which visual, auditory, gustatory, olfactory, and other sensory memories may be incorporated: the smell of corpses masked by incense, the taste of *tô mainty*, the sound and feeling of songs sung only in the presence of royal spirits.

These bodily memories are not simply of and through places, but memories of and through beings created from the conjunction of people-present-in-places, elaborated on in agricultural images and actions, so that placing becomes planting, and (at)tending becomes clearing, cultivating, and growing; and so that people-present-in-places merge into trees, and finally one tree, rooted in the ground.

In commemorating these beings in bodies made of people-present-in-places, workers remake their own bodies. Like the preceding hypothesis, this could not be confirmed without further research on what Bronislaw Malinowski called the "psychophysiology"[25] of mind and memory. Nevertheless, it does accord with local Malagasy ideas and practices about how images and words, especially names, associated with deceased persons are buried not only in the ground but also in the bodies of their mourners, and with the popularization of memories about ancestors through spirits who "come down" to move and speak through the bodies of living people, especially those who claim not to believe in their existence.

Drying up, chopping, cutting, and burying—acts of forgetting—are important features of this process, but finally the emphasis is on the re-union of elements—human beings, trees, rocks, earth—that participants themselves see as living-and-dead. Whether or not *hadino*, or "forgotten," is linguistically related to *hadina*, meaning "to be dug, to be made into a trench" is debatable. In any case, the root *hady* is itself complex, meaning not only to dig, perhaps to bury, but also to dig in order to unearth, to investigate. The linguistic emphasis in "remembering" is on the reemerging of connections, literally, "making-not-set-apart" *(mahatsiaro)*.

In the practices of people in northwestern Madagascar, the embodiment of memories occurs in counterpoint with speech. The royal tomb is rebuilt to repair the unspeakable death of a living ruler. Or perhaps more accurately, royal followers serve to make a past event that was unspeakable as well as unseen not only visible and palpable, tastable, smellable, but also *nameable* once again. As in Western popular notions of conscious, preconscious, or unconscious forms of thought, or as Malinowski observed in the Trobriands,[26] there is here too a stratigraphy to the psychophysiology of mind and memory, in which verbal images—names, in this case—are the first to go and the last to reemerge, only after their bodies have been remade.

The re-creation of these beings, the re-presentation of these "lost" and now "found" people-present-in-places, is inescapably historical and political in Western terms as well, involving the reassertion of identities among people upon themselves, as well as the attempted imposition and extirpation of social identities upon the bodies of others. Formal theories about memory, derived from the work of Plato and Aristotle, seem to substantiate a divide between people who are predominantly literate and those who are not. Greater attention to the bodily processes of remembering should help to refocus the attention of scholars on sociocultural and historical variations in what may be universal processes, for example, in the spatialization exemplified in mnemonic practices dating back to the Greeks and Romans of imagining the mind, located in the head, as a house in which an orator moves from room to room. "His belly is a tabernacle of magical force,"[27] says Malinowski, echoing biblical scripture in summarizing Trobriand accounts of an elderly man famed for his memory of magical acts and sayings. The interdisciplinary, cross-cultural research that Küchler and Melion advocate in this volume would provide the ideal grounds for this new scholarship on memory.

ARTHUR G. MILLER

Transformations of Time and Space: Oaxaca, Mexico, circa 1500–1700

By all appearances conquest is a one-sided act. When the battles are over, the winners impose, and the only choice open to the losers is between submitting or seeking to renew the battle. Students of the Spanish conquests in America have begun recently to accumulate evidence to the contrary. Choice, negotiation, and creative adaptation are among the features of postconquest cultural change that belie the image of passive reception. The introduction of European symbolic systems and modes of representation into Mexico during the early part of the sixteenth century triggered a variety of interactive processes of change affecting Mexican memory, cognition, and production of images and texts. I am concerned in particular with the development of two colonial genres—native calendars and maps—in which form and content are interwoven in new ways, and the relationship between image and text is given new meaning.

This paper presents initial considerations about the influence of European writing and spatial representation on indigenous memorial practices, as evident in selected calendars and maps produced during the first two centuries after conquest. It is a preliminary statement of an ongoing project, restricted to a two-century period from A.D. 1550–1700, focusing on the mountainous zone north of the Valley of Oaxaca in south central Mexico, a region known as the Zapotec Sierra (fig. 29).[1] Because the extant Zapotec data is sparse and not yet analyzed, I also consider relevant comparative material from elsewhere in Mesoamerica.[2]

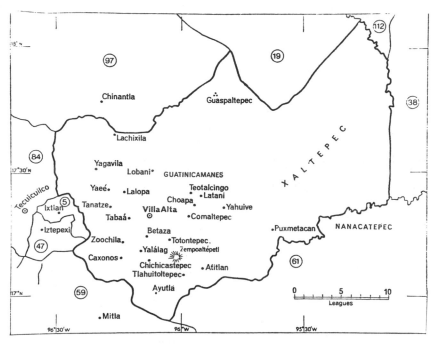

Figure 29. Map of the Zapotec Sierra Region. After Peter Gerhard, *A Guide to the Historical Geography of New Spain* (Cambridge, 1972), p. 368.

Colonial period calendars and maps record on paper changing native solutions to the tasks of keeping time and charting space under European influence. During the pre-Hispanic period, glyphs from "ritual calendars" were used to date historical events and for divination purposes, and they formed an essential part of Zapotec funerary practice. Examples survive on stone and stucco architecture, free-standing carved monuments, and especially ceramic offerings and sculpted and painted tomb walls. But nowhere do they exist as complete timetables.[3] By the end of the seventeenth century, ritual calendars were written using the Latin alphabet and Arabic numerals for ancient divination purposes that were specifically prohibited by the colonial regime. No longer partially represented in stone, clay, or paint, colonial calendars were written on European paper as complete timetables, disclosing the entire system as linear template. Ordinarily hidden from Spanish eyes, examples of colonial ritual calendars survive in the colonial archives in Spain, discovered and sent to the Spanish Crown to substantiate the continued existence of idolatrous practices in the colonies.

While calendars changed form and became more complete, maps, in the European sense, were invented. Unknown in pre-Hispanic America, where other means of depicting spatial relations existed, maps were devised by native draftsmen early in the colonial period as a means of complying with specific requests for territorial records and of arguing land disputes before Spanish judicial authorities. These survive in various archives as part of the colonial records of land tenure and jurisdictional boundaries. The maps evolved over a two-century period, influenced by alphabetic literacy as well as European map-making conventions. A direct influence appears in the written glosses on spatial terms and representations. A less obvious, yet perhaps more significant, influence is the solitary nature of alphabetic writing, in which writer and reader are isolated from the traditional interchange of oral discourse. This kind of isolating textual quality (which I call here European literacy or writing) marks a major break from "oral literacy" in which texts were read aloud to a literate audience.[4] I propose that the adoption of European literacy in the form of colonial calendars undermined the traditional power of those who wielded calendrical knowledge in Zapotec society. Furthermore, the special kind of script involving solitary reading of a discrete text also induced a particular kind of spatial organization of images in native drawing practices, where space is shown to have a fixed and isolated relationship with the map "reader," resulting in the secularization of native territories in accordance with Spanish administrative and judicial authority.

The calendars and maps were produced for highly contrasting social contexts: strict secrecy and public judicial contest. Together they provide unique direct evidence for the effects of colonial domination and European influence on indigenous modes of thought and representation. The case of calendars and maps reveals a dual process of incorporating the European in order to preserve the pre-Hispanic, at the cost of limiting action in the future. The colonial calendars inscribe a new political and economic significance on the Zapotec conception of temporality. Incorporation of European writing into the form of the ancient calendar perpetuated the concealing of sacred knowledge, while at the same time it undermined the ancient structures of authority. Similarly, the native map tradition was a response to the European secularization of land ownership, while it also tended to destroy land ownership's ancient sacred connotations.

Calendars and Maps

This preliminary exploration of postconquest ideational change focuses on two native genres closely resembling European models but with significant formal differences and radically different genealogies. My goal is to trace and, as far as possible, begin to explain the development of colonial calendars and maps. They are colonial products not only by virtue of chronology but also because they were forged by specifically colonial processes of interchange. Rather than a syncretic mixture of European and pre-Hispanic traits, these two genres are material evidence of creative responses to new social realities forged by the intermingling of two vastly different cultural systems.

The two processes in question are far from simple parallels. The genealogy of the written calendars is relatively easy to trace but difficult to explain, while the maps have obscure antecedents but a relatively obvious functional explanation. The motives of the Zapotecs for adopting European writing when seeking to communicate with the Spanish rulers are self-evident. Why they should have done so when recording information that was proscribed by the Spanish and meant to be hidden from their eyes is puzzling.

Although European alphabetic script is held to be more efficient than other forms,[5] the Zapotecs' own pictographic system (with possible phonetic aspects) was perfectly serviceable for the task of recording calendrical information. Nor did the new system enhance the elite's control over ritual knowledge. The ancient image form and the new Latin script were equally esoteric and restricted: information was as nearly inaccessible to the masses when encoded in painted glyphs as it was in written calendars, if not more so. To suggest that knowledge of the pictorial mode died out merely begs the question of why the form but not the content should have lost cultural currency. We have to assume that, in the Zapotec view, the new form came to acquire some kind of efficacy that the old one lacked.

In contrast, maps seem to have emerged precisely because the Zapotecs (and other Mesoamericans) had to communicate with the Spanish, but their pre-Hispanic origins are far from clear. Maps in the sense of two-dimensional projections of three-dimensional "reality" (that is, landscape) seem to have been European imports, although we cannot really doubt that the Zapotec had some means of recording a whole range of geographical information aside from the place glyphs that identified particular sites—most likely through a variety of other glyphic forms that we do not yet understand.[6] I postulate, then, a complex genealogy for the postconquest native maps: overall European form with written glosses, on the one side, joined, from the local tradition, to a combination of glyphs and drawing conventions developed in pre-Hispanic mural paintings and polychrome pottery.

Memory

Pre-Hispanic calendrics and territorial management strategies fashioned memory as a process of selective remembering and forgetting, governing patterns of labor and loyalty. When inscribed and "fixed" in European text, memory did not become accessible and constitutive of knowledge, as one might assume given the Western experience. Rather, the process served to conceal indigenous political economy from Spanish influence by arresting mnemonic practice in script. Texts of indigenous and Spanish authority both shared similar physical, social, and philosophical experience in the colonial period. But the new textual form of memorial practice had a marked impact on indigenous authority by enfeebling power traditionally wielded by those who controlled calendrical knowledge.[7]

"Memory" as the history of conquest in the Americas is, of course, a Western construct. The history has been written largely from European perspectives; very little is known of how native Americans regarded their conquerors. This is due to the nature of the sources; records of the inter-action between Old and New Worlds were made by Europeans. Never-theless, some important work has been done to reconstruct the native view of the conquest. For Mesoamerica, Eric Wolf, Gonzalo Aguirre Beltrán, and Charles Gibson are major figures in the history of Indian societies. Nancy Farriss has combined anthropological concepts with archival and ethnographic research in an attempt to uncover structures of meaning as well as social patterns in native society under colonial rule. James Lockhart has concentrated on native language texts and linguistic analyses in looking at how native Americans perceived their conquerors and how they used European ideas for their own purposes. Serge Gruzinski has examined native American spatial conventions in colonial maps; his focus, however, is the Valley of Mexico, and he examines only a sampling of the Oaxaca material. While many of the maps that are without provenience and un-dated (that is, located outside the national archives) have been published, these have not been ordered stylistically as a whole by a trained art historian to evaluate change over time. Nor have they been systematically evaluated for changes that occurred in the Amerindian system of recording space under European influence. Donald Robertson's 1959 work on colonial period maps is a ground-breaking beginning, but much remains to be done.

Using ethnographic data, Eva Hunt attempts to link time and space, arguing that Mesoamerican calendars encapsulated the meaning of what she calls the "time-space continuum," which she describes as an essential aspect of their religion. However, exactly what is the Mesoamerican view of the relationship between time and space is never made explicit in Hunt's work. Barbara Tedlock's study of calendars in contemporary highland Maya communities provides valuable ethnographic background for this research, which can be used for comparative purposes. Given the scarcity of sources to study Amerindian modes of thought in the past, it is an extraordinary privilege to be able to glimpse how European traits were seen through Amerindian eyes. Such is the opportunity afforded by the two remarkable sets of native American documents that are the focuses of this study.

The theoretical and comparative literature on cultural change under colonial rule is vast, as is the literature on the shift from oral to literate traditions in Western societies. So far, the only studies I know that deal with the impact of European literacy on colonized groups are the works of Jack Goody, and of Caroline Bledsoe and Kenneth Robey. More general discussion of colonial changes in non-Western thought can be found in Phillip Curtin and in Robin Horton and Ruth Finnegan. Already cited above, Gillian Feeley-Harnik's sensitive study of the transformation of power in colonial Malagasy society is most pertinent to my investigation.[8]

The Sources

The sources that may reveal how European forms influenced Zapotec temporal and spatial renderings fall into two main temporal units: pre-Hispanic and colonial. Most pre-Hispanic calendrical representations in the Zapotec region have been found on architectonic or free-standing carved monuments and in tombs, primarily in the vivid wall paintings that line elite funerary monuments. As part of a long-term project to record and analyze ancient Mexican mural painting, I have photographed and supervised the drawing of this Zapotec material. The richest and most complex collection has recently been discovered in the so-called Tomb 5 at the site of Huijazoo to the north of Oaxaca City.[9] Eight other painted tombs located at Monte Albán and near Mitla, excavated earlier in this century, yield the rest of the preconquest calendrical notations in which glyphs appear, painted both separately and within figurative compositions. These murals and the archaeological contexts in which they appear provide the original matrix out of which the colonial transformations emerged.

The major colonial source of Zapotec calendrical material and contextual data is a series of idolatry records sent by the Bishop of Oaxaca to the Spanish Crown at the beginning of the eighteenth century and preserved in the Audiencia of Mexico section of the Archivo General de Indias.[10] In addition to the recorded confessions and reports attesting to the persistence of Zapotec religious rituals, the dossiers contain 103 *librillos* (little books) confiscated from the "masters of idolatry," which are in fact the ritual calendars written in European script referred to earlier.

Already worn with use when confiscated, these calendars date from between the middle and the end of the seventeenth century. Long hidden in the Seville repository, the calendars are the only extant examples of recorded ritual produced specifically by and for Amerindians living under Spanish rule. They contain written columns of the twenty Zapotec day names facing thirteen sequentially ordered Arabic numerals usually, but not always, repeated twenty times. The names do not remain constant with the numbers, but shift progressively every thirteen days. Several of these books also contain glyphlike drawings reminiscent of pre-Hispanic calendrical representations, suggesting possible glosses or equivalences of glyph and written version. These unique documents not only bear witness to the persistence of native beliefs after more than a century and a half of European contact, they also provide an unprecedented opportunity to study the interaction between European and native American solutions to recording time.

The period between the last pre-Hispanic tomb images on the eve of the Spanish encounter and the late seventeenth-century calendar texts is crucial to an understanding of how the Zapotec regarded writing and how the Spanish viewed traditional imagery. No comparably rich source exists for this intervening period. Nevertheless, the calendar was so intrinsic a part of the Zapotec ritual system that a considerable amount of evidence can be assembled from references, direct and indirect, in other idolatry trials.[11]

So far no Zapotec maps have been found that can be dated before the Spanish conquest. This lack of material is a significant datum in itself, suggesting that other representative forms may have been used to encode space. Maps, as we understand the term, appear to be a uniquely colonial genre responding to new colonial needs. The extant examples were produced throughout the colonial period and are found either in their original location in Zapotec villages or scattered in national and foreign collections that have been catalogued and many of them published.[12] But a larger number remain unedited. These are the pictorial records, which we call maps, preserved in the Tierras section of the Archivo General de la Nation as part of the "títulos" or titles submitted as evidence in land claims and territorial disputes. The particular value of these maps is their association with contemporary documentary evidence. All of them accompany verbal testimonies supporting the parties' claims. The date of their use, if not always of their production, can be clearly established, as well as their provenience; information on their meaning and function can be teased out of the documentary matrix surrounding them.

From both the Zapotec and Spanish perspectives, the function of the maps was to make clear to a variety of audiences—Indian allies and opponents as well as Spanish judges—what territories were at stake in the particular disputes. This dual audience helps to account for the mixture of techniques. The early maps exhibit pre-Hispanic conventions for rendering space on a flat surface, such as hierarchical ordering of figures. For example, a mountain or tree will be rendered larger if it is more important, regardless of its distance from the picture plane. There are examples of bird's-eye-view landscapes combined with profile view. Sometimes these pre-Hispanic conventions are mixed with European ones, such as two- or three-point perspective.

Yet the colony's power structure tipped the balance in favor of European conventions, at least for communicating with Spaniards. Ultimately Spanish courts and Spanish judges decided the merits of the conflicting claims; success, then, depended on the ability to convey spatial information to them. It seems that the written glosses on traditional depictions and the increasing use of European conventions respond to this need.

Both the Seville calendars and the Mexico City maps are embedded in judicial records that date the sources, provide essential interpretive clues to their meaning, and help link these two indigenous genres. The idolatry trials explicitly related sacred time to sacred space by the use of the calendars to regulate the timing of rituals in particular locations. Moreover, the written records are accompanied by maps of the "idolatrous" parishes commissioned by the ecclesiastical authorities but obviously prepared by Indian draftsmen and incorporating some indigenous conventions. Less explicitly, the written "títulos" accompanying the Tierras maps contain narratives relating territorial claims to temporal sequence, and sacredness of time to sacredness of space—for example, foundation myths based on the erection of churches.

Calendars

In pre-Hispanic contexts, specific dates from the Zapotec calendars appear carved in stone or painted on walls, as well as molded, carved, or painted on pottery. Yet none of these demonstrably preconquest calendrical references can be understood as an entire calendrical system. This fact has two major implications: a preconquest "reading" would have required the presence of persons with knowledge of the calendar as an entirety to understand how the date or dates in question fit into the system; and our "reading" will require that we reconstruct that lost knowledge. How?

By piecing together the puzzle of the pre-Hispanic "timetable" from all of the extant Zapotec glyphs, we can reconstruct the lost system. Alfonso Caso began this task in 1928, assigning letters of the Latin alphabet to nonnumerical signs from the twenty deity-days then known, which were largely understood from the better documented Mexica culture that had dominated much of Mesoamerica (including Oaxaca) by the time the Spanish arrived in the New World.[13] Recently, Gordon Whittaker, in "The Hieroglyphics of Monte Albán," has restudied Zapotec calendrics, proposing alternate readings for those examined by Caso, as well as some new ones. Whittaker cites the trecena or unit of thirteen days as an especially important time period in Zapotec calendrical notation.[14]

Sources for the Zapotec Calendar

There is an important colonial source describing the calendar in use in the valley of Oaxaca shortly after conquest. But at least one archaeologist has argued that the so-called Zapotec calendar described in 1578 by the Dominican friar and student of Zapotec language Juan de Córdova is not

Zapotec, but, rather, one used by the Mixtec peoples originally from the mountainous zone to the west of the valley.[15] Nevertheless, it seems clear that the calendars described by Córdova were those used in the Valley of Oaxaca in the middle of the sixteenth century, whatever the ethnic identification of its practitioners. According to Córdova's *Arte del idioma zapoteca*, the colonial Zapotec (in use, if not in derivation) calendars can be understood to be a complete ritual cycle of 260 days. Based on repeating permutations of 20 days and thirteen numbers, the 260-day cyclical calendar, called the *pije* in Zapotec, served as a divinatory device for calendar specialists. In the *pije*, these 20 days combined with thirteen numbers (which also had sacred connotations) were shown in a bar-and-dot manner so that each dot represented one unit, and a bar five. The *pije* was also used to select—more accurately, to determine—the names of newborn children, and to order the temporal existence of the community and the individual by establishing when it was appropriate to hold ritual sacrifices, plant, harvest, build, marry, travel, or engage in any but the most routine activity. In addition to the *pije*, there was another calendar, *yza* in Zapotec, based on the solar year and concurrent with the 260-day count.

Córdova's description of the calendars in use in the valley of Oaxaca shortly after conquest cannot stand for the system in use more than a millennium earlier. But if the actual physical remains from the archaeological past showing calendrical glyphs tend to support Córdova's descriptions, I see no reason to throw them out only because they represent a much later time period. Obviously, caution is advisable. Many of the Zapotec glyphs—most of them calendrical—known from the pre-Hispanic period, are associated with the so-called Danzantes carvings from the major Zapotec site of Monte Albán, dating from as early as 500 B.C.[16] Among the painted tombs, the earliest glyphs appear on the walls of Tomb 72 from Monte Albán (fig. 30). Dating from the early part of the valley of Oaxaca mural chronology,[17] about A.D. 200, the tomb bears calendrical notations painted in two tones of red. In figure 29, the calendrical notations read "8L,10J" according to the system developed by Alfonso Caso in *Las estelas zapotecas* and "Zapotec Writing and Calendar." Each of the three pairs of numbers and pictographic glyphs (number-letter combination in Caso's system) shown on the Tomb 72 walls probably refers to a trecena (thirteen-day period) or a single day, defined by the *pije* and concurrently by the *yza* (solar year).

Calendrical notations occur also in paintings of later periods (A.D. 300–1500), but always in a subsidiary context as part of a headdress or an

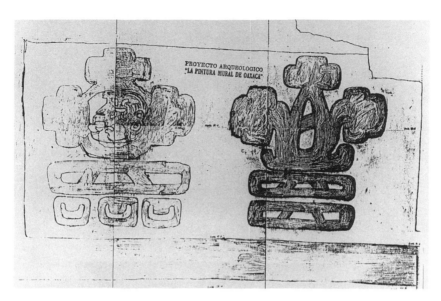

Figure 30. Author's field drawing of south wall, east end of Tomb 72 at Monte Albán. Shown here are pictographic glyphs for day and bar-and-dot number combinations from the 260-day ritual calendar known as the *pije*.

isolated glyph column fronting a standing figure (fig. 31).[18] When calendrical glyphs appear in association with figures' headdresses and clothing, as in figure 31, we may infer a naming function. But when calendrical glyphs appear alone, as on the walls of Tomb 72 (fig. 30), we can read either a date standing for an event, such as time of death, or the calendrical name of the deceased. In any case, it is clear that dates from the calendars, however used, were an integral part of Zapotec funerary ritual. Most striking is the fact that the calendrical notations on the walls of Tomb 72 form the walls' entire design. In contrast to later murals, no figures are associated with these dates. Yet it is probable that the dates refer, in some way, to the person buried in the tomb. If these glyphs and numbers are the deceased's calendrical names or those of his ancestors or descendants, and even if they stand for an event such as time of death, the anonymity of such glyphic representations is remarkable, for no image of the individual is depicted, only his calendrical signs.

From Córdova's 1578 account, it is clear that knowledge of how to "read" the calendars remained the exclusive province of the calendar spe-

Figure 31. Author's field drawing of the north wall, west end of Tomb
105 at Monte Albán. The four figures shown wear headdresses displaying
pictographic naming glyphs for the *pije*. Each figure faces a glyph column
including calendrical dates. The upper band is a stylization of the upper
maw of a supernatural jaguar known as "jaws of the sky."

cialist at the time of the conquest. This suggests the possibility that the
Zapotec calendar may not have existed in pre-Hispanic times as a complete
system. Rather than all examples being destroyed by the conquerors or, for
some other reason, not surviving, perhaps they were never rendered in any
form in the first place, but instead carried in living memory. If so, their
memory would have been carried from generation to generation by chosen
families, and the genealogies of calendars would correspond with those of
persons charged with such sacred knowledge within Zapotec society.

It also seems clear from Córdova's description of calendar use that a
schedule of events was in itself not enough to ensure success in ritual and
agricultural activities. Timely ritual action had to be performed in designated sacred places in order to be efficacious. The coordination of ritual
activity in appropriate sites required a sacred geography that was carried in
living memory or recorded by means of a map-making convention that
designated the time and place for ritual action. These are the documents
produced by the preconquest Zapotec that come closest to the European
"map." The form such records may have taken are discussed in the section
on sacred geography below.

As we have seen, the pre-Hispanic Zapotec data currently available clearly suggests that while specific dates exist in recorded form—referring to events or names—the complete calendar itself (either the 260-day *pije* or 365-day *yza*) is not known to exist in any material form. Why not? I suspect that prior to European influence, complete calendars were not recorded because the Zapotec calendar, like all Mesoamerican calendars, was a fluid, constantly changing concept. Since it ran continuously as a chronological count based on permutations of thirteen and twenty, a record of any single 260-day cycle would be of no use alone as a divinatory device, for a calendar specialist would be needed to interpret the timing of events. Knowledge of how to evaluate the day-number combinations of the *pije* was not inherent in the system. Rather, it was carried in the memory of calendar specialists. Indeed, the most extensive record of calendar use in the early colonial period (associated with the 103 confiscated colonial Zapotec calendars discussed below) makes it clear that even after two centuries of European influence, the Zapotec calendar's meaning depended on specialists who were knowledgeable of how the *pije* functioned and what it meant in changing contexts and times.[19] What this evidence suggests is that the Zapotec calendar was in pre-Hispanic times not a discrete document painted or carved on a surface as glyphs, but rather a form of discourse involving persons who had knowledge of the calendar, their clients, a setting, and a specific day. It was the interaction of these factors, themselves in constant flux, that determined meaning.

Another clue for characterizing the significance of calendar use lies in the special way in which its divine actors were viewed. The colonial sources make it clear that Zapotec supernatural beings controlled the destiny of each day in the 260-day count. They were truly pantheistic beings:[20] supernatural, fluid entities that changed identities, altering the days that composed the calendars. In constant temporal movement, these fluid entities imbued with meaning the sequential permutations of thirteen numbers and twenty days. These day-number combinations could signify positive or negative connotations for any given event. In other words, to use a grammatical analogy, there was no fixed lexicon of deities. Rather, like the output of a grammar, there was a very broad, variable discourse of gods.

The fatalistic predictability of life inherent in the Zapotec calendars had little to do with the individual predestination envisioned by Calvin. The future had both inevitable and alterable qualities, to which the Zapotec responded in a manner that could be characterized as passively active.

Cosmic catastrophe threatened if appropriate ritual action was not taken in response to a predictable sequence of days. Births, deaths, good or bad agricultural yields were events which, when considered in context of the calendar, were fixed with a prescribed fate. While the calendars provided a predictable schedule of positive and negative days, it also had a certain flexible quality. It was the role of the calendar specialist and his memory to manipulate that schedule. For example, the calendar specialist would give a newborn child a name based on the day-number combination in effect at the time of birth. But the parents and the calendar priest had a certain amount of leeway in assigning the child a name. The *maestro* could counsel the parents to wait a few days until a favorable sign occurred if the child was born on a negative day.[21]

Ritual action could be prescribed to postpone the naming event. Thus, the calendar was mutable when used in conjunction with appropriate sacred memories of ritual action residing in personages charged with interpreting and applying the calendars to specific situations. On the one hand, the ritual calendar seemed to be fixed in its relentlessly shifting permutations of the 20 days and thirteen numbers, repeating again after the cycle of 260 days was completed. And when the 260-day calendar (*pije*) permutated with the solar calendar (*yza*), inevitable combinations occurred until a total of fifty-two solar years was completed, when the same cycle would repeat again, on and on until the end of time. On the other hand, the calendars were not fixed, because their link to human actors was variable. Thus the "beginning" of a biography, as in the naming of an individual, was subject to human agency. In fact, without the act of naming the child, in the context of a *maestro* consulting the *pije*, the child could be said to be not yet human, in Zapotec terms. Thus the naming act, like the modern birth certificate, registered the individual in Zapotec society. This is hardly a discrete esoteric use of the calendar. The initiation of the recently born into the body politic is a function of enormous significance. In the practice of naming, we see what may be a typical pattern in a discourse between an inevitable fate, inherent in the day-number combinations of the *pije*, and potentially altering ritual action orchestrated by the calendar specialist.

When a recorded calendar is used to explain an event, there is a certain dissonance: an arbitrary form is applied to action which is anything but arbitrary. The prescribed linear character of the recorded calendar and the multidimensional aspects of an event in time were for the Zapotec incompatible. For the sixteenth-century Spanish, calendars and their use were more fixed; Europeans viewed time as a linear series of events with cyclical characteristics in liturgical observations.[22] The linear narrative of the Passion was repeated every cycle of the Christian year; the Mass reenacted the sacrifice of Christ in ritual action. Unlike Amerindian cyclical calendars, European cyclic rituals were inflexible, repeating virtually similar patterns every cycle. Cyclical ritual in the Americas constantly varied according to current realities and may have even varied from place to place.[23] Zapotec calendars, formed in the past to predict the future, effectively responded to present needs through human action.

When Spain intruded into the Zapotec present, threatening the future survival of the calendars, the response was to take action, not only in ritual, but also on the very form of the calendar itself. Thus, the Zapotec transliterated their calendars into the Latin alphabet (fig. 32), adopting a new communication mode perceived to be more powerful than their own, a form that might preserve a concept of time that was being destroyed by

Figure 32. A page from one of the 103 late-seventeenth-century written calendars now kept in the Archivo de Indias, Seville, Spain (Mexico 882). Arabic numerals displace Zapotec bar-and-dot numeration; transliterated Zapotec words displace pictographic glyphs signifying deities.

Europeans. In so doing, they diminished the role of the calendar specialist. They crystalized what had been fluid, weakening an essential component of their timely discourse.

The Seville Calendars

More European than Mesoamerican, the Seville calendars suggest how a new script influenced temporality notions in the Oaxaca Sierra. Alphabetic writing combined with Arabic numerals to chart out days and names in linear format, serving to gel (and to preserve) what had been subject to ritual practice (which was now forbidden). This does not mean that the calendar became a frozen linear template, unalterable by ritual action. But it implies that, two centuries after conquest, there was an interest in making firm what had been conceived of as being fluid. It also seems that this change in form undermined the future viability of calendrical practice by tending to disengage the parties involved.

Disengagement of actors in calendrical discourse is evident in the isolation of text from reader visible in the form of the Seville calendars themselves. Their format is not that of the Mesoamerican screenfold (the traditional textual form),[24] but rather that of the European codex—with pages sewn on one side. The screenfold had enabled cyclical dates appearing on one page to be placed beside virtually any other page on both sides of the screenfold. Such flexibility of page ordering meant that dates appearing on separate pages could be combined in any number of ways, literally positioning appropriate past events alongside current ones. Thus, the way in which the Mesoamerican screenfold was read depended in part on the manipulative action of the reader. Calendrical notations and the time they represent were therefore not inscribed by an unalterable scribed sequence as in the European codex, where reading order is fixed as firmly as the threads that bind the pages' sides.

In one sense, adoption of the European codex format on the part of the Zapotec is evidence for their interest in incorporating European views of time into their own. And it can be interpreted as an attempt to appropriate those forms for their own use. In any case, we have to assume that, since the Seville calendars were made, not as a result of coercion or any process of active conversion on the part of the Europeans, but rather as a totally indigenous product, the Zapotec hoped to gain something positive by incorporating foreign forms into their ancient knowledge. Something of what they hoped to achieve can be teased out of the wordy testimonies surrounding the Seville calendars, representing direct commentary on calendar use among the Sierra Zapotec two centuries after the conquest.

When the fact that Zapotec ritual calendars were recorded as a complete system in an alien script came to the attention of the energetic bishop of Oaxaca, Fray Angel Maldonado, he consequently instigated one of the most extensive and intensive idolatry trials ever carried out in Oaxaca. Aimed at weakening the competitive authority of the missionary Dominican friars by showing that their policies had failed, the investigation probed the idolatrous practices of the Zapotec inhabitants of the Villa Alta district, located in a mountainous region to the northeast of the valley of Oaxaca. The proceedings of these investigations, consisting of translated trial testimonies from native informants, were sent to the Crown as proof that the Dominicans were ineffective missionaries, along with statements to the effect that they should be recalled and control of the region be placed in the bishop's capable hands. These verbatim testimonies of Zapotec religious practices were accompanied by late seventeenth-century "ritual books," which are in fact calendars. Maldonado's informants described the contexts of these ritual books within the Zapotec communities from which they were confiscated. In the over eight hundred manuscript pages of trial testimonies are accounts of how the books were used, who owned them, and under what circumstances they were passed on to succeeding generations. The Maldonado testimonies are the most detailed account of calendrical use in Mesoamerica yet available.[25]

According to the idolatry testimonies collected by Bishop Maldonado, a "maestro de idolatría" knew the significance of each day in the 260-day cycle. It was knowledge of the meaning of the day-number combinations that gave meaning to the calendar and power to a *maestro*. Support for this view derives from trial testimony, including references to individuals who did not own ritual books but had committed the calendars to memory and carried out calendrical rituals. This is evidence of shamanic performance encoding time, a practice that has been observed in colonial Yucatecan material as well.[26] Cited also are instances of individuals owning calendars but ignorant of their use. Such testimonies suggest that it was not the written calendars themselves that were crucial, but rather their memory. They also suggest that the power of the calendar specialist had diminished since earlier times. Clearly, the combination of day names and numbers and how these numbers and names shifted over a repeating 260-day period had become, through the reproducibility of texts, more accessible and commonplace and were capable, therefore, of being memorized by almost anyone.

That the Zapotec calendar may not have existed in recorded form in pre-Hispanic times is therefore comprehensible. Recorded calendars were not essential to the work of a calendar specialist and would be useless without knowledge of the calendar's workings, knowledge that was carried in living memory. Also, knowledge of the calendar could have been encoded in any number of partial or total forms whose mnemonic devices were spatial. For example, a procession through space involved principals knowing temporal corollaries of sacred places, which were marked by natural features. Thus, sacred geographies were inextricably tied to calendrical practice. Such practice is not only reported in the testimonies, but is also evident in ethnographic accounts of the Sierra Zapotec.[27] Comparatively, processions through space in which principals knew temporal corollaries are reported for the colonial and ethnographic Yucatec Maya.[28]

Why, then, did the Zapotec go to the trouble of transliterating into a foreign script what had been consigned to memory? They clearly had no intention of showing these calendars to Europeans. In fact, they knew they would be punished if the calendars' existence was discovered by their conquerors.

The Attraction of European Literacy

The Seville calendars are hardly simple examples of European influence on native forms. Instead, they are best understood as documents created in reaction to European attempts to destroy memory of native ritual. The Seville calendars represent a Zapotec attempt to appropriate European script and numeration into their own concepts of temporality. They hoped to profit by the power of European texts. But the foreign script had a very different effect on Zapotec social organization from that described for it in Max Weber's model of typical bureaucratic structure in *On Charisma and Institution Building:* from 1500 to 1700 the production of alphabetic writing in the form of calendars did nothing to reveal the role of calendars in Zapotec society. On the contrary, European writing concealed their function from the community at large, which remained illiterate. Displacement of image by text continued to conceal knowledge, for both image and text can be esoteric, but the new relatively rigid form—deemed more powerful—at the same time undermined the structures of authority that resided in the calendar specialist's facility in manipulating flexible image. The Zapotec turned the new technology of the word—alphabetic writing—to their own clandestine uses to preserve their memory. But they thereby rendered that memory less potent by restricting its applicability to actual social situations.

In spite of the probability that in pre-Hispanic times the Zapotec calendar had never been recorded wholly in material form, by 1700 it had appeared as a complete recorded form in the alien European script, signaling an attempt on the part of the Zapotec to incorporate the European power inherent in the written word. Rather than being an example of native alignment with Spanish culture, the Seville calendars are instead concrete evidence of Zapotec resistance to European spiritual authority. But the new form in a sense substituted for, and therefore fundamentally undermined, the very authority of those wielding calendrical knowledge.

Bishop Maldonado clearly saw these calendars as the threats to the Spanish church the Zapotec intended them to be. For the bishop, it was not graven images he had confiscated, but words directed to false gods. That idolatry should have been transformed into written form must have been anathema to him and perceived as a greater threat than images. Idols can be smashed and thereby false gods dispatched. Of course, an "idol" (what Marx called a "fetish") is by definition a token of false religion; the notion that destroying an image of a god in the other's belief system in fact does away with that god may be as unfounded as the thought that smashing a Catholic crucifix would dispatch Jesus Christ. The point is that Maldonado and Europeans like him in colonial situations tended to regard images of "false" gods as vulnerable to destruction.[29] Whether or not they could in fact be annihilated by the act of physical destruction is less important than the belief that they could be. In any case, an image tends to be unique, and its destruction is therefore inevitably tied to eradication of its substance. Words on the other hand are, as Saussure tells us in *Course in General Linguistics*, abstractions of something else, which cannot be destroyed by eliminating its form. Maldonado's iconoclastic zeal is firmly based in Western attitudes toward deity-images, stretching back to Moses's destruction of the Golden Calf. We cannot doubt that Maldonado saw holy scripture as directly linked to divine power.

It seems that the literate pre-Hispanic Zapotec did not write down their calendar in a complete form because a written text—be it pictographic, phonetic, syllabic, or alphabetic—limits the authority of those who are charged with wielding sacred power. If the textual calendar literally restricts the range of possibilities of action on the part of calendar specialists, then this may explain why sacred knowledge of the calendars was never recorded in material form by the pre-Hispanic Zapotec. Like the most classified secrets of modern states, their sacred calendrical knowledge was too precious to take material form. Its vulnerability may have been protected by the prohibition against its being rendered manifest.

Because the Zapotec had a writing system perfectly capable of inscribing their calendars, it is not so much the adoption of European script that separates pre- from post-Hispanic calendrical use as it is the act of scriptural encoding of complete calendrical information, thereby limiting its interpretation. Because the act of writing down complete calendrical timetables enfeebled the traditional power of personages wielding sacred calendrical authority, Maldonado should have been ecstatic when he saw evidence of this process of weakening native "idolatry." But Maldonado did not see it this way. Nor did the Zapotec, for they not only encoded in script their complete calendar, thereby restricting its traditional use, but they did so by adopting the alien alphabetic script of their conquerors. Why? The answer lies buried in the mass of colonial documentation in which the calendars are imbedded, a data source currently being mined for answers to this important question. In the meantime, certain hypotheses seem worth testing during the course of our ongoing research.

One lies in the possibility that the Zapotec thought that by both transforming their calendar from image to text and rendering it as a complete scriptural record, they could preserve it in the conquerors' memory template and thereby partake of that template's attendant power. The European written word and its powerful role in judicial and religious matters was one of the most striking innovations confronting the conquered Zapotec. Their earliest exposure to the power of foreign texts was most dramatically presented to them in the formal delivery of the *Requerimiento* (the "Requirement") of 1512—a royal proclamation read from a Spanish text that was subsequently notarized, requiring that all who heard it should accept Spanish spiritual and secular authority or submit to the sword.[30] The Requirement was recorded speech of Europeans that intruded a new memory template into the New World. It stated that from the moment of its reading, the past of the conquered was that of the conquerors. The Requirement opened with the proclamation that a common narrative history now bound the American aborigines to the exigencies of European memory as set forth in text: "The Lord our God, Living and Eternal, created heaven and earth, and one man and one woman, of whom you and I, and all men of the world, were and are descendants, as well as all those who came after us."[31] With a stroke of the pen, the indigenous peoples of the Americas became subject to the Pope and, by his concession of America to Spain, to Ferdinand and Isabella and their royal policies of government. Since the essence of Spanish spirituality was presented to them as text (the word presented as God), the subjugated peoples of Oaxaca were also exposed to the association of sacred power with written texts.

Another possible explanation for the Zapotec's adopting the conquerors' alien script lies in the fact that alphabetic text's facile reproducibility seemed to ensure the survival of crucial past knowledge. If their written calendars were burned, they could be reproduced. As with the bible and the textual knowledge of the ancient Western world, the likelihood of survival could be increased during hard times by the production of multiple copies. Also, the power of European texts evident in judicial and spiritual matters presented the native occupants of Oaxaca with a model which could preserve important aspects of their community identity in the future. The appearance of such power in written words was seductive. Perhaps the new form would revitalize their sacred knowledge. Whatever the reasons, in accepting the illusion that the memory of ancient sacred knowledge could be ensured by adopting alien ideas, the Zapotec seemed oblivious to the fact that writing down such knowledge undermined the calendar specialists' power, for their power depended on their ability to manipulate a secret unrecorded calendar. This paradoxical effect of text to preserve and, at the same time, to destroy traditional uses of temporality is evident also in the colonial transformation of pre-Hispanic space.

The Secularization of Sacred Geographies

Map-making, as we know it, is linked to the colonialization of territories; transforming three-dimensional space onto a flat surface aids in the domination of one group by another. Maps reduce spatial reality to documents that are useful in the colonial penetration of the indigenous landscape. We know that Roman cadastral maps inscribed conquered lands for purposes of redistribution and taxation.[32] It also seems clear that the Spanish expansion into the New World brought with it the need to encode territories onto flat surfaces, so that the quality and quantity of conquest could be measured, assessed and redistributed.[33] Unlike the Romans, however, the Spanish conquerors did not draw the maps in question. Instead they had the Zapotec do it for them. In the process, the Zapotec isolated their land from pre-Hispanic associations, the most salient of which was temporal.

In the beginning of the colonial period, maps were produced by Zapotec draftsmen because they were demanded of them. Maps showing communities under Spanish rule were produced in response to one of the questions asked by the Crown of local populations in the 1578–85 *Relaciones Geográficos*.[34] These Relations were quite specific in the spatial information required, and the native populations complied by producing maps to the satisfaction of the royal representatives. Maps of this sort aided in the breakup of traditional land-use patterns by disrupting preexisting land management strategies exercised by Zapotec nobility (*cacicazcos*), thereby facilitating the establishment of new centers of population (*congregación*).[35] It is not surprising, therefore, that the Zapotec, along with other Mesoamerican groups, came to regard maps with a wary eye.

When asked to encode their traditional lands, the Zapotec (as well as other Mesoamerican groups) responded by producing *pinturas* (paintings), many of which appear to be clumsy attempts to approximate European map-making and landscape conventions, fettered, as it were, with the residue of pre-Hispanic stylistic traits.[36] But there are alternate explanations for early colonial maps or *pinturas*. One is that their style reveals that the Zapotec had no previously existing tradition of schematically rendering, in the European manner, three-dimensional space on a flat surface. Even maps made in the latter part of the colonial period depict this characteristic. Another explanation relates to the practice of willful deception on the part of Indian map-makers. Like the verbal record, maps in the *Relaciones* were produced as a result of a complex discourse that was far from direct.

Consider what we know of the way in which the inquiry was carried out. First, local authorities in colonial towns were ultimately responsible for answering the questionnaires. Some they could answer, no doubt, based on their own experience in the area. Others, they may have had no idea how to answer, particularly if recently arrived in the jurisdiction. Take, for example, queries dealing with the comparative values of preconquest and postconquest life, differences in dress and hygiene, in food and drink, in domestic houses and burials, among other traits not easily discernable.[37] If the local administrator could not answer the questions, he had two choices: he could make up the answers, or he could engage the aid of Indian informants. How did these native informants respond to inquiries into practically every facet of their life, an inquiry posed by local officials, many of whom had not won the confidence of their charges? What was the session with the informant like? In many cases questions were originally formulated in Spanish. Then they were presented directly in the native language; on occasion, the questions were translated into the Mesoamerican lingua franca, Nahuatl, and then into Zapoteco. Replies were translated back into Spanish. A good deal could have been lost or misunderstood in the process. On top of the formidable translation barriers, the *Relaciones* also include evidence in their replies of intentional deception on the part of the Zapotec.[38] Given these circumstances, the *Relaciones* are certainly problematic historical documents. The pictorial replies, too, cannot be taken at face value.[39] We know that at least six of the ninety-two extant *pinturas* were made by Indian informants, who are named in the text, and a seventh one was executed by an unnamed "yndio pintor."[40] The majority were most likely executed by Indian informants. Some of them were probably made with deceptive purposes, for we can be sure that the Zapotec were not anxious to lose what they themselves considered precious, even sacred. These maps may show more what the Spanish wanted to see than they do native territories. The awkward appearance of the *Relaciones* maps seems to have less to do with style than with meaning. They may well, in fact, serve as direct evidence for the Indians' reluctance to convey information about their territories in their own terms.

Deceit or concealment to stem territorial disintegration was not the only motivation for manipulating foreign forms. The Zapotec also willingly adopted the European map for purposes of resolving their own long-standing land conflicts.[41] But maps used in colonial courts as evidence in territorial disputes contributed to the gradual altering of the perception of land in Zapotec society. No longer an entity subject to traditional authority, land use yielded to the alien authority of the Spanish judiciary system. When lands were transformed into European-style maps, their sacred quality became secularized and thereby subject to colonial government. Encoding space in the European manner, abstracting lands to cartographic conventions tended to isolate territories from those who lived in them.

Like the written calendars, post-conquest maps in the New World were colonial inventions responding to new situations. But intent did not jibe with content: their purpose was to conserve, but their effect was to erode the native landscape.

Pre-Hispanic Maps

The nature of land tenure and how it was recorded in pre-Hispanic Zapotec society is a complex and poorly understood aspect of their culture. In her work on Mixtec place signs and maps, Mary Elizabeth Smith explicitly states that "no pre-conquest maps of community lands have survived from Mixtec-speaking or any other region of Middle America."[42] Nevertheless, there are references to the existence of pre-Hispanic maps in the literature of early colonial book production.[43] But the fact that no maps recognizable as such have survived is a significant fact that cannot be attributed to the accidents of preservation. Surely the Spanish would have kept any extant preconquest territorial records as an aid to colonial administration. Renderings of territories would not have been tainted with proscribed idolatrous practices as were calendrical notations, and some of these had survived into the colonial period despite their prohibition. Given the evidence, the inescapable conclusion is that maps, as Europeans understood the term, never existed in the pre-Hispanic past. The lack of surviving maps implies that, in preconquest times, the Zapotec did not make scale reductions of landscape on a flat sheet of drawing material in the European manner. It does not mean, however, that they had no means for or interest in recording space.

The highly structured Zapotec society must have had some way of keeping track of lands that were such a vital part of their economic, social, and political identities. Surely there was a need to demarcate sacred territories, to delineate agriculturally favored lands, and to keep records of taxable regions, as well as to record spatial information on trade routes, borders of hostile territories, and other such geographical features. As Zapotec centers, such as Monte Albán, gained regional hegemony, it seems that this kind of geographical information would have become indispensable. Using data collected from Monte Albán, Richard Blanton compares the settlement pattern at what he calls the "disembedded" capital to what he describes as a three-part territorial structure (that is, the three arms) of the surrounding valley of Oaxaca.[44] Recently, I have argued in "The

Painted Dead" that administrative control over the territories in the valley of Oaxaca is replicated in the architecture and site planning at the site of Monte Albán. While it may be difficult for us to conceive of spatial records in the form of huge templates such as settlement patterns or site layouts, we can not rule out such a possibility simply because it is beyond our ken.

Comparative evidence that architecture and city planning may have served as territorial records comes from outside the Oaxaca area. Tatiana Proskouriakoff was the first to point out that site plan layout may replicate in miniature the layout of a site's territories. In 1962 Proskouriakoff linked Mayapan's site plan with the polity it ruled as reconstructed from documentary sources.[45] The sources compared to the material remains of Mayapan are, of course, colonial in date. The correspondence is, nevertheless, suggestive of how the postclassic Maya may have architecturally expressed control over territories.

David Freidel and Jeremy Sabloff make a similar connection between site planning and political control in their San Gervasio report, comparing the quadripartite structure of elite housing in San Gervasio to a four-part territorial division on Cozumel Island. For late postclassic Highland Guatemala, Robert Carmack links the site plan of Utatlan with a tripartite territorial division of the Quiche Basin, reconstructed from documentary sources.[46] Recently, Olivier de Montmollin has analyzed the site plan of the Maya site of Tenam Rosario in light of its hinterland. Montmollin suggests that there is a purposeful replication of surrounding territories in the planning of the site-center: "The Rosario polity's regional hierarchical and territorial arrangement appear to be reproduced in microcosm within the capital's civic-ceremonial zone."[47] While the sources used to link the material remains of site planning to the territories that site may have controlled are, in the cases of Freidel and Sabloff and Montmollin, based on material remains alone, and, in the cases of Proskouriakoff and Carmack, based on linking material remains to ethnohistorically reconstructed patterns, the approaches taken together represent an attempt to find evidence for some kind of physical record of the territories controlled by preconquest polities.[48]

In support of my contention that pre-Hispanic maps took various forms, Joyce Marcus has argued that "territorial boundaries were frequently given as geographical landmarks such as named mountain peaks or rivers. This tradition of delimiting Zapotec territory by named topographic features persisted in the early Colonial period," and "These landmarks were referred to in settling disputes." Marcus further suggests that early colonial maps from Oaxaca reveal "that the territorial boundaries of the Zapotec realm were conceived of as a series of mountains or rivers with hieroglyphic names, a pattern of perhaps 2000 years' standing."[49]

Although it is a European-style map drawn by Zapotec native draftsmen, the Lienzo of Guevea[50] reveals the pre-Hispanic tradition of linking spatial with temporal information. Eduard Seler, in "Das Dorfbuch von Santiago Guevea," pointed out that the upper portion of the Guevea is more than a "map." He perceptively demonstrated that it could also be read as a list of the "months" in the Zapotec calendar (as described by Córdova), an argument reiterated by Blas Pablo Reko in *Mitobotánica zapoteca* and more recently by Joseph Whitecotton in "Zapotec Pictorials and Zapotec Naming." Another early colonial period map from the Mixtec area of Oaxaca, known as the Lienzo de Jicayán,[51] shows exactly fifty-two place signs surrounding Jicayán, suggesting a calendrical association[52] with spatial orientation, a practice I have argued is quintessentially pre-Hispanic. A "native style" pictorial screenfold, known as the *Codex Vindobonensis Mexicanus I* (Vienna) is composed of fifty-two pages, probably related to the fifty-two-year cycle. Jill Furst has presented cogent arguments for seeing parts of the Vienna as a sacred map of day and year date combinations that refer to places and events, rather than Western-style calendrical dates.[53]

References to land and its representation in colonial-period documentary sources on Oaxaca are also suggestive of possible ways in which the Zapotec may have recorded their territorial domains prior to the conquest. Juan de Córdova's 1578 work on Zapotec language and calendars makes it clear that in the Zapotec world, every event and every thing was governed according to relations to space by the powers ruling the four directions. Córdova's evidence indicates that, for the sixteenth-century inhabitants of the valley of Oaxaca, space was an idiom in which independent events could be organized for purposes of social control. Thus, the demarcation of territories may have included a sophisticated system of codified map-making, unlike that of Europeans, involving the calendar. For example, the Zapotec referred the ritual calendar to the four directions, dividing it into four sections of sixty-five days each. Glyphs may have both calendrical and directional meaning in certain contexts. The success of this approach depends on the survival of the original contexts of glyphic representations. The opportunity for exploring such a promising line of research has been enhanced greatly by the rich glyphic corpus from the Suchilquitongo Tomb Number 5 investigations, currently in progress.[54]

Charting Time and Action in Space

Pre-Hispanic spatial records may not have been recognizable as maps to colonial period Europeans or modern investigators. No extant clearly pre-Hispanic maplike or landscapelike pictorials come from Zapotec-speaking regions of Oaxaca. Nevertheless, map-making compositions are not unknown in pre-Hispanic screenfolds from the Mixtec area of Oaxaca.[55] The ways in which these preconquest documents differ from European map-making and landscape-making conventions serve to illustrate how unlike are pre-Hispanic and colonial spatial renditions.[56] Robertson cites page 2 of the Codex Zouche-Nuttall screenfold as "close to landscape." Five temples are arranged around a plaza with a fire drill in the center and another temple and a ball court to the left, suggesting that they depict "the Mesoamerican religious center." Because the temples, fire drill, and ball court in these scene are depicted as "formalized signs," Robertson states that this is not a "'picture' of a religious center; it is a symbol of one."[57] More recently, the Vienna screenfold has been described as a map of part of the Mixteca Alta, despite its distinctly noncartographic appearance in Western terms.[58] Refining this view, Furst has pointed out that the "generalized maps" of the introductory pages of the Codices Laud and Fejérváry-Mayer ("presenting the cardinal directions with associated gods, trees, birds, day signs, colors, and perhaps even years") are better characterized as "a mental construct, or an abstract concept of a map, rather than a description of a specific area." She sees that the postconquest maps, "painted on a square or rectangle of woven material, are largely derived from this prehispanic convention."[59]

The link between place and events can be read in the native-style Codex Zouche-Nuttall, where other examples of symbolic spatial renderings are evident. For example, page 19 of the Codex Zouche-Nuttall (fig. 33) portrays the space within a single place sign, where the wedding of Lord 12 Wind "Smoking Eye" and Lady 3 Flint "Jeweled Quechquemitl" is depicted.[60] Since ritual activity is depicted within this space, an appropriate designation for the kind of spatial rendition shown may be *sacred geography*. Shown in bird's-eye view are the limits of the space within

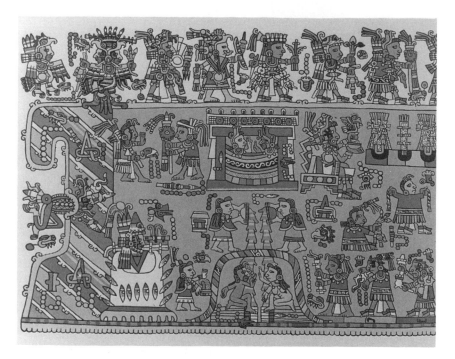

Figure 33. Page 19 of the Codex Zouche-Nuttall, left side.

which figures shown in profile view perform ritual acts. While the spatial relationship between figures is not signified, temporal information is carried in calendrical notations that both provide calendrical names and date the figural scenes. Because the dating of events depicted is carried by specialized calendrical glyphs associated with the figures engaged in ritual activity, the scene is more properly characterized as a diachronic rendering of events within a single space, rather than a synchronic portrayal of figures within a defined space at a single moment in time.[61] The passage of time may also be conveyed by the undulating segmented baseline on which five figures within the scene walk, bearing offerings. The footprints shown within the segmented baseline may serve as distance markers. Thus viewed, this scene is again not a rendition of a space at a particular time, but rather the conflation of several events that take place within a sacred space. Included within the precinct is another place sign at the lower left, another place within a place, possibly conveying information about the destination or origin of some of the participants shown in the scene. In this sacred geography, information conveys the effect of time within a precinct. What is shown, then, is not a plan or map as we understand it, but rather a depiction of the range of activities that regularly occur within a defined space, that is, the interdigitation of space and time and their mutual regimentation.

Early colonial cadastral records of community lands also suggest how Mesoamericans conceived of spatial records. Like the sacred geographies of pages 2 and 19 in the Codex Zouche-Nuttall, Mexican pictorial cadastral registers are more than records of spatial dimensions; they are packed as well with information about land ownership and use. They contain more kinds of information than do Roman cadastral maps, their obvious prototypes, which were conveyed to the New World by the Spanish. This embellishment of the cadastral format is reported by Alonso de Zorita: Indian principales commissioned records of cultivated lands which were "pictures on which are shown all the parcels, and the boundaries, and where and with whose fields the lots meet, and who cultivates what field, and what land each one has."[62] The sources and the early maps themselves suggest that spatial renderings were never simple symbolic depictions of space, but rather conflated with many other kinds of information, such as ownership and land use in changing seasons. The pre-Hispanic map, then, may have been a far denser kind of record than the contemporary European one. Cadastral maps appear to be close in concept to the pre-Hispanic map because they include the kind of information referred to by Zorita. Of course, we know that extant cadastral maps are not pre-Hispanic in date, for they are drawn on European paper. Also, the cadaster is a Western format for recording lands. We therefore cannot see these colonial versions as being pre-Hispanic in form. Nevertheless, the embellishment of information on the European format—the tendency to pack information about space with temporal data—I would suggest is indicative of pre-Hispanic attitudes toward their territories.

When the lands are sacred, such as those depicted on pages 2 and 19 of the Codex Zouche-Nuttall, temporal information about the proper execution of ritual is included. Such an interpretation of sacred geography, linking spatial and temporal information, is supported by recorded oral testimonies of Zapotec witnesses describing ritual activities under investigation.[63] When witnesses were asked what in fact happened during idolatry practice, a description of action and place would inevitably follow.

Such testimonies indicate that action was meaningful only when carried out at the appropriate place and at the appropriate time. Documentary sources inevitably provide information on where and when ritual activity took place, as if the two were inseparable in the Zapotec mind. The sum of the available evidence, visual and verbal, points to a native conceptualization of sacred space itself as an animate being, the vital forces of which are inherent in its essential characteristic of movement in both time and space.

While the parts of these scenes in the Codex Zouche-Nuttall may be interpreted in various ways, this much seems clear: these pre-Hispanic drawings include complex aspects of space along with temporal information and depictions of action. It is also clear that they contrast with later colonial maps produced by native draftsmen that attempt to show the spatial layout of one place, at one time, devoid of action. In contrasting pre-Hispanic spatial concepts with those of Europeans, we are not comparing apples and oranges. Rather, the two systems overlap, and it is this convergence that made possible the native assimilation of foreign forms. Western-style maps do depict places that may be considered monuments of events. In such a document, time would be a "map," even if not obviously so. Extant evidence for indigenous spatial concepts seems to suggest that representations of territories were incomplete without direct reference to other factors such as time, because place, like time, was conceived of as constantly changing during the course of action. The European map, then, must have appeared to the Zapotec as a strangely incomplete form of spatial rendering. Similarly, the pre-Hispanic recorded sacred geographies may not have been considered proper maps in European eyes. What are known as the pictorial narratives of colonial-period Mexico, then, are results of mutual accommodations on both sides.

The Europeanization of Native Spatial Conventions

Maps recognizable as such by Europeans were drawn in pre-Hispanic style by native draftsmen early in the colonial period. In fact, this native early colonial map production has been cited in the literature as evidence for the existence of similar spatial renderings in pre-Hispanic times. Robertson, in *Mexican Manuscript Painting of the Early Colonial Period*, argues that early colonial maps give a clear indication of pre-Hispanic map-making. But if the pre-Hispanic "map" encodes a diachronic view of several spaces and times at once, if its nature is to include several dimensions of experience at once in a single dense recorded form, how can we account for the in-digenous production of simplistic European-like maps showing spatial relations without obvious reference to time, so early in the colonial period?

Part of the answer, of course, lies in the fact that the Spanish directly introduced European maps into the native consciousness by specifically requesting them, as in the case of the *Relaciones* discussed above. Cortés and Bernal Diáz refer to a map supplied by Montezuma.[64] Cortés specifies that is was especially made for an expedition in search of gold. He makes no reference to an archive. Bernal Diáz merely says that maps were given to Cortés, with no information on the source. Robertson states that, "If Cortés phraseology is accurate, he meant that it was drawn up especially for Montezuma by someone with a knowledge of the terrain or that it was compiled from existing maps."[65] I propose a third possibility: Montezuma had the map drawn up after finding out what was required. This map was never described, beyond the fact that the Spanish found it accurate for their purposes. It is unlikely that either Montezuma or anyone in his court would have easily understood what Cortés wanted, for European map-making conventions were surely alien concepts. If the documents Montezuma produced were like the spatio-temporal renderings shown on pages 2 and 19 of the Codex Zouche-Nuttall, it is unlikely that Cortés would have recognized them as maps. The simplicity of Cortés's request must have perplexed and even amused Montezuma and his court. That anyone could conceive of territories in such uncomplicated terms must have convinced them that they were not giving any significant information away by pro-ducing what was to them a curiously simplistic geographic rendering. It is likely, then, that the invention of the colonial map-making genre as we know it may have begun with Cortés's request. The production of native maps may be one of the earliest material manifestations of what one could call a "culture of conquest," that is, the process of native adoptive and adaptive manipulation of new social realities introduced by a colonial regime.

Forgeries

It rapidly became clear that the European map played an essential part not only in colonial government, but also in local land disputes.[66] Most early colonial manuscripts "were prepared for one general purpose: to protect the lands of the community and of the native nobility."[67] One means to defend territories from Spanish encroachment was the manufacture of land title documents known as *títulos*. Another was to "create" the desired temporal requirements for a map that would appear more venerable and therefore more valid in colonial courts. Documentary evidence demonstrates that colonial maps were sometimes dated earlier than they were drawn and that an "older" map-making style was employed in conformity with the forged date. Some assert that they were done prior to the conquest. Since Spanish judges followed the principle of honoring older land claims before more recent ones, the motivation for the forging of "old" (that is, what the Spanish would have perceived as old) maps is understandable. In fact, so pervasive was the forging of land documents that colonial courts eventually rejected all maps prepared by natives as evidence.[68] Forgers would not have reproduced spatio-temporal conventions similar to those shown on pages 2 and 19 of the Codex Zouche-Nuttall because they would have been totally unintelligible to Spanish judges. Nor could they totally depart from the traditional spatial renderings, because they had to address Indian allies in land disputes as well as Europeans.

Colonial map-makers were faced with the double task of producing land claims in the form of maps that would appear venerable and comprehensible to Indian and European alike. Such a scenario may account for the invention of the early colonial map-making genre. It is an example of an active response to new social realities introduced by the conquest, rather than the passive result of a latent indigenous drawing style spiced by European map-making conventions to produce the material cultural stew known as colonial maps. While there is currently insufficient evidence to confirm this hypothesis, I predict that the data will reveal the actively creative role of native Americans in the formation of colonial society. I view postconquest cultural change as a process of choice, negotiation, and creative adaptation that belies the image of passive reception.

Conclusions

Under siege, the Zapotec took extraordinary measures to preserve their sacred memory and at the same time endeavored to become full participants in the colonial system. This is manifest in their abandonment of the spatio-temporal devices which had portrayed sacred geographies that had no meaning in Spanish courts and were imbued with sacred meanings proscribed by the colonial regime. Under Spanish rule, ownership of land became a secular issue. The Zapotec themselves contributed to making it so. Their maps produced for the *Relaciones* deliberately excluded information about the temporal dimension of their territories. This invented genre of map-making also enabled them to claim ownership of territories in colonial courts. In fact, when they introduced the temporal dimension into their territorial renderings, it was not for purposes of qualifying space, as in sacred geographies, but rather to deal with the new colonial need to quantify the document's chronology, that is, to establish legitimate ownership in land disputes—or illegitimate ones by making forgeries. As participants in colonial society, they relinquished sacred geographies for the pursuit of physical ones. The sources make it clear, however, that knowledge of sacred geographies was not lost. No longer recorded, they were carried in living memory. The testimonies of idolatry trials reveal that timely ritual sacrifices in sacred places continued well into the colonial period.[69] Indeed, ethnographic studies report their continuance up to the present day. And these are not carried out only in remote places. The remains of chicken sacrifices at Monte Albán, just outside of Oaxaca City, are visible today.

While sacred geographies remained unrecorded, the ritual calendar was alphabetically transformed in order to incorporate the evident power of the European script. But in the process of transforming their calendar into a new scriptural mode, the Zapotec fundamentally altered both its form and function. It seems paradoxical that the most developed type of scripture, alphabetic writing, was also the most effective at eliminating options for the future. Considered a more advanced mode of recorded communication than image making and pictographic systems of writing, the alphabetic script of European civilization displaced images as a tool employed by native Americans to preserve the memory of ancient sacred knowledge.[70]

In Oaxaca, the displacement by text of images also imposed severe limitations on the interpretation of the past for future use. When memory became scripture, the past was cast as linear narrative, delimiting the future within the scope of previous events. In their written form, the identities of deities overseeing days in the 260-day cycle became less fluid and tended to crystalize. They no longer retained the essential mutability conveyed by pre-Hispanic images. With the calendar fixed in a recorded form, the calendar specialist became less crucial to its function, because his interpretive role was limited and his power thereby decreased in Zapotec society. With a shift from image to text and from spatio-temporal to uniquely spatial renditions, the Zapotec concepts of time and space had changed. With meanings fixed by the written word and beginnings and endings of time periods clearly marked, the calendar assumed a linear narrative quality it had previously lacked.

The enforced orthodoxy imposed by scripture at once preserved the past and contributed to its eventual demise as a major factor in native community life. The role of the calendar specialist, with his vast store of sacred memory about how to mediate the effects of the calendar, became less crucial. As text displaced image, the memory of time was transformed from a template of infinite mutability capable of responding to everyday needs to that of a fixed linear sequence whose meanings became historical and esoteric when consulted in the changing present. Land no longer was subject to the timely rituals that defined its sacred character but was portrayed as devoid of temporal meaning and nothing more than a secularized physical entity.

Constant change of repeating cycles of time had offered Zapotec society hope in times of deprivation. Bad times could become good when time itself changed identity with positive and negative divine forces. Once the possibility of mutability was cut off by enshrining time in a linear template, hope for change became severely restricted. For example, the calendar specialist had been able to recommend ritual action that might alter the effect of negative calendrical signs occurring on a given event. Land that suffered from the negative effects of drought at one time could, following prescribed ritual action, become well watered at another. This sort of flexibility was more difficult to achieve when dealing with the kind of fixed records characteristic of European modes of thought. With the calendar rendered as text, the "inconvenient parts of the past"[71] could no longer be forgotten, because of the exigencies of the continuing present. With maps rendered as only records of space, devoid of temporal data, sacred geography could no longer be recorded as timely activities performed in proper places. Text and the mode of thought it represents had undermined the sacred power of calendar specialists and the bases of sacred geographies.

Displacement of Zapotec concepts by European concepts of time and space resulted in the concealment of political economy within apparently readable and accessible modes of communication (alphabetic script and

European map-making conventions). Because script was a shared experience between the two worlds of conquerors and conquered, it served to veil and disguise, but also eventually to restructure, the ways through which relationships of labor and loyalty were formed and transmitted onto the conquered landscape. Perhaps this is an explanation for the seemingly paradoxical speed with which the Zapotec culture embraced the colonial one, without ever becoming indistinguishable from it.

The Seville calendars and native colonial maps are evidence of the Zapotec strategy of aligning their traditional authority structures with the Spanish, which necessitated adjustment and innovation in those traditional forms. By transforming sacred knowledge of time and place into the new alphabetic script and European-style maps, the Zapotec confronted a dangerous present and a problematical future with something close to equanimity, without relinquishing their sense of authority. But the incorporation of the conqueror's script and space altered the Zapotec conception of time and territories. Displacement of glyph by European script and indigenous sacred geographies by European secular maps effectively served to incorporate Zapotec society into the colonial orbit more profoundly than had been achieved by two centuries of missionary and governmental policies. These fundamental changes were not imposed by force, but rather willingly, even enthusiastically, wrought by the Zapotec themselves.

RICHARD VINOGRAD

Private Art and Public Knowledge in Later Chinese Painting

The introduction of anthropological perspectives to the study of Chinese painting is welcome, because Chinese visual phenomena have often suffered distortions that are, ironically, invisible by reason of transparency: they are viewed as either mirror or as shadow of things Western. A greater self-consciousness about the relativity of cultural standpoints may moderate both the projection of Western interests and paradigms onto Chinese cases and the relegation of Chinese phenomena to a nether realm of cultural otherness and opposition. The clear definition of even fundamental terms and problems in Chinese cultural phenomena remains troublesome, however, in some respects as much hindered as helped by the special status of Chinese literature and painting among non-European traditions as arts endowed with a sophisticated system of critical and historical discourse.[1] The promise of parallelism, or the accessibility of underlying concepts such as truth and imitation, often proves illusory, although here also the supplementation of textual research with anthropologically oriented studies of art as deprivileged social practice may offer useful insights.[2]

Among the most pernicious attitudes has been the tendency to view Chinese cultural phenomena in unitary terms, as characteristic equally of all periods and groups. Chinese writers have been as liable to such formulations as Western observers, in part because of culturally self-centered attitudes and a tendency to define Chinese phenomena in terms of opposition to external things. In the realm of pictorial art, at least, a broad continuity of technique and terminology has often obscured a rich plurality of orientations and a historical dynamic of change that affected even the most fundamental concepts and practices. It is thus important to stress that the discussion which follows, couched in terms of contrast with European pictorial art, is meant to apply, not to Chinese painting as a whole, but to a particular, though quite broad, era and arena of pictorial practice. This qualification is not only for reasons of accuracy, but because the concepts and approaches involved took on a good part of their significance through contrast with, or rejection of, alternatives within the Chinese horizon.

The attitudes to be discussed are broadly representative of Chinese scholar-amateur painting, which emerged in the late eleventh century A.D. very much as a minority critical-artistic complex, as an alternative to prevailing representationally oriented trends and criteria.[3] From around the beginning of the fourteenth century down to the end of the imperial age in the early part of our own century, scholar-amateur painting was in the ascendancy in the critical and historical arena, though never free of competition from alternative orientations toward decorative, illustrative, or otherwise functional values in painting, nor ever independent of a context of competing social and esthetic modes.

Moreover, diversity and divisions appeared within scholar-amateur ranks over the long historical course of the movement, sometimes as the result of evolving social or historical conditions that shifted the ground of critical positions and pictorial practices, more or less out of sight of contemporary commentators. For example, early scholar-amateur painting and theory contained orientations that might easily be termed avant-garde in their disengagement of critical standards from criteria based on representational fidelity or technical skill, and in the relative social autonomy of its practitioners from patronage pressures by the imperial court, the academies, or the marketplace. In later times, some branches of scholar-amateur painting might fairly be considered profoundly conservative in their orientation toward the past and their espousal of an iterative mode of painting. Such tendencies were, in their turn, challenged by reactions in part from within scholar-amateur ranks. The presentation that follows thus requires both general and historically specific accounts. Broadly based orientations within Chinese scholar-amateur painting toward the commemorative, descriptive, and cognitive status of painting, and toward problems of criticism and evaluation are first outlined. Then follows a discussion of a particularly dynamic episode of Chinese painting in the seventeenth century that reflects revisions of the imagistic status of painting and the changing conditions of painting's participation in memory and public knowledge.

Witness and Commemoration

We should first consider the implicit claims of Western and Chinese paintings as objects and as images, and what such a comparison reveals about underlying paradigms of knowledge and memory as related to the pictorial realm. For the sake of coherence, and so that the discussion should not be too cumbersomely hedged around with qualifications, we shall limit the comparison to the still vast territory of European painting after the medieval and before the modern period, and to Chinese scholar-amateur painting from around the same time—after the Song dynasty and up to the end of the imperial age, roughly the mid-thirteenth century through the nineteenth.

European paintings from this era, whether religious or secular, often claim the status of a witnessed scene. Masaccio's early-fifteenth-century *Trinity* (fig. 34) and Rembrandt's *Syndics of the Cloth Guild* of 1662 (fig. 35) exemplify this conception. The claims of the paintings extend beyond changing standards of lifelikeness or realism, and even beyond the vividness or adequacy of the pictured scenes as re-presented events, though all those aspects are at issue in some ways. Both these paintings take pains to verify the presence of witnesses, in divergent ways. In Masaccio's fresco, the onlooking donor figures comprise one set of witnesses, and the elaborate specification of an illusionistic spatial theater for the sacred figures, and of an exact viewing position, make the viewer a kind of captivated veridical witness to the event. Rembrandt's painting acknowledges and embroils the viewer as witness in subtler ways. The rising postures and the distracted glances of the figures toward the viewer imply a kind of complicity or obligation of courtesy on the part of the viewer as witness. The status of witness does more than suggest an esthetic fiction; it implies a network of roles and obligations that have specific existence within the religious, legal, or social spheres.

These images may seem to be extreme examples in the clarity of their invocation of the viewer in the role of witness, but there are even more explicit cases, such as van Eyck's *Arnolfini Marriage Portrait*. It is useful to

Figure 34. Masaccio, *Trinity*, fresco, early fifteenth century. S. Maria Novella, Florence. Courtesy Alinari/Art Resource, 62966.

follow some of the extended corollaries of this conception of painting.[4] First, in supplementing the emphasis on *representational* processes in much recent theoretical and critical writing, this conception of painting insists rather on the *presentational* aspect of painting: the scene or event as actually present, and the presence of the viewer as witness demanded equally.[5] The related implication that the artist witnessed or imagined the scene and reproduces or represents it for the viewer is only a weakened version of this claim. Second, the specificity of the painting both as image and as object is heightened. Spatial exactitude, simulation of light and texture, and other illusionistic devices particularize the image; while being accorded a special location, if a fresco, or an individual, often elaborate, frame, if an easel painting, accentuates the uniqueness of the painting as object. Third, the publicity of the painting is acknowledged. Frescoes,

altarpieces, paintings for guildhalls or government offices, and even paintings intended for private collections were oriented toward long-term display, and some degree of public or social access to them was maintained
within varying regulations and limitations. The truth-status claims of this
kind of European painting are very strong, not only because the painting
is held up as a window or mirror to the world, but also because a specific
witness is implied, and the witnessing is publicly repeatable and verifiable.
Furthermore, the image-object has an authority that exerts a measure of
control over the viewer. This control may range from subtle manipulation
through visual intrigue, to blatant seduction, arousal, or captivation of the
viewer, to heavy-handed exertions of scale or visual structures that operate
at the perceptual or visceral levels.

Finally, we should examine the implications of this kind of painting
for processes of memory. If a European painting serves as an object of
witness, it must be memorable in order to permit testimony about the
painting, or the scene, event, or world which it presents. The memorability
of a European painting is enhanced by its double specificity: both the
detailed illusionistic world of the painting and the unique setting or frame

Figure 35. Rembrandt, *The Syndics of the Cloth Guild*, oil on canvas, 1662,
191.5 × 279 cm. Courtesy Rijksmuseum-Stichting, Amsterdam.

for the painting as viewed object locate the painting in a specific matrix of experience. The European conception of painting as image implies imitation, as in mirroring, and a parallel conception of memory as captured or stored reflections. Ideally, the image-imitation as well as the memory reflection should be transparent, immediate, and flawless: the presented scene will then have the status of truth and will be able to serve as an instrument of knowledge. The European conception of a painting as a transparent window or a flawless mirror showing a witnessed world may imply a deobjectification of the acts that produced it, and a wiping away of the traces of production.[6] The image may be an aid to memory as a captured moment or event, but seldom does it evoke the extended temporality of the event of painting itself.

A comparative examination of a representative work from the world of Chinese scholar-amateur, or literati, painting reveals radical differences in the status of the painting-object and its involvement with processes of memory. A late fifteenth-century Ming dynasty Chinese literati painting by Shen Zhou (1427–1509), titled *Watching the Mid-Autumn Moon* (fig. 36), datable to around 1488, shifts the emphasis from a represented witnessed scene to a recollected event, with temporality, duration, and memory interwoven in both the act of painting and the act of viewing, in complex ways. Instead of the all-at-once, transparent illusionism of the European image, the Chinese painting has a pronounced sign-character, with featureless faces on the schematically depicted guests and visible graphic formulas for the cottage enclosure and landscape elements. This mode introduces temporality in two different dimensions: the formulas mediate the representation and draw attention to the process of depiction, and they require the viewer to make an extended effort in order to recognize them.

The physical properties of the painting in themselves have some interesting temporal implications, most pronounced in the horizontal scroll—or handscroll—format of Shen Zhou's painting. The format implies some deferral of the experience of the scene: handscrolls are customarily viewed sequentially, in sections, as the scroll is rolled out and rolled up by the viewer, and even short handscrolls imply some directed travel of the gaze in surveying the painting. The Chinese scroll retains clear traces of its status as the product of a complex series of events, for example, in the case of Shen Zhou's *Mid-Autumn Moon*, the painted depiction, the artist's explanatory or poetic inscription, and the accompanying literary responses by other members of the moon-viewing party and by later view-

Figure 36. Shen Chou (Shen Zhou), *Watching the Mid-Autumn Moon*,
paper makimono, late fifteenth century, Ming dynasty, 30.4 × 134.5 cm.

ers of the painting.[7] These and other elements, such as the title calligraphy,
are part of the physical fabric of the painting, laid out sequentially from
right to left, outside to inside, as the scroll is unrolled. Some of the
elements, for instance the title frontispiece, have to be gone through before
the painting can be reached; the colophons following the painting might be
left unviewed, but the momentum and suspense involved in the process of
looking at a painting usually induce at least a cursory examination. Looking
at a scroll painting requires some visual travel and travail on the part of the
viewer, though these can easily be withheld, for example by viewing a
painting cursorily or leaving it partially unrolled. This gives the viewer
some direct power over the painting.

The duration of the act of viewing a Chinese painting is a direct
continuation of the extended series of events that produced it; the process
is more like a *reexperiencing* of those events of production through the
record of textual and visual traces than like the witnessing of a presented
or simulated scene. For instance, behind the texts and depictions of Shen
Zhou's scroll lie precipitating events: gathering to watch the mid-autumn
moon, and the traditions, customary rituals, and protocols associated with
such occasions; the friendships and chains of meetings to which the inscriptions refer; and later occasions of viewing and commenting on the
painting. The Chinese scroll painting does not serve as just a record of the

Chinese and Japanese Special Fund, 15.898. Courtesy, Museum of Fine Arts, Boston.

precipitating events—especially not in the form of a perfect mirror or window as European paintings often imply themselves to be—but instead becomes part of the very fabric of an extended occasion. The handscroll is the physical site where the poetic, calligraphic, and pictorial activities that are part of the gathering are deposited. The painting collects traces of a series of events and allows a re-collection of them in the viewing process.

In the case of Shen Zhou's scroll the events are cooperative and coauthored: Shen Zhou's painting and the first and later inscriptions—the colophons and poems added by other participants and viewers. Memory is evoked on many levels: the nostalgia and regret that were part of the conventional aura surrounding the festival of the mid-autumn moon; the memory of a particular gathering depicted in the painting; and the memories of the painting and poetry writing that were part of, or followed upon, the gathering.[8] The painting is the site of a commemoration, not only by the participants in the gathering but by later viewers of the painting.

Even Chinese works that were less thoroughly cooperative than the "Mid-Autumn Moon" handscroll in their precipitating events and execution were customarily embedded in a memorializing context of conception, event, or reappraisal by the artist's own inscription. Furthermore, the techniques of Chinese painting and calligraphy permit a retracing and re-creation of the activities of painting and inscription-writing in ways usually erased by the painting process in the West. European painting is often presented as a way of witnessing, knowing, and memorizing a world; Chinese scholar-painting is bound up with reexperiencing or commemorating events.

Chinese literati painting of this kind is relatively participatory and consensual; not so much concerned with asserting a veridical or authoritative version of a scene, but rather with permitting recognition and re-creation. From a nonprivileged, extra-artistic perspective, we might characterize Chinese scholar-painting as an occasion for small-group communion.[9] The artist formulated a codification of a site, gathering, or natural element that was imbued with personal style or historical reference. Use of the painted sign permitted the audience to show recognition in the form of written, frequently poetic colophons. The responses often referred either to common personal memories or to cultural memory in the form of shared literary competence. The painting was usually portable and personal; it had no dedicated location or distinguishing frame, and the painting proper was liable to be encroached upon or edged aside by the textual additions of the artist or other writers. The scroll-complex passed from hand to hand, painter to dedicatee, owner to guest, viewer to viewer, acquiring traces of its passage in the form of inscriptions and seals. The painting was thus visibly altered by the act of viewing, becoming a vehicle for cultural bonding, and it claimed communion that could extend across centuries. This was commonly referred to as *shen-hui*, or "spirit-communion," which on a refined level implies a kind of meeting of congenial minds; a more prosaic and somewhat anthropological perspective would note that it also involved handling the same tangible object in a kind of ritual coparticipation across time.[10] The function of Chinese literati painting thus had less to do with capturing or asserting a veridical version of a scene and its attendant symbolic power than with serving as the occasion and site of re-creations, recognitions, and commemorations. The viewer was not the passive witness of a finished image, but rather was an active participant in the extended event of the painting.

Image and Description

The status of painting as object and event in the Chinese scholar-artist context outlined here has some more or less direct relevance to theories of knowledge and to issues of privacy and publicity. Chinese concepts of knowing have sometimes been classified as "knowing how" or "having acquaintance with," as opposed to Western concepts of "knowing of the content or substance"; Chinese knowing in philosophical terms is bound up with practice and the application of social conventions, as contrasted with the knowledge of reality or essence.[11] A European painting that claims to present or mirror the outer world, exactly, fully, and flawlessly might be seen as both the counterpart and the visual demonstration of Western concepts of the knowledge of essence. Chinese paintings that apply conventional systems of signs in recognizable ways suggest a visual corollary of theories of knowledge that focus on the application of social conventions. Moreover, the content of many Chinese scholar-paintings can appropriately be understood as visualized methods of procedure, for invoking or revivifying the style of a practitioner from the past, for example, or for reformulating a traditional landscape theme.

The terminology of Chinese literati painting points most often to processes of "delineation" (*hua*), "depiction" (*tu*), and "description" (*xie*), rather than to image-making.[12] The concept of the image implies imitation or the making of a replica, and seems connected to theories of knowledge as a mental picture. The closest counterpart in the realm of Chinese pictorial art would seem to be *xiang,* or "image-likeness," which relates to the theory of counterparts of model heavenly portents. In later Chinese painting, the concept of *xiang* was most relevant to the practice of portraiture as the capturing of a physiognomic likeness, or the making of an effigy,[13] and the practice of that approach was largely the province of portrait specialists, whose work was for the most part ignored or denigrated by the literati critics.[14] Instead, it was the concept of painting as description that was prominent in the writings of scholar-artists and their apologists. Description implies a deferral of the presence of the object through transposition into language, as well as a process carried out over time.[15] The cognitive processes associated with pictorial description, understood as a counterpart of verbal description, may involve recollection, metaphorizing, and comparison of distinguishing elements. European image-making, on the other hand, would seem to imply cognitive models of captured perception, imagination, or knowledge of fixed or mathematically absolute theoretical paradigms of proportion, perspective, and iconography.

A Chinese literati painting in the descriptive mode was oriented toward rendering in terms of something else, rather than having an image-based orientation toward capturing an object. The terms of its pictorial description often involved a vocabulary, whether personalized or conventional, of texture-strokes, type-forms, and the like, that were given explicitly metaphorical designations.[16] The techniques of literati painting usually permitted a reprisal by the viewer of the brush-acts of the painter, and so the description unfolded over time, like a linguistic description, rather than being manifested all at once, in the way of images. Descriptions imply at least a submerged narrativity, and the pictorial descriptions of Chinese literati painting betray a narrative of process and intention—often restated in the artist's accompanying inscription—though rarely an explicit pictorial narrative of action. Literati paintings permit a retracing of the events of the painting process, and that sequentiality is often extended by written inscriptions and colophons on the painting to encompass the pretext or occasion for the painting as well as its reception.

The assertion that Chinese scholar-amateur painting is not fundamentally concerned with the image-status of the painting may require some amplification, if only because the vocabulary and conceptual apparatus of the image have become so thoroughly ingrained in Western theories of painting that only with some difficulty can a discussion be couched in other terms. The concepts of image, imitation, and memory have become intertwined and can provide an avenue of approach to the problem. To say that Chinese scholar-painting is not oriented toward an image-status does not mean that there are no images to be found in such paintings, in the sense of memorable forms or structures that can be imitated. Scholar-paintings did make use of compositional structures, especially of distinctive and memorable type-forms and schemata for elements such as trees, foliage, rocks, and water. Indeed, there was a substantial body of theoretical and manualistic writing devoted precisely to outlining imitable procedures for producing motifs and compositions in memorable and recognizable stylistic modes. However, the subject or content of such paintings does not offer itself as directly capturing or replicating an object or scene. Instead, the painting displays procedures for the production of styles or categories of motifs that are mediated by reference to historical manners of rendering or to acknowledged codes.

We might refer to some types of modern Western painting that are more or less imageless to clarify the point. Jackson Pollock's drip paintings lack images and are, in a literal sense, unmemorable because of the complexity of the viewing experience, which involves durational processes of perception.[17] However, one can follow relatively simple procedures of production to make a recognizable imitation of such a work. Chinese scholar-paintings are not imageless in the same sense of lacking recognizable motifs, but they do share a reliance on and a manifestation of durational processes that require an active reexperiencing and retracing to be fully memorized. Some of the conceptual, instructional designs of Sol LeWitt suggest illuminating analogies to Chinese literati paintings. LeWitt provides general rules of procedure for drawings that can be executed by others (or conceivably by many groups of others), that might differ in scale, color, and conformation, and yet still be familialy related by their obedience to the original rules.[18] LeWitt's conceptual pieces of this sort imply a sharing that erodes the authority of the work, in a fashion analogous to the cooperative sequence of events that contributes to a handscroll production. Furthermore, the visual manifestation of LeWitt's pieces is the product of a description, a series of guiding rules that permit variation in the details of execution, just as a series of literati paintings might show a distinct range of variations of individual manners while still obeying the guiding rubric of a given stylistic mode. LeWitt's formulations can yield recognizable structures that lack the specificity of an image but still permit discrimination of types and categories, in the fashion of Chinese scholar-paintings.

The descriptive mode of Chinese scholar-painting, it is important to recall, first appeared within—and constituted a reaction against—a context of strongly representational, visually oriented, and imagistic modes of painting that predominated during the Song dynasty and were just reaching the zenith of technical capability never to be matched in the later course of Chinese painting history. The reaction of the literati may have been motivated in part by discomfort with the potency and authority of such iconographic and representational paintings, which threatened to unravel the fabric of a textually based order and supplant it with the seamless and immediate attractions of an image-realm. The descriptive mode of the literati made painting a less immediate and more associative art, not only by the cooperative production of painting and texts, but also by drawing painting into metaphorical, historical, memory, and lineage relationships. The social basis of painting became, not the obligation of veridical witness, but the recognition and reconstitution of affiliative relationships, with the viewer playing an active and powerful role.

Evaluation and Affiliation

The epochal change that occurred in the direction and nature of Chinese painting during the transition between the Song and Yuan dynasties in the late thirteenth century—leading to the predominance of literati or scholar-amateur values and esthetics of the sort discussed above—had many dimensions. It has often been characterized as a shift in orientation from realism to self-expression.[19] Perhaps equally significant was an institutional shift: from the imperial court, its bureaus of painters, and its collections, as the center of gravity in the world of painting, to private painters and collectors as the focus of importance, following the disruption and diminution of court-painting institutions and the dispersal of imperial collections.[20] The thoroughness of this shift should not be overstated: the boundaries of public versus private realms of painting and patronage can be subtle and problematic. There were a number of significant movements or schools of painting during the Song dynasty and earlier centered outside the imperial court. These included some kinds of Buddhist religious image-making, professional painters serving the popular urban market, and the beginnings of an amateur movement in painting and art criticism.

Nonetheless, a survey of surviving art-historical writings from the Song and earlier suggests that most important painters and movements at least partially intersected the orbits of one of the major dynastic court centers of painting. Painters could be born into these realms, as members of one of the nearly hereditary clans of court artists or as aristocrat-painter relatives of the imperial family, or they might be drawn in as if by gravitational attraction, their talents recognized and rewarded by invitation to join the acknowledged center of the art world.[21] Most of all, the values and standards of the court-connected academies, collections, and critics tended to become normative, so that those painters and movements outside the court either engaged in some kind of elliptical or intermittent linkage with the court scene or imitated academic styles from a distance to avoid the danger of being consigned to (Chinese) art-historical irrelevancy and oblivion, as were some schools of Buddhist painting, professional or Chan (Zen).[22]

Conversely, court-centered painting activity certainly continued under the Mongol rulers of the Yuan dynasty in the late thirteenth century—including patronage, painting, and collecting—and it touched on the careers of both minor artists and specialist artisans as well as leading literati painters and critics.[23] But the weight of innovative and self-critical painting and thinking about painting and its purposes had shifted to venues outside the court.[24] When court-centered painting was revived on a larger scale under the Ming, it was carried out largely by inarticulate practitioners. The center of critical discourse resided firmly with the amateurs, whose involvement with the court was largely peripheral or explicitly political.[25] Court painting, of course, is not simply identified with public painting, though the literati circles can be termed private without much qualification. Court collections were very much the property of the imperial family, and court patronage resulted often in works that remained hidden in the forbidden precincts of the imperial palaces and residences. In early times, such as the Tang dynasty, there was a genuine intermingling of court and public venues of painting, as court-centered artists undertook such projects as the fresco decoration of the great Buddhist and Taoist temples of the capital.[26] By the Song dynasty, such intersections of activity were rarer, but court painting continued to be at least normative. It set the standards and modes for much of the painting of the dynasty, and its styles were disseminated through school works and imitations on a broad and genuinely public scale.[27] Court painting continued to be linked to public and even popular art under the Ming dynasty, but by then it was no longer the art centrally connected to critical values and discourse.[28] It was especially in the domination of the terms of criticism and evaluation that the court painting of the Song and earlier can be said to have been public in focus.

Some genres of art-historical writing were pervasive in all periods of Chinese painting history, especially artistic biography and painting catalogues. However, the preoccupying issues and key critical concerns seem to shift markedly after the Song, in ways that appear linked to the shift of the center of painting and critical activity from the court to private realms. In painting texts from the Song and earlier, there is a continual search for terms of critical evaluation and of the ranking of artists and paintings. The change of the site of evaluation from the temperament of the artist to the resonance or structure of the painting and then to faults of representation should not obscure the common presupposition that all these projects of

critical evaluation share: that there are public standards of critical evaluation and it is the business of criticism to define and apply them.[29] The
distinctive aspect of Song dynasty criticism is its focus on qualities of the
painting-as-representation as the locus of evaluation. Thus texts by court-
affiliated writers such as Guo Xi (post-1000–ca. 1090)—whose major
surviving work, which displays a complex representational ambition,
marks one side of the gulf that separates Song academic painting from
post-Song literati painting—and Han Zho (active ca. 1095–ca. 1125) list
the faults and proprieties of organization, representation, subject matter,
and the like.[30] This presupposes both a broadly representational project for
the painting of the time and the kind of common training in and understanding of painting aims and techniques most efficiently fostered by the
systems of the court bureaus of painting. Visual access to and knowledge
of paintings may have been largely limited to artists, officials, and critics
who circulated in court environments, but the subject of discourse covered
a broad, commonly shared field of artists and paintings.

After the fall of the Song dynasty, painting and collecting became
largely private, and much of the writing about painting shifts to cataloguing
activity, including informal collections of notes on paintings seen, along
with the biographical compilation traditions continued from earlier
times.[31] Catalogues and notes on paintings might embody criticism and
evaluation, but the terminology of discussion tended toward vaguely
defined qualities of temperament, spiritual resonance, intent, and the like,
along with the historical affiliations of painters and styles.[32] The relationship of collecting to recollecting or reconstituting a canon of paintings
remains to be explored, but the direction of emulation among the literati
painters shifted toward the more generalized styles of the so-called Southern masters, in part perhaps because of the difficulty of seeing, studying, or
transmitting more particularized techniques. In any event, scholar painting
became something private, restricted to a limited in-group of friends and
associates of like background and tastes. Scholar painting was a shared and
communal activity, but with a limited circulation, and with knowledge of
both old paintings and contemporary productions constrained strongly by
circumstance. Scholar-painters did not paint in public arenas; notorious
problems of authenticity in both ancient and modern times probably had
much to do with a lack of public standard works in permanent and sta-
tionary formats, corresponding to the frescoes or altarpieces that appeared
in the West. Scholar-paintings often served as imperfect and largely private

aides-memoires: a way of notating, preserving, or reexperiencing inaccessible works.[33]

Painters could imitate or copy antique or more recent works, but were limited by the difficulty of access to rich collections and by the private nature of painting formats, as well as by the conception of knowledge as consensual, shared, and practical.[34] Because the imitations, as well, had only limited circulation, there was a tendency for the public record of paintings to be lodged in literary forms such as published editions of comments on paintings seen, notes on painting, or catalogues of objects owned or viewed. Since written records of painting could be circulated and published, unlike the painted imitations or reconstitutions, the tendency for post-Song scholar-painting to become "literary," "calligraphic," or "unpictorial," as it has been variously characterized—or "descriptive" in my formulation above—may have had something to do with the desirability and efficiency of painting achieving a condition in which it could intersect with written accounts of styles.[35]

Textual descriptions of painting were couched in fairly general terminology during the first major phase of literati painting dominance, the Yuan and much of the Ming dynasties, from about 1300 to about 1600. The classification system then developed was formulated in terms of school styles, themselves organized according to a gradually evolving rubric of amateur versus professional, scholarly versus academic, southern versus northern oppositions.[36] This system had a certain mnemonic value, but also allowed readers to associate or project into the texts their own varied experiences of specific paintings in the manner of a given master or lineage, even while providing a comforting reassurance of commonality and ideological correctness. Instead of observable qualities of technique or representation, artists were evaluated and categorized based on lineages of affiliation, stylistic inheritance, or association. Acknowledgment of the proper sources and models, even if largely in the form of written citation and only perfunctorily in visual and stylistic terms, was enough to assure placement in the critically prestigious camp of literati discourse.

Publicized Pictorial Knowledge

The literati painting system outlined above—largely privatized, descriptive, textually transmitted, and affiliative in purpose—dominated the world of scholar-amateur painting from around 1300 to around 1600. This system gave rise to schools of literati painting that were at least nominally art-historical, characterized by brushwork, compositionally and visually unadventurous, and closely linked by common concerns and mutual awareness among their members. During the seventeenth century, coinciding with the end of the Ming dynasty (1368–1644) and the early years of the Qing (1644–1911), a number of artists emerged whose educational and social status and background broadly matched or surpassed those of the literati, but who as painters followed quite different pictorial strategies. They have been variously characterized by art historians, but under whatever heading, have generally been accounted the most important painters of the century. Included among their number are Chen Hongshou (1598–1652), Hongren (1610–64), Kuncan (1612–74 or later), Gong Xian (ca. 1619–89), Zhu Da (1626–1705), and Shi'tao (1642–1707).[37]

Western art historians have most often termed them individualists, which, despite abdicating any attempt at classification, at least has the virtue of suggesting their only shared characteristic: that their painting styles pursued radically disparate directions, marked by a certain experimentalism that could lead to extremes of specialization, along with novel kinds of compositional and imagistic power.[38] Chinese historians have tended to classify these artists as *i-min* or "loyalist" painters, because their lives and artistic careers overlapped the politically and socially traumatic years of the fall of the Ming dynasty—to which their primary loyalties remained attached—as well as the conquest by the Manchu rulers of the Qing. Consequently interpretation of the motivations and significance of their paintings has often centered on political factors.[39] Japanese scholars have preferred to emphasize the Buddhist monk identities adopted by many of the group, in part in an effort to avoid potential persecution or entanglement in political affairs. The difficulty with classifications that point to shared life, or political or religious orientations, however, is that they are no help in explaining the radical diversity in visual styles and orientations among members of the group, while "individualists" is self-contradictory as a group name.

In this context, it may be helpful to recall that the emergence of these painters also coincided with some major events and changes in the visual culture of the time, the importance of which deserves further consideration. It may be that any links between the so-called individualists are to be discovered at a deeper level than surface manifestations of style and theme.

Figure 37. "Mi Yuren Style
Mountains," from the *Mustard
Seed Garden Manual of Painting*
(1782 edition), chap. 3. Courtesy
Library of Congress, Washington,
D.C.

We might hypothesize that what their art held in common was a profundity
of response, albeit response manifested in a variety of forms and directions,
to some nearly structural alterations of the imagistic, public, and cognitive
status of painting. These alterations would seem to have been occasioned
by a couple of newly important factors in the visual culture of the age: the
rise and increasingly broad distribution of the woodblock medium of illustration and instruction, and the intrusion of European pictorial imagery
into the seventeenth-century Chinese visual consciousness.

　　The seventeenth century saw a visual publicizing of pictorial styles in
published woodblock manuals of painting such as the *Ten Bamboo Studio
Manual on Calligraphy and Painting*, published between about 1627 and
1644, and the *Mustard Seed Garden Manual of Painting*, published in two
installments, in 1679 and 1701 (fig. 37).[40] These provided both a mnemonic and a cognitive system of painting, since works were broken down
categorically into motifs and elements that collectively constituted a kind
of visual encyclopedia and classifying system. The painting manual illustrations had accompanying written tags and explanatory notes that allowed

the systematic acquisition of formulas representing various canonical styles of elements, from rocks, trees, foliage, and figures on up to compositional arrangements.[41] The private transmission and painstaking recollection of visual artistic knowledge was being superseded by publicly accessible systems in both visual and linguistic form.[42] Catalogue descriptions of paintings in the seventeenth and early eighteenth centuries become more systematic and circumstantial than earlier ones, as well, including not only records of measurements and transcriptions of inscriptions, but often also fairly extensive and specific accounts of compositions, subject matter, and brush manners.[43] In addition to the illustrated manuals such as the *Mustard Seed Garden Manual* and the *Ten Bamboo Studio Manual*, encyclopedic projects of various kinds appeared, such as the *Pei-wen-chai* encyclopedia of painting and calligraphy, from around 1708.[44] The *Pei-wen-chai* art encyclopedia was compiled under the general editorship of the painter Wang Yuanqi (1642–1715), whose position as an art advisor at the Manchu court of the Kangxi emperor represented the terminal stage of co-optation of the affiliative strategies of the literati painters into a state-validated, truly orthodox school.

The reverberations of this publicizing of pictorial knowledge in what had been largely private spheres of painting were pronounced. Serial paintings that undertook a limited encyclopedic project—for example, a series of landscapes in the styles of a dozen or so ancient masters—become increasingly common. The tendency toward constructed and formulaic renderings, perhaps based on a kind of artistic catalogue-shopping, has sometimes been blamed for an ossification of certain modes of Qing dynasty scholar-painting, such as the orthodox school, whose adherents tended more than most to conceptualize and paint in categorical terms.[45]

Although publication of pictorial knowledge seemingly reinforced some conservative tendencies toward consensual formulations in literati painting, the spread of painting knowledge profoundly altered the basis of that art in privately shared events. It may be that the provocative power of this publicizing of painting in the seventeenth century has not been sufficiently acknowledged as contributing to a reaction in the art world that included some of the most interesting painting of the time, that of the individualists.

Another intrusion into traditional visual culture in seventeenth-century China was the appearance of European religious imagery brought by Jesuit missionaries, including religious icons of a powerful visual presence, vividly plastic forms, and strong chiaroscuro effects in both figural and landscape elements.[46] European images were publicized by inclusion in such woodblock compilations as the *Cheng Family Manual of Ink-Cake Designs* of 1606, in the company of traditional Chinese figural and landscape motifs and compositions.[47] Such examples of European imagistic power had an undeniably powerful impact on the Chinese scholars and painters who saw them from as early as the beginning of the century, and who commented on their sculpturelike plasticity or mirrorlike verisimilitude.[48]

An equally powerful reaction was the denial of any interest or esthetic value in specifically European representational techniques and imagery.[49] Instead, the impact of European pictorial practice emerged in disguised forms or partially transformed devices. Some seventeenth-century Buddhist figure-painting betrays the influence of European practices of pictorial modeling and plasticity, while drawing on a tradition with its own history of vividly iconic production.[50] Similarly, European recessional devices and heavy textural and chiaroscuro effects in landscape prints seem to have been refashioned to accompany traditional Chinese themes and styles revived from the Song dynasty age of representational orientation in painting.[51]

The introduction of these two elements—published pictorial knowledge and European imagery—had the potential to alter profoundly conceptions of pictorial practices, values, and functions. The strongest impact of these factors seems to have been upon the painting of the so-called individualists. The variety and innovativeness of their pictorial formulations does not necessarily indicate a progressive orientation, if by that is meant a wholehearted embrace of the values of publicity and imagistic force. Indeed, some aspects of their practice and outlook might fairly be termed reactionary, asserting the value of private imagery and significance. Most of all, these painters were characterized by both a deep engagement with issues of the imagistic and public status of painting and a thoroughgoing ambivalence in their attitudes toward those issues.

One of the early painters in this group, who maintained an extremely ambiguous position in regard to issues of the private and public in art, was Chen Hongshou (1598–1652). His involvement was far more than theoretical, because he produced substantially in pictorial forms that were both public and popular, such as woodblock designs for playing cards and illustrations of drama.[52] His figural themes often embraced the world of

Figure 38. Chen Hongshou,
Immortal Companions, vertical
scroll, late Ming dynasty.
Chingqing Municipal Museum;
after *Yi-yuan duo ying*, 7
(Shanghai, 1979), p. 44.

characters and heroes from popular novels and plays, and even his favored
subjects of idiosyncratic recluses such as Tao Yuanming were broadly
understood cultural types. Even so, his figures often manifest a strained
theatricality and self-consciousness that foreground the tension between
public roles and private integrity. His subjects characteristically appear

distracted, with averted gazes or brooding inwardness of attention that suggest isolated subjectivities. The powerful idiosyncracy of Chen's figure-painting manner also has the effect of eliding distinctions between the historical/literary and contemporary/personal identities of his seemingly familialy related figures.

Chen Hongshou's painted images often have an uneasy reality status, blurring the distinction between pictorial and present. He was prominently concerned with the device of images within images, pictures within pictures, in which the viewer's presumptions of orderly pictorial conventions are questioned. Most vividly, the icons he portrays often seem half-animate, as if to manifest in an uncanny way the potency of images (fig. 38).[53] Though Chen has not been much linked to the influence of European imagery, his paintings suggest an awareness of the potential iconic power of images, while maintaining a certain deliberate ambiguity as to their own reality status. Chen seems to withdraw his images from accessibility of interpretation even as he presents culturally familiar types, so that they remain simultaneously public and private images.

The Nanking area painter Gong Xian (ca. 1618–89) is another interesting case of an artist who straddled the realms of private art and publicized pictorial knowledge. Gong Xian was active in the same period and area as the *Mustard Seed Garden Manual* was produced, and was a teacher of Wang Gai (active ca. 1677–1705), the artist who served as editor for that publication's designs.[54] Gong Xian himself seems to have produced sketchbooks for his own and student use, with close similarities to the format and approach of the *Mustard Seed Garden Manual*—analytically presented components of landscape with accompanying notes and explanations scattered around the album pages.[55] At the same time, the sketchbooks belong to the tradition of private artistic practice and training, with only the survival of the illustrations unusual.[56] Gong Xian's mature paintings display a relentless personalization of style, apparently uncongenial to imitation for the paradoxical reason of its extreme simplicity. Against the background of the contemporary painting manuals, Gong Xian's style seems to lack the categorized distinctiveness of lexicon that made other manners imitable; it is withdrawn from the kinds of appropriation current at the time, through an endless reiteration of uniform brushstrokes that seem to transpose painting from a graphic language into a world of light and dark tonality and texture (compare figs. 37 and 39). Some of the powerful plastic, textural, and chiaroscuro effects of Gong Xian's land-

Figure 39. Kung Hsien (Gong Xian), *Village on a Mountainous Lakeshore*, one of ten album leaves in *Landscape Album (Shan-shui ts'e)*, ink and color on paper mounted as a hanging scroll, 1671, Qing dynasty, 24.1 × 44.7 cm. The Nelson-Atkins Museum of Art, Kansas City, Missouri, Nelson Fund 60–36/6.

scapes have been persuasively linked to the impact of northern European landscape engravings introduced into China by the Jesuits, but Gong Xian himself never acknowledged the influence, instead attributing the qualities of his imagery to the private sources of dreams and visions.[57]

The monk-painter and descendant of the Ming imperial house Shi'tao (1642–1707) is generally accounted the most notable of the individualist painters of the seventeenth century. He was a theoretician of painting and a habitual, nearly compulsive, experimenter with changing stylistic modes. He moved at intervals throughout his career, living for

Figure 40. Shi'tao, *Ten Thousand Ugly Inkblots*, handscroll, ink on paper, 1685. Suzhou Museum.

varying periods at most of the major centers of painting, collecting, and patronage of the time, including Anhui, Nanking, Peking, and Yangzhou.[58] He lived in Nanking in the early 1680s, just after the appearance there of the *Mustard Seed Garden Manual of Painting*. By 1682, he was writing:

> It may look like Dong Yuan, but it isn't Dong.
> It may seem like Mi Fu, but it isn't Mi.
> The rain passes over the autumn mountains,
> creating a brilliance as though the world were washed clean.
> Nothing but "coming out," nothing but "going in"—
> All it is is an essential turning and twisting of my brush.[59]

Dong Yuan and Mi Fu were the originators of influential style-types from the tenth and eleventh centuries whose designs were prominent as models in the woodblock printed manuals of the seventeenth century.[60]

In the same vein, Shi'tao claimed an even more aggressively antitraditional and unrulebound stance a few years later, in 1685, when he wrote on an extant painting (compare figs. 37 and 40):

> Ten thousand ugly ink dots to scare Mi Fu to death!
> Some fibers of soft traces to make Dong Yuan roll over laughing!
> From afar the perspective doesn't work—it lacks a landscape's winding
>   ways.
> Close up the details are all confused—you can barely make out a few
>   simple cottages.
> Once and for all cut off the "heart's eye" from conventional molds,
> Just as the immortal who rides the wind has freed his divine spirit from
>   the bounds of flesh and bones![61]

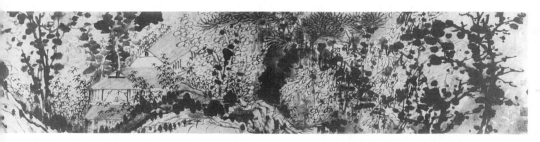

Shi'tao's later theoretical writings are still more metaphysical in tone, but even these early writings convey the transcendent aspirations and the claims of a nearly cosmic originality that have made it tempting to characterize Shi'tao as the supreme individualist of his era, however unsatisfactory and evasive that kind of art-historical labeling may be.[62] Shi'tao's preoccupation with changing styles may indeed have had much to do with a profound and determined originality, but it may also have been prompted by artistic circumstances much nearer at hand: the reductionist labeling of representative styles that was implied in the painting manuals' categorizing system of art-historical knowledge. Shi'tao may have had a very real and reasonable fear of artistic capture by classification. His vociferous disdain for imitation, similarly, may have come not so much from the pursuit of a theoretically profound individuality as from a much more concrete recognition of the stereotyping dangers attendant upon public access to stylistic schemata. Later in Shi'tao's career, he returned often to themes of reminiscence, of travels and occasions reconstituted, as if to assert the value of specific personal memories.[63] At an opposite extreme, but with related implications, Shi'tao also explored themes of forgetting, both in late works such as his illustrations of the myth of the Peach Blossom Spring, and with his concern with the concept of "no method"; in such cases, Shi'tao repudiated the systematized knowledge and classified artistic memory implied by the painting manuals.[64]

Finally, in the life and paintings of Zhu Da (1626–1705), another relative of the fallen Ming imperial family active in the early Qing period, we observe a combination of personal behavioral eccentricities and disconnected, cryptic, or incoherent pictorial images that have been seen as signs of neurosis. At times, seemingly incongruous motifs are scattered about the surfaces of his pictures, as if subject to unseen pressures and carrying implications of an underlying psychological fragmentation (fig. 41).[65] The cryptic logic of his thematic associations and the stark isolation of his motifs suggest affinities with Chan (Zen) Buddhist painting traditions. Like much of the earlier Chan imagery from the Song dynasty, Zhu Da's plants and creatures convey the iconic potential of the everyday object, along with an evident imagistic fragility, in the manner of visions or hallucinations. In other ways, however, such images are reminiscent of the scattered, disconnected motif-images found in the pages of the painting manuals, although presented in the mode of a supple calligraphy that is inescapably personal (compare fig. 41).[66] Whatever the psychological im-

Figure 41. Chu Ta (Zhu Da),
*Mynah Birds and Rocks (Ch'u-yu
shih pi)*, hanging scroll, ink on
satin, Qing dynasty, 204.6 × 54
cm. The Nelson-Atkins Museum of
Art, Kansas City, Missouri, Nelson
Fund, 67–4/1.

plications of his imagery, Zhu Da may also have been engaged in a kind of visual parody of the prevailing system of pictorial knowledge classification by heightening incongruous juxtapositions and pictorial illogic. The resulting suggestion of privatized meaning through cryptic imagery and writing may imply a fear, or realization, that the last refuge of private art lay not in the shared memories and understandings of literati groups, but in the hidden realms of the personal psyche.

Notes

Introduction

1. For a recent text on bark painting that is sensitive to its pictorial status, see P. Sutton, ed., *Dreamings: The Art of Aboriginal Australia* (New York, 1989).

2. For alternative approaches to Rembrandt, which focus on his manipulation of social and commercial protocols, see S. Alpers, *Rembrandt's Enterprise: The Studio and the Market* (Chicago, 1988) and G. Schwartz, *Rembrandt: His Life, His Paintings* (New York, 1985).

3. II. Morphy, "From Dull to Brilliant: The Aesthetics of Spiritual Power among the Yolngu," *Man* 24 (1989): 21–41.

4. Alpers explores these interpretative strategies in *Rembrandt's Enterprise*, 58–122.

5. E. Casey, *Remembering: A Case Study* (Chicago, 1987), 2.

6. F. C. Bartlett, *Remembering: A Study in Experimental and Social Psychology* (Cambridge, 1932); J. Piaget and B. Inhelder, *Memory and Intelligence*, trans. A. J. Pomerans (New York, 1973).

7. F. Yates, *The Art of Memory* (Chicago, 1966).

8. G. Bateson, *Naven: A Survey of Problems Suggested by a Comparative Picture of the Culture of a New Guinea Tribe Drawn from Three Points of View* (Stanford, 1958).

9. See J. Cahill, *The Compelling Image: Nature and Style in Seventeenth-Century Chinese Painting* (Cambridge, Mass., and London, 1982) and in this volume, R. Vinograd, "Private Art and Public Knowledge in Later Chinese Painting."

10. See B. Jewsiewicki, "Collective Memory and Its Images: Popular Urban Painting in Zaire—A Source of 'Present Past,'" *History and Anthropology* 2 (1986): 389–96, and by the same author, "Collective Memory and the Stakes of Power: A Reading of Popular Zairian Historical Discourses," *History in Africa* 13 (1986): 195–223.

11. On perspective and the art of gauging, see M. Baxandall, *Painting and Experience in Fifteenth-Century Italy* (Oxford, 1972), 29–108; on painting and the Latin period, M. Baxandall, *Giotto and the Orators* (Oxford, 1971), 121–39; on German calligraphy and carving, M. Baxandall, *The Limewood Sculptors of Renaissance Germany* (New Haven and London, 1980), 145–52.

12. E. Gombrich, *Art and Illusion* (Princeton and New York, 1960), especially 181–241, and by the same author, "The Renaissance Theory of Art and the Rise of Landscape," in *Norm and Form* (Oxford and New York, 1966), 107–21.

13. S. Alpers, *The Art of Describing* (Chicago, 1983), especially 26–71.

14. C. Geertz, *The Interpretation of Cultures* (New York, 1973), especially 3–30 and 87–125, and by the same author, "Art As a Cultural System," *Modern Language Notes* 91 (1976): 1473–99.

15. P. Bourdieu, *Outline of a Theory of Practice* (Cambridge, 1977); D. Sperber, "Anthropology and Psychology: Toward an Epidemiology of Representations," *Man* 20 (1985): 73–89, and by the same author, *Rethinking Symbolism* (Cambridge, 1975).

16. A phenomenological account such as E. Casey, *Remembering: A Phenomenological Study* (Bloomington, 1987) would focus on materiality rather than on the material act of representation and would posit the essential "being" of remembering itself.

17. A similar distinction would have been made between *handelingh* and *teyckeningh*, that is, rendering and drawn representation, and *handelingh* and *schilderij*, that is, rendering and painted representation. Dutch and English share the term *print*, which can designate an engraving, etching, or woodcut. On Van Mander's biography of Goltzius, see W. Melion, "Karel van Mander's 'Life of Goltzius': Defining the Paradigm of Protean Virtuosity in Haarlem around 1600," *Studies in the History of Art* 27 (1989): 113–33.

18. The drawing measures 230 × 322 mm. and is inscribed "HGoltzius. fecit. Anno. 1588." On this and a second drawing of Goltzius's hand, also executed in pen and brown ink, see E. K. J. Reznicek, *Die Zeichnungen von Hendrick Goltzius* (Utrecht, 1961), 1: 305–6.

19. "T'leven van Henricus Goltzius," in Karel van Mander, *Het Schilder-Boeck* (Haarlem, 1604), folios 281v–282r. The *Schilder-Boeck* or *Book on Picturing* was the seminal text establishing the Netherlandish canon of fifteenth- and sixteenth-century masters that remained central throughout the seventeenth century. It assembled a firmament of painters, draftsmen, and engravers that later theoreticians might accept or dispute, alter or expand, but that remained fundamental to their efforts. Van Mander juxtaposed three historical constructions—the histories of ancient, Italian, and Netherlandish art—through which he articulated critical categories pertinent to the project of northern art.

20. The engraving measures 353 × 232 mm. and is one of a series of ten plates published in Haarlem in 1586 with a dedication to the Holy Roman Emperor Rudolf II. The series' martial theme and its appropriation for the engraver of the rewards of valor would have appealed to Rudolf, who was a celebrated supporter of northern masters. On the series, see O. Hirschmann, *Verzeichnis des Graphischen Werks von Hendrick Goltzius* (Leipzig, 1921; rpt. Brunswick, 1976),

nos. 161–70, and W. Strauss, *Hendrik Goltzius 1558–1617: The Complete Engravings and Woodcuts* (New York, 1977), nos. 230–39.

21. See "T'leven van Henricus Goltzius," fol. 284v. As the heroes exercise *pietas*, sacrificing themselves to save the nation, so Goltzius devotes himself to the strenuous task of engraving, securing the artistic fame of the Netherlands.

22. The story of Mucius Scaevola appears in book 3, chapter 3 of Valerius Maximus, *Dictorum factorumque memorabilium*, and book 2, chapter 13 of Titus Livius, *Ab urbe condita*. In a large drawing of *Venus, Bacchus, and Ceres* executed in 1606, Goltzius allegorizes his love of art by holding his left or drawing hand above a sacrificial flame, converting Mucius Scaevola's deed into an assertion of his own devotion to the pen. He holds burins positioned to resemble compasses in both hands, alluding to his ability to draw freehand the kinds of circular lines for which his engravings were famed.

23. See "T'leven van Henricus Goltzius," fol. 284r: "En dit heb ick van hem te segghen, dat hy van jongs aen niet alleen en heeft de schoonheyt oft verscheyden ghedaenten der Natueren gesocht nae te volghen: maer heeft oock seer wonderlijck hem ghewent verscheyden handelingen der beste Meesters nae te bootsen, alsnu Hemskercken, Frans Floris, Blocklandts, dan Fredericks, en eyndlinghe des Spranghers."

24. Vasari's magnum opus, the *Vite* of 1550, traces the revival of the visual arts in Italy from Giotto to their contemporary flowering in Florence and Rome. Underlying Vasari's history of art is the ideology of the *Accademia Fiorentina*, which aimed to justify the cultural superiority of the Tuscan vernacular. Ortelius, Lampsonius, and other Netherlanders responded by formulating regional canons in opposition to Vasari's. It was Karel van Mander who consolidated the northern position by publishing his comparative critical histories of ancient, Italian, and Netherlandish art in the *Schilder-Boeck*.

25. On *ekphrases* see S. Alpers, "*Ekphrasis* and Aesthetic Attitudes in Vasari's *Lives*," *Journal of the Warburg and Courtauld Institutes* 23 (1960): 190–215, and Baxandall, *Giotto and the Orators*, 85–87, 90–96, and 135.

26. For documents on the book's publication, see M. Rooses, "De Plaatsnijders der *Evangelicae Historiae Imagines*," *Oud-Holland* 6 (1888): 277–88; for the complicated history of illustration and engraving, see M.-B. Wadell, *Evangelicae Historiae Imagines: Entstehungsgeschichte und Vorlage* (Goeteborg, 1981), especially 9–17; on the Wiericx family of engravers who finally received the commission, see M. Mauquoy-Hendrickx, "Les Wierix illustrateurs de la Bible dite de Natalis," *Quaerendo* 6 (1976): 28–63.

27. For a sixteenth-century precis of the letter offering Goltzius these perquisites, see Rooses, "Plaatsnijders," 284. By 1580 Antwerp had become a European center for the publishing of reproductive prints. Goltzius seemed to the Jesuits the unqualified heir to the tradition of northern reproductive engraving. He had been trained in the mid-1570s by Dirck Volckertsz Coornhert, who specialized in the reproduction of drawings by Martin van Heemskerck and had previously trained Philip Galle, one of the most gifted engravers affiliated with the publishing house of Hieronymus Cock. Founded by at least 1550, Cock's Antwerp establishment, known as *Aux quatre vents*, introduced the Netherlands to print publication

on an unprecedented scale that matched and then superseded the Roman operations of Salamanca and Lafrery. In the 1560s Galle, along with Cornelis Cort, another engraver who often worked for Cock, standardized a mode of rendering suited to the execution of reproductive figured prints. Goltzius worked for Galle early in his career, when he assimilated the executory means promulgated by Galle and Cort. He adjusted their burin-hand to fashion the rendering characteristic of his engravings in the 1580s and 1590s. On the operations of Cock's publishing house, see T. Riggs, _Hieronymus Cock (1510–1570): Printmaker and Publisher in Antwerp at the Sign of the Four Winds_ (New York, 1977).

28. The series had come to be known as the _Meesterstukjes_ or _Little Masterpieces_ by the eighteenth century. The six episodes from the early life of the Virgin are _The Annunciation_, 1594, Hirschman, 9 and Strauss, 321; _The Visitation_, 1593, Hirschman, 10 and Strauss, 318; _The Adoration of the Shepherds_, 1594, Hirschman, 11 and Strauss, 319; _The Circumcision_, 1594, Hirschman, 12 and Strauss, 322; _The Adoration of the Magi_, 1594, Hirschman, 13 and Strauss, 320; and _The Holy Family with the Infant St. John the Baptist_, also known as _The Rest on the Flight_, 1593, Hirschman, 14 and Strauss, 317.

29. See "T'leven van Henricus Goltzius," fol. 285r: "Al dees verhaelde dinghen t'samen bewijsen, Goltzium eenen seldsamen Proteus oft Vertumnus te wesen in de Const, met hem in alle ghestalten van handelinghen te connen herscheppen." Van Mander's use of the Proteus metaphor arose from the earlier conviction, shared by members of the Ortelian circle, that the mid-sixteenth-century master Pieter Bruegel had succeeded in recuperating the art of the early-sixteenth-century master Hieronymus Bosch. To Ortelius and his friends, Bruegel's status as "the second Bosch" justified his place in the northern canon.

30. See "T'leven van Henricus Goltzius," fol. 285v. Goltzius tells his peers about the pictorial accomplishments of the Lombard, Venetian, and Roman masters whose works have particularly impressed him. Van Mander's formulation is that "he had imprinted his experience of Italian painting as if in a mirror" ("hadde de fraey Italische schilderijen als in eenen spieghel soo vast in zijn ghedacht ghedruckt").

31. My account of the terms _nae t'leven_ and _uyt den geest_, which I take to be cognitive categories, expressive of the relationship of sight to the execution of images, is based on a reading of the _Schilder-Boeck_, fol. 9v (stanza 16), 37r–37v (stanza 37), 233r, 241v, 275v, 292v, and 294r–294v.

32. The details of Goltzius's procedure come from H. Miedema, "Het Voorbeeldt niet te by te Hebben; Over Hendrick Goltzius's Tekeningen naar de Antieken," in _Miscellanea I. Q. van Regteren Altena_ (Amsterdam, 1969), 74–78. _The Farnese Hercules_, 405 × 294 mm., published 1617, Hirschman 145 and Strauss 312, is one of a set of three engravings of antique effigies seen by Goltzius during his visit to Rome. The Haarlem publisher Herman Adolfz issued the set in 1617, soon after Goltzius's death, perhaps in homage to the master. In "T'leven van Henricus Goltzius," fol. 283r, Van Mander recounts the intensity of Goltzius's concentration when drawing antiquities _nae t'leven_. He seemed "to forget himself completely," as if "disembodied" by the acts of seeing and transcribing. So complete was his absorption in Roman statuary that he failed to note the effects of the

plague, whose victims littered the city's streets, encroaching upon the places where he sat to draw.

33. On this drawing, executed in pen and red-brown ink, washed in red-brown and gray, and heightened with white, 295 × 536 mm., see Reznicek, *Zeichnungen*, 1: 442–43.

34. On Matham's print of 1598, inscribed *J. Matham sculp. Ao. 1598*, 316 × 425 mm., see F. W. H. Hollstein, *Dutch and Flemish Etchings, Engravings, and Woodcuts* (Amsterdam, 1955), 11: 231. On the print of 1601, inscribed *Maetham. fecit et excud.*, 310 × 425 mm., see Hollstein, 231. On Saenredam's print of 1602, inscribed *Joannes Saenredam inve. et sculptor ano. 1602*, 407 × 596 mm., see F. W. H. Hollstein *Dutch and Flemish Etchings, Engravings, and Woodcuts, ca. 1450–1700*, vol. 23, ed. K. G. Boon, comp. G. S. Keyes (Amsterdam, 1980), 94; and A. B. van Deinse, "Over de Potvissen in Nederland Gestrand tusschen de Jaren 1521–1788," *Zoologische Mededeelingen* 4 (1918): 22–50, especially 24, 36–40. Unlike Matham's prints of 1598 and 1601, which undoubtedly issued from Goltzius's Haarlem workshop, Saenredam's print may have been published in Amsterdam. The figure of the Maid of Amsterdam was added to the second state, and the third state, issued posthumously in 1618, includes the name of the Amsterdam dealer and publisher Joannes Janssonius.

Matham's widowed mother Margaretha Jansdochter married Goltzius in 1579. Van Mander states in "T'leven van Henricus Goltzius," fols. 282v and 286v, that Goltzius trained his stepson assiduously, applying him to *Plaet-snijden* (engraving) from an early age. Matham continued the operations of Goltzius's engraving workshop after the master retired from the strenuous work of engraving around 1600; through Matham, Goltzius continued to exercise his burin-hand. In "Het leven van Iacques de Gheyn," fols. 294v–295r, Van Mander identifies Jan Saenredam as a student of Goltzius's protégé Jacob de Gheyn. In 1593 Goltzius contracted for the services of Saenredam, who replaced Matham during his journey to Italy. By 1601 Saenredam had established his own workshop in the nearby town of Assendelft, but his burin-hand would have been perceived as an extension of Goltzius's. On Goltzius's relations to Matham and Saenredam, see Reznicek, *Zeichnungen*, 1: 33, 51, 118, 120, 175–76. On Saenredam, see also I. Q. van Regteren Altena, *Jacques de Gheyn: Three Generations* (The Hague, 1983), 1: 31–33, 50, 123. The imperial privilege Goltzius procured for his plates in 1595 documents the speed and expertise with which he and his collaborators produced engravings. Besides referring to the diligence, industry, and excellence exemplified by these plates, the privilege praises the celerity with which the workshop "brings forth varied images in the space of a day" ("varias in dies imagines edere"). For a transcription of this privilege granted by Rudolf II, see Reznicek, *Zeichnungen*, 1: 94–95, n. 18.

35. Notwithstanding the plea to the gods, Screvelius refrains from allegorizing the whale, choosing instead to dramatize its battle with the elements: "Ingens caeruleo iactatus gurgite cetus/ (Dij prohibete minas) Catthorum littora vidit,/ Qualis Atlantiaci terror, Ballaena profundi,/ Quum vento motuue suo telluris ad oras/ Pellitur, et sicca subsidit captus arena:/ Quem chartis famaeque damus, populoque loquendum."

36. "Monstrum horrendum, informe, ingens, membrosius ipso/ Hellespon-
tiaco genitali pube Priapo,/ Qua Bavarum vicus Lemi Neptunius urbem/ Pronus ad
occasum, rutilo prospectat ab ortu,/ Immanis pelagi populator, littoris oras/ Rasit,
et attonito fatalibus haesitaremis/ Corpore; at impresso mox rumpitur ilia ventre/
Theodorus Screvelius Anno 1601."

37. "Bij wijck op see, na t'west, Desember neghentien/ t'Jaer sestien hondert een, op t'strant de See quam ruijmen/ Potwalvisch groot/ ghelijck in druck
men hier mach sien, Lanck drij en t'sestich voet, en elck voet van elf duijmen.

"Dick achtenderlich voet: maer Ocean int schuijmen/ heel pekelich wat
brenght u borgher ons aenboort?/ ist dreijghing, of waerschouw, of ijdel volx
constuijmen/ hem hier verschricken in, welck niet gheschieden hoort?

"Godt waerschouwt al ghenook ons in sijn heylick woort/ Daer elck goet-
willich most ghehoorsaem onder buijghen/ Den lof sijns hooghen naems verbreijdt
sij voort en voort/ wiens wonder wercken groot sijn heerlijckheijt betuijghen."
The poem on the print of 1598 reads: "De soute golven wreed afgrondich omghe-
woelt/ door onwedersche locht, met winden stijf ghesmeten/ hebben dusch eenen
visch bij Catwijck aenghespoelt/ ons t'wonder werck van Godt wt diept der Zee
doen weten.

"Elf duijmsche voeten ses en viijtich langh ghemeten,/ en drij en dertich dick,
in sporckel derden dach/ Sestien hondert min twee men schreef, maer hoe ghe-
heten/ onder walvisch gheslacht men sulcke tellen plack.

"Met een verwondert hert hem menich oogh aensach,/ des menich tongh en
mont den heere most loven:/ want nemmermeer ghenoegh men hem gheprijsen
mach/ wiens hooghste weerd' alleen, gaet alle lof te boven."
These prints should be contrasted with an early broadsheet of 1579, 223 × 160
mm., Strauss, 106, in which Goltzius broadcasts information about an abnormal
birth that took place in Haarlem in February of that year. In the long inscription
below, he provides the two-headed child's date and place of birth, describes his
internal and external anatomy, and notes that he saw him and made the drawing
on which the plate was based in June of 1579. However, he closes by invoking the
child as a portent, calling it a mirror of God's wrath against a sinful Netherlands.
In 1579, the Dutch suffered several military setbacks, including the loss of Maas-
tricht and Mechelen to the forces of Alexander of Parma.

Van Mander's interest in the kinds of information conveyed by whales goes
back to at least 1596, when he received a city commission to paint a *gedachtenisse*,
an inscribed plaque commemorating Jan Linschoten's donation to the town of
Haarlem of a whale's jawbone. Linschoten, a native of Haarlem, had found the
jawbone on the coast of Nova Zemblon, while on an exploratory arctic voyage.
Still displayed in the Haarlem town hall, Van Mander's painted inscription
identifies the specimen suspended above it, cites its place of origin, and names its
donor. Van Mander chose a letterhead appropriate to the historical function of his
descriptive plaque: broken Gothic capitals codified in Germany and the Netherlands around 1550 for use in civic and family chronicles and books of heraldry.

Indeed Van Mander's plaque, which inscribes the jawbone, corresponds
precisely to the verses inscribed on the print: as we learn from Linschoten's *Twee
Journalen van Twee Verscheyde Voyagien*, the chronicle of his exploratory arctic

voyages of 1594 and 1595, the jawbone formed part of a whale beached on the "eastern coast of Vaygats between Twisthoeck and Kruyshoek." Linschoten records the measurements of the jawbone, noting its extraordinary size and plotting its location by reference to *teyckenen*, "cartographical diagrams." The term *teyckenen* can signify "portents," but Linschoten restricts its meaning to "maps," just as he limits the record of the whale to descriptive data. His aim, as he notes in the title to his book, is *beschryvingh*, "description" of terrain, the arctic coast, the ships' route, the peoples encountered, and the goods they produce. He adds later that his purpose is "to commit his experiences to memory in order to report them to the States General upon his return." In brief, Van Mander's inscription fulfills these functions, attaching Matham's print to the descriptive mode exemplified by Linschoten's *Journal*. See J. Huygen van Linschoten, *Twee Journalen* (Amsterdam, n.d.), 27, 37.

38. For the full transcription from this booklet of 1598, entitled *De Potvisch van Berkheij*, see Van Deinse, "Potvisschen," 36–38. The title reads: "Walvisch van Berckhey: Dat is, Eene beschrijvinghe des grooten Vischs, die tot Berckhey ghestrandet is Anno 1598. den 3. Februarij, met eene verclaringhe der dinghen die daer naer ghevolght zijn: Met noch een cort verhael der geschiedenissen, die van den lest Augusti 1598, tot nu toe verloopen zijn int Vorstendom Cleve ende omliggende vrije Landen, door de aencomste van den Spaenschen Leger, hare ongehoorde wreetheyt tegen de Cleefsche ende hare Steden, die sy als vyanden inemen voor den Conick van Spagnen. T'samen eenen Brief van des Keysers Ghesant, met d'Admirants antwoordt." The first verse of the author's poem on the stranding reads: "Ick sweegh vast still', ick hielt mijn penn' end' oock mijn mondt,/ Hopende dat de Heer' soud' toonen t'sijner stondt,/ Dat hy dit monster groot hadd' in Hollandt doen stranden,/ Niet als een voorspoeck, dat hij woude dese Landen/ Brenghen onder het groot, wreet, en bloet-dorstich dier,/ Dwelck niet ander en soeckt, dan door het zweert en vyer,/ Ons edele Nederlandt, woest ende leech te maken,/ Als een Walvisch, die t'gheen dat hy crijght in sijn kaken,/ Verscheurt, inswelght, verteert, en gantschelijck vernielt." For a short history of the kind of allegorical reading advanced by this poem, see H. van de Waal, *Drie Eeuwen Vaderlandsche Geschied-Uitbeelding* (The Hague, 1952), 1: 19–20, 2: 8–9, esp. n. 4.

39. In the account that follows, I take issue with the analysis of Saenredam's print in S. Schama, *The Embarrassment of Riches: An Interpretation of Dutch Culture in the Golden Age* (New York, 1987), 137–40. Schama positions the print within a Netherlandish tradition that depicts the whale stranding as an "oracular signpost," pregnant with implications for the political future of the fledgling Dutch state. He notes that each of the calamities invoked by the allegorical frame—the lunar and solar eclipses and the earthquake—actually occurred between the dates of the stranding and the print's publication. Later the figures of Death shooting the Maid of Amsterdam with an arrow were added to allude to the plague that decimated Amsterdam during the midwinter of 1601–2. Additionally, a series of military setbacks made the martial tone of the dedication to Court Ernst Casimir, future Stadholder of Friesland and Groningen, all the more relevant. Schama's conclusion is that Saenredam has engraved a "disaster print," mingling symbol and

fact, "oracle and description," and playing upon the anxieties of Dutch citizens conflicted about the wealth of their nascent republic.

Schama enriches our understanding of the specificity of Saenredam's allegory, but he attaches the print to a community of popular images neither as finished nor as ambitious in their execution, which function something like political broadsheets. I have focused on the earlier state of the print to underscore its links—of format, rendering, subject, and I believe, function—with the beached whale images precipitated by Goltzius's drawing of 1598. Within *this* community of images, the print claims its place by commenting on the distinctive potentialities of Goltzius's burin-hand, its interpretative and descriptive aspects. The print's pictorial organization, its division into frame and scene, compels us to acknowledge that oracular allegory, while it can overlay and enframe the event of stranding, is not intrinsic to it. It is precisely this categorical distinction that the print articulates.

40. My thanks to Professor William Tronzo for his translations from the Greek. The dedication reads: "Illustri generoso Ernesto Comiti de Nassau et fortissimo Heroi, et Belgicae Libertatis vindici acerrimo D. suo clementissimo hoc monstrum νεοχαρακτον monstroso hoc saeculo DDD. Saenredam."

41. The use of the transliterated Greek *ectypoma*, along with the Greek *characteron*, calls attention to these terms, which imply the coincidence of oracular engraving and portentous event. The term *character* appears in C. Plantin, *Dictionarium Tetraglotton* (Antwerp, 1562), fol. 49v, where it denotes the two senses of *sign*: a thing that signals something else, and a mark inscribed on a surface. In French and Dutch, Plantin's entry reads: "Marque, Signe, Forme. Fasson. Een Marck/ Teecken/ Forme/ Fatsoen." *Ectypoma*, a Greek term that would have been known to the humanist Screvelius, does not appear in the *Dictionarium*, but the two Latin terms on which *ectypoma* puns are clearly defined: *eiectio*, "throwing forth," and *pomum*, "fruit." Applied to the whale, the combination of these terms connotes "the fruit of God's wrath, ejected upon the beach at Beverywyck." For *eiectio*, see fol. 104v; for *pomum*, fol. 236r. On fol. 197r, Plantin defines *monstrum* as "a strange and unnatural thing, whose occurrence contravenes the order of nature."

42. The inscription reads: "Ano. 1601 exspirante. XIII Cal. Januarijs. portentosi Neptuni monstri in littus Hollandiae Bevervicanum eiecti plagam meridionalem versus, cuius longitudo pedum 60, altitudo 14, corporis ambitus 36, cauda 14, rictus oris 12 pedum spatium adaequabant secundum proportionem membrorum et musculorum Geometricam exactiss. delineatio."

43. The essential discussion of the nexus among seeing, picturing, and knowing, occurs in S. Alpers, *The Art of Describing* (Chicago, 1983), 73–84. Her prime example is the polemical *Apple-Core* etching by Pieter Saenredam, the son of Jan. Saenredam's print repudiates an earlier etching that purported to see the effigies of Roman Catholic priests in the blemishes found in the core of an apple tree on a farm near Haarlem. The blemishes had been publicized as portents of the hostile intentions of Catholic Spain against the Protestant Netherlands. Saenredam's print rejoins by representing the conditions of unbiased sight that restore the blemishes to themselves. I believe that the series of beached whales by Goltzius, Matham, and Jan Saenredam constitutes the founding moment of this assertion.

The Haarlem series of beached whales concludes with three etchings: two of 1614 by Willem Buytewech and Esaias van de Velde recording a whale stranded on 28 December of that year near the town of Noordwijk; and a third by Buytewech, recording the stranding of 21 January 1617 between Scheveningen and Katwijk. All three etchings revise the format and rendering of the earlier engravings of Goltzius, Matham, and Saenredam. The vantage point is lowered so that the beholder shares the view of the assembled witnesses, and Goltzius's burin-hand has been exchanged for the looser hatches of the etching needle. Both the viewpoint, which incorporates us as witnesses, and the rendering, which resembles the kind of drawing one would have done on the spot, argue that this is an image done *nae t'leven*. Van de Velde's print carries an inscription affirming that it is a "true image" ("ware afbeeldinge") and conveying the place and day of the stranding and the measurements of the whale. Buytewech's print of 1617 is inscribed similarly. These prints share the descriptive function explored by Goltzius and his followers, but they dispute the claims made for the transparency of his burin-hand, advancing instead the *handelingh* of an on-site sketch along with an on-site vantage point. On Van de Velde's print, see L. Burchard, *Die Holländischen Radierer vor Rembrandt* (Berlin, 1917), 151; on Buytewech, see M. van Berge, J. Giltay, C. van Hasselt, and A. W. F. M. Meij, *Willem Buytewech 1591–1624*, exhibition catalogue, Museum Boymans-van Beuningen, Rotterdam and Institut Néerlandais, Paris (Paris, 1975), 38–39, 101–3.

44. This case study is based on two years of anthropological fieldwork in Northern New Ireland, carried out between 1982 and 1984. Uncredited quotations were recorded during this period.

45. For analyses of Malangan art, see P. Lewis, *The Social Context of Art in Northern New Ireland* (Chicago, 1969); G. Wilkinson, "Carving a Social Message: The Malangans of Tabar," in *Art in Society*, ed. M. Greenhalgh and V. Megaw (London, 1978), 227–43; E. Brewer, *A Malangan to Cover the Grave* (Ph.D. diss., University of Queensland, 1980); and M. Gunn, *Tabar Malangan* (Unpublished report on fieldwork in Tabar, 1982).

46. I am using *social memory* to allude to the inscribed modality of remembering. The activation of social memory in performances, specifically in commemorative ceremonies and bodily practices, has recently been elaborated in P. Connerton, *How Societies Remember* (Cambridge, 1989).

47. *Port Moresby Patrol Report*, May 1956; see also, P. Biskop, *Memories of Dampier* (Canberra, 1975).

48. The functions of Malangan correspond closely to what G. Feeley-Harnik calls "the political economy of death"; see G. Feeley-Harnik, "The Political Economy of Death: Communication and Change in Malagasy Colonial History," *American Ethnologist* 11 (1984): 1–19. In both cases, the economy goes underground and comes to be inspired by "common historical roots in experiences of the body and its labor that are inseparably physical, social, and philosophical experiences" (2).

49. The sacrifice is made to the gods *Merulie* and *Moroa*, who are associated with an imaginary land behind the horizon called *Karoro*. This land is addressed in one of the most important magical performances—*wangam a musung*, or "the calling of smell"—which provides the cosmological foundation of Malangan.

50. There is a connection between sacrifice and social memory, as noted by Nietzsche, who writes: "Es ging Niemals ohne Blut, Martern, Opfer ab, wenn der Mench es nötig hielt, sich ein Gedächtnis zu machen." See F. Nietzsche, "Zur Genealogie der Moral: Eine Streitschrift," in H. Heinz Holz, ed., *Studienausgabe* (Frankfurt am Main, 1968), 4: 60–61. On sacrifice in the Pacific region, see C. Gregory, "Gifts to Men and Gifts to God: Exchange and Capital Accumulation in Contemporary Papua," *Man* 15 (1980): 626–52, and V. Valeri, *Kingship and Sacrifice: Ritual and Society in Ancient Hawaii* (Chicago, 1985).

51. See H. Codere, *Fighting with Property: A Study of the Kwakiutl Potlatching and Warfare* (New York, 1950).

52. See E. Wolf, *Europe and the People without History* (Berkeley, 1982).

53. Remembering the image during carving can take the form either of projection or selection; see S. Küchler, "Malangan: Art and Memory in a Melanesian Society," *Man* 22 (1987): 238–55. Each method assures that what is transferred onto others in the exchanges concerns the image but does not cancel the right to produce the image. *Projection* implies the enlargement of a detail, which is translated into another dimension—vertical to horizontal, or horizontal to figurative. *Selection* implies the reduction of motifs that are carved into a sculpture. The shape is varied when the image is transferred between villages, whereas image-transference within the village inspires changes in the selection of motifs. See S. Küchler, "Malangan: Objects, Sacrifice and the Production of Memory," *American Ethnologist* 15 (1989): 625–37.

54. As Bartlett argues in *Remembering*, the mnemonic processing of visual information requires the formation of image-schemata; condensation and redundancy are symptoms of their operation. Stressing the importance of interest and attitude, he notes how remembering transforms material. On the active construction of schemata in relation to child development, see J. Piaget and B. Inhelder, *Memory and Intelligence*, trans. A. J. Pomerans (New York, 1973), and on the schemata and social-historical process, see A. Luria, "Towards the Problem of the Historical Nature of Psychological Processes," *International Journal of Psychology* 6 (1971): 259–72.

55. See H. Hubert and M. Mauss, *Sacrifice: Its Nature and Functions* (Chicago, 1981), 19–49.

56. Ibid., 20–21.

Memory, Imagination, Figuration

1. I owe special thanks to Claire Farago for her excellent criticism, and to Martin Kemp, who was kind enough to read and comment on an earlier version of this paper. I have also benefited from the timely advice of Ann C. Peterson and Catherine M. Soussloff. In addition, Andrea Bolland has brought valuable information to my attention, and Beth Mulvaney has been a most helpful research assistant. My work has been assisted by a Faculty Council Grant and a Junior Faculty Development Grant at the University of North Carolina, Chapel Hill.

2. On the tradition of mnemotechnics, to which painting may have contributed at various times, see Frances A. Yates, *The Art of Memory* (Chicago, 1966), 1–105. As will become apparent, this essay is not so much concerned with the storage and retrieval of information as with the productive function of memory in Renaissance art.

3. In Isidore of Seville's seventh-century definition, the role of memory is already emphasized: "Pictura autem est imago exprimens speciem rei alicuius, quae dum visa fuerit ad recordationem mentem reducit." See his *Etymologiarum sive originum libri XX*, ed. W. M. Lindsay (Oxford, 1911), 19, 16. For the textual connection, which was certified as early as the sixth century by Pope Gregory the Great, see L. G. Duggan, "Was Art Really the 'Book of the Illiterate'?" *Word and Image* 5 (1989): 227–51, and the references cited by Hans Belting, *L'arte e il suo pubblico: Funzione e forme delle antiche immagini della Passione* (Bologna, 1986), 47–72.

4. See Michael Baxandall, *Painting and Experience in Fifteenth-Century Italy* (London, 1972), 40–41, and also above, n. 3.

5. On the Thomistic recommendations for the exercise of memory as a part of the virtue of Prudence, and their applicability to late medieval religious painting, see Yates, *Art of Memory*, 74–81.

6. Isidore, *Etymologiarum*, 19, 16, completes his definition of painting thus: "Pictura autem dicta quasi fictura; est enim imago ficta, non veritas. Hinc et fucata, id est ficto quodam colore inlita, nihil fidei et veritatis habentia."

7. Belting, *L'arte e il suo pubblico*, 73–102.

8. David Summers, *The Judgment of Sense: Renaissance Naturalism and the Rise of Aesthetics* (Cambridge, 1987), 317–20, addresses the Renaissance conception of point of view in relation to style. For the implications of the optically based naturalism of Renaissance art, one should still consult the conclusions of Erwin Panofsky, "Die Perspektive als symbolische Form," in *Vorträge der Bibliothek Warburg* (Hamburg, 1924–25), 258 ff.

9. Alberti's analogy borrows from Cicero's *De amicitia*, 7, 23: "Seeing that friendship includes very many and very great advantages, it undoubtedly excels all other things in this respect, that it projects the bright ray of hope into the future, and does not suffer the spirit to grow faint or fall. Again, he who looks upon a true friend, looks, as it were, upon a sort of image of himself. Wherefore friends, though absent, are at hand; though in need, yet abound; though weak, are strong; and—harder saying still—though dead, are yet alive; so great is the esteem on the part of their friends, the tender recollection and the deep longing that still attends them." Roland Barthes, *Camera Lucida*, trans. R. Howard (New York, 1981), 76–89, makes a sharp distinction between photography ("an emanation of *past reality*") and painting (which "can feign reality without having seen it"); but a strong argument could be made that Alberti—who had no way of anticipating the possibility of an image that was literally "an emanation of the referent"—understood the optical certainty of the perspective image much as Barthes understands the chemical certainty of the photographic, as an irreducible trace of the real. The key phrase in the Ciceronian passage is "he who looks upon a true friend, looks . . . upon a sort of image of himself," an idea glossed in Alberti's identification—a few lines further—of Narcissus as the inventor of painting.

10. Alberti, *De pictura*, pars. 25–26. In the Latin version, Alberti's two anecdotes about portraiture are more clearly stated as counterexamples. Cassandrus is overwhelmed by the recognition, in a portrait, of a spiritual quality, his deceased commander's majesty. By implication, then, King Agesilaus's refusal to be portrayed has less to do with the ugliness of his features than with the negative moral interpretation to which it will be subjected after his death. In either case likeness is affectively and ethically charged, but where Alexander's portrait conveys a truth about the sitter that can be certified by those who knew him, Agesilaus—famed for his sense of personal honor and love of family—fears the opposite, the image's giving rise to a truth of its own that will compete persuasively with the other memories of his achievement. Alberti implicitly recognizes (though it does not lessen his enthusiasm) that the veristic image must be interpreted: by itself it will not give access to anything other than an apparent truth.

11. Alberti here deliberately ignores the distinction between painting and sculpture, which he observes elsewhere, no doubt because his principal subject is the power of illusionistic representation as such. It bears noting that for Alberti there is no conceptual difference between a sculpture and a modeled image on a flat surface. Like *Della pittura*, Alberti's *De statua* resolves the spatial properties of the three-dimensional image into outline and volume (*finitio* and *dimensio*, as he calls the instruments he has devised for their transcription in sculpture; or "border" and "surface-variation," for the painted image).

12. Baxandall, *Giotto*, 70–71.

13. See Barocchi, ed., *La Vita di Michelangelo nelle redazioni del 1550 e del 1568* (Milan, 1962), 1: 124, 4: n. 727: "E stato Michelagnolo di una tenace e profonda memoria, che nel vedere le cose altrui una sol volta l'ha ritenute si fattamente e servitosene in una maniera che nessuno se n'è mai quasi accorto; né ha mai fatto cosa nessuna delle sue che riscontri l'una con l'altra, perché si ricordava di tutto quello che aveva fatto. Nella sua gioventù, sendo con gli amici sua pittori, giucorno una cena a chi faceva una figura che non avessi niente di disegno, che fussi goffa, simile a que' fantoci che fanno coloro che non sanno et imbrattano le mura. Qui si valse della memoria; perché, ricordatosi aver visto in un muro una di queste gofferie, la fece come se l'avessi avuta dinanzi di tutto punto, e superò tutti que' pittori: cosa difficile in uno huomo tanto pieno di disegno, avvezzo a cose scelte, che ne potessi uscir netto." Barocchi, 4: 2074–76, cites Vasari's source for the first part from *Vita di Michelangelo Buonarroti raccolta per Ascanio Condivi da la Ripa Transone* (Rome, 1553): "E stato di tenacissima memoria, dimanieraché, avend'egli dipinto tante migliaia di figure, quante si vedono, non ha fatto mai una che somigli l'altra o faccia quella medesima attitudine, anzi gli ho sentito dire che non tira mai linea che non si ricordi se più mai l'ha tirata; scancellandola, se s'ha a vedere in publico."

14. Raymond Klibansky, Erwin Panofsky, and Fritz Saxl, *Saturn and Melancholy: Studies in the History of Natural Philosophy, Religion and Art* (London, 1964). The full title is indicative of the book's extraordinary scope. On the connection between memory and the melancholy temperament, see pages 67ff.

15. In Summers, *Judgment of Sense*.

16. Baxandall, *Painting and Experience*, 29–108.

17. See Ernst H. Gombrich, "Leonardo's Method of Working Out Compositions," in *Norm and Form* (London, 1966), 58–63.

18. There is still much uncertainty surrounding the dating of some of Leonardo's most important theoretical statements, because they come from manuscripts that have been dismembered, scrambled, and recomposed (such as the *Codex Atlanticus* in Milan; hereafter cited as C.A.), or because the autograph texts are lost—as in the case of the *Treatise on Painting*, Codex Urbinas 1270 (Vatican Library; hereafter cited as C.U.), compiled under the supervision of Leonardo's pupil and heir, Francesco Melzi. The latter, in particular, is an invaluable source for Leonardo's ideas about the psychological impact of painting. Though only about a third of its chapters can be matched to surviving manuscript material, it is a scrupulous compilation; for an edition with comments of the first part of C.U., which contains most of the material on the comparison of the arts and their means of sensory appeal, see Claire Farago, "Leonardo da Vinci's 'Paragone,' a Critical Interpretation: The 'Parte Prima' of 'Codex Vaticanus Urbinus 1270,'" Ph.D. diss., University of Virginia, 1988. An index of the chapters in C.U., with a suggested chronology and concordance with the corresponding manuscript material is in Carlo Pedretti, *Leonardo Da Vinci on Painting: A Lost Book (Libro A)* (Berkeley, 1964), 177–225. Most of my arguments are based on the contents of Leonardo's MS B.N. 2038 of 1490–92 (Institut de France, Paris), a volume originally part of MS A, also in the Institut de France. Unfortunately, I have not been able to consult a diplomatic transcription of the text, but it is reproduced almost entirely in Anna Maria Brizio, *Scritti scelti di Leonardo da Vinci* (Turin, 1968), 187–237 (hereafter cited as Brizio). Brizio, 35–36, provides an index and chronology (which sometimes differs in its details from Pedretti's) of Leonardo's manuscripts. My references to B.N. 2038 are drawn from Brizio and from Jean Paul Richter, *The Literary Works of Leonardo da Vinci* (London, 1939; hereafter cited as Richter), supplemented by Carlo Pedretti's commentary of 1977. Pedretti, *The Literary Works of Leonardo da Vinci: A Commentary to Jean Paul Richter's Edition* (Berkeley, 1977), 1: 92ff., gives a more exhaustive list than Brizio's of Leonardo's surviving manuscripts, also with proposed chronology. Of these, *Madrid Codex II* (MS 8936, Biblioteca Nacional, folios datable 1503–5), the reconstructed *Libro A* (Pedretti, *Libro A*, datable 1508–10), and MSS E and G at the Institut de France (datable 1510–15), contain sustained discussions of painting, though without the emphasis on elementary instruction evident in B.N. 2038.

19. For Cennini, painting consists of drawing and coloring, with drawing as the foundation because it is the proper means of mastering light and shadow. As far as I know, he never discusses pure line drawing, as Alberti does. Cennini's chapters 1–34 (on *disegnare*) set down the essentials of apprenticeship. See also Francis Ames-Lewis, *Drawing in Early Renaissance Italy* (New Haven, 1981), chap. 1, where Cennini is read somewhat more restrictively than here. For the transmission of imitative learning based on drawing to the sixteenth and seventeenth centuries, see also *Children of Mercury: The Education of Artists in the Sixteenth and Seventeenth Centuries* (Providence, R.I., 1984), passim, and Elizabeth Cropper, *The Ideal of Painting: Pietro Testa's Düsseldorf Notebook* (Princeton, 1984), chap. 3.

20. Cennini, *Libro*, chaps. 27–28, following the chapters on making and using tracing paper. Cennini recommends tracing works (unless they are of difficult access and have to be "eyeballed") by one good artist rather than several, because of the danger that too many models will derail the young artist's innate *fantasia* (or, as Cennini puts it make the artist *fantastichetto*). While the accent on mechanically transferring the model's contours seems stronger than in later periods, one should bear in mind that Cennini's *disegno* is explicitly conceived as the tracing with shadow of an object's contour. Moreover, Cennini deliberately confines his instruction to the technical basis of painting. Thus, drawing "in one's head" is left unspecified in the measure that it is not, of itself, a technique.

21. Richter, no. 484 (B.N. 2038, fol. 33r; see also Brizio, 235): "ORDO DEL RITRARE. Ritrai prima desegni di buono maestro fatto su arte sul naturale e non di pratica, poi di rilievo in compagnia del disegnio tratto da esso rilievo, poi di buono naturale, il quale debbi mettere in uso." Pedretti, *The Literary Works*, 1: 326, claims there is an obliterated letter, possibly an *a*, after the *su* in "disegni di buono maestro fatto su arte sul naturale e non di practica," and translates the phrase as "drawings by a good master who has formed his art on nature, not on practice." He takes "nature" to mean "theoretical study." I do not follow this reading; in the literature *pratica* is consistently associated with "drawing in one's head," but also with working *di natura* rather than scientifically. A variant of the learning schema on an earlier page of the same manuscript (Richter, no. 485: B.N. 2038, fol. 10r; see Brizio, 191–92) calls attention to the element of manual training as such which is inseparable from the training of judgment: "The painter should first habituate [*suefare*] the hand through the copying of drawings by the hands of good masters, and having achieved such habituation [guided by] his instructor's judgment, he should next train himself [*suefarsi*] by copying choice things in relief, following such rules as shall be given below."

Leonardo does not deal with the hand's intrinsic contribution to the form of the image. From his references to sensory activity, it would seem that he regarded the craftsman's hand as a passive instrument, which is not to say that its products were inexpressive, but that they were virtually direct records of the artist's will. For Leonardo's advice to the apprentice, to learn diligence first, that he may develop exactitude in applying light and shade and in following the contours of forms, see Richter, no. 492 (B.N. 2038, fol. 27v; see Brizio, 224). Pedretti, *The Literary Works*, 1: 11, reproduces Paolo Giovio's account—based on firsthand acquaintance with the artist—of Leonardo's teaching methods.

22. See above, n. 20. See T. M. Greene, *The Light in Troy: Imitation and Discovery in Renaissance Poetry* (New Haven, 1982), chaps. 4 and 5, for a nuanced analysis of the imitative method of literary apprenticeship, which received heightened attention in the trecento and seems to have been adapted in the more complex variants of Renaissance pictorial training. Beyond the training stage, imitation was a habit of conscious dialogue with received tradition. The issue is investigated in terms relevant to this essay by Ernst H. Gombrich, "Ideal and Type in Italian Renaissance Painting," *New Light on Old Masters* Studies in the Art of the Renaissance 4 (Chicago, 1986).

23. Richter, no. 483 (B.N. 2038, fol. 17b; see Brizio, 199): "Il giovane debe prima imparare prospettiva, poi le misure d'ogni cosa, poi di mano di bon maestro per suefarsi a bone membra, poi di naturale per confermarsi le ragioni delle cose imparate, poi vedere uno tempo l'opere [Brizio omits *l'opere*] di mano di diversi maestri, poi fare abito al mettere in pratica e operare l'arte." By "training in perspective," I take Leonardo to mean all three "perspectives" in his system (of size or linear, of color, and of disappearance or finish); see Richter, no. 14 (B.N. 2038, fol. 18r; see Brizio, 200). See also Richter, no. 18 (C.A., fol. 221v–d; dated to ca. 1490 by Pedretti, *The Literary Works*, 1: 114), for Leonardo's argument that such rules are specifically for the purpose of assisting the judgment in its corrective acts, "For if you wished to employ these rules in composition you would never see the end of it, and you would produce confusion in your works."

24. Richter, no. 531 (B.N. 2038, fol. 26r; see Brizio, 214–15): "DEL MODO DEL BENE IMPARARE A MENTE. Quando tu vorrai sapere una cosa studiata bene a mente tieni questo modo, cioè quando tu ài disegnato una cosa medesima tante volte, che te la paia avere a mente, pruova a farla sanza lo esempio e abbi lucidato sopra uno vetro sototile e piano lo esemplo tuo e porrailo sopra la cosa, che ài fatta sanza lo esempio, e nota bene dove il lucido non si scontra col disegnio tuo e dove truovi avere errato li tieni a mente di non errare piu, anzi ritorna allo esemplo a ritrare tante volte quella parte errata che tu l'abbi bene nella imaginativa." The link between this literal memorization of forms and Cennini's advice on tracing is evident. It is as if the apprentice's image-making faculty were formed by physically ingesting and absorbing the approved model. As Cennini puts it, "[your style] may not be anything but good, since (as your intellect is always in the habit of picking flowers) only with effort might your hand pick thorns."

25. Richter, no. 496 (B.N. 2038, fol. 26r; see Brizio, 220): "DELLO STUDIARE INSINO QUANDO TI DESTI O NANZI T'ADORMENTI NEL LETTO ALLO SCURO. O in me [Brizio has *Hòime*] provato essere di non pocca utilità, quando ti truovi allo scuro nel letto andare colla imaginativa repetendo i liniamenti superfitiali delle forme per l'adrieto studiate, o altre cose notabili da sottili speculatione comprese, ed è questo propio uno atto laudabile e utile a confermarsi le cose nella memoria." The suitability of darkness for memorization points back to the medieval mnemonic tradition, and chiefly Albertus Magnus; see Frances A. Yates, *The Art of Memory* (Chicago, 1966), 68.

26. Richter, no. 497 (B.N. 2038, fol. 27r; see Brizio, 223): "DI CHE TEMPO SI DEVE STUDIARE LA ELETIONE DELLE COSE. Le veglie della invernata devono essere da' giovani usate nelli studi delle cose aparechiate l'estate, cioè tutti li nudi che ài fatti l'estate, convienti riducierli insieme e fare eletione delle migliori membra e corpi di quegli e metterli in pratica e bene a mente."

27. Cicero, *De inventione*: 2, 1, 1. On the Zeuxian topos and its implications for Renaissance figuration, see Elizabeth Cropper, "On Beautiful Women: Parmigianino, Petrarchismo, and the Vernacular Style," *The Art Bulletin* 58 (1976): 374 ff.

28. Giorgio Vasari, *Le vite de' più eccellenti pittori, scultori e architettori, nelle redazioni del 1550 e 1568*, ed. Rosanna Bettarini and Paola Barocchi (Flor-

ence, 1976), text vol. 4: 3–4. Vasari's five components of good artifice (recovered in the quattrocento) are rule, order, measure, design, and style (*regola, ordine, misura, disegno, maniera*). The progression from measure to manner—from the more general and abstract to the more specific and individual—encodes the key phrases of the quattrocento apprenticeship (at least as presented in Leonardo's sequence cited in n. 23, above).

29. On the rhetorical aspect of style, see David Summers, "Contrapposto: Style and Meaning in Renaissance Art," *The Art Bulletin* 59 (1977): 335–61.

30. Richter, no. 497 (B.N. 2038, fol. 27r; see Brizio, 223). The passage follows directly after the one cited above in n. 26.

31. This accords with the late medieval model of the psyche in which memory is the repository of intentions (meanings or purposes) inherent to the things apprehended in the fantasy. The memory-image is an interpreted one with respect to the initial visualization provoked by the perceptual act. See F. Guichard Tesson's rich examination of the role of memory as presented in a fifteenth-century commentary on the allegorical "Echecs amoureux," in "Le pion Souvenir et les miroirs déformants dans l'allégorie d'amour," *Jeux de mémoire: Aspects de la mnémotechnie médiévale*, ed. B. Roy and P. Zumthor (Montreal, 1985), 100 ff., especially 101. Of even greater importance for memory as a source of judgments and rules for procedure is its inclusion, in Scholastic philosophy, under the cardinal virtue of Prudence; see Yates, *Art of Memory*, 57–81.

32. For Leonardo's recommendations about training young students additively, one step at a time, see Richter, no. 491 (B.N. 2038, fol. 28r; see Brizio, 226). The passage may be indebted to Alberti's advice in *Della pittura*, Book 3, par. 55 (Leon Battista Alberti, *De pictura*, ed. Cecil Grayson [Rome and Bari, 1975], 94). In his approach to composition as the organic integration of active figures, Leonardo innovatively developed the ground-breaking prescriptions in *Della pittura*, which are drawn, in turn, from rhetorical theory. See Michael Baxandall, *Giotto and the Orators* (Oxford, 1971), pt. 3.

33. See Richter, no. 571 (B.N. 2038, fol. 27v; see Brizio, 224): "DEL MODO DELLO IMPARARE BENE A COMPORRE INSIEME LE FIGURE NELLE STORIE. Quando tu avrai imparato bene di prospettiva e avrai a mente tutte le membra e corpi delle cose, sia vago e spesse volte nel tuo andarti a spasso [Brizio has *sollazzo*, which seems closer to the original] vedere e considerare i siti e li atti delli omini in nel parlare, in nel contendere o ridere o zuffare insieme, che atti fieno in loro, che atti faccino i circumstanti, i spartitori, i veditori d'esse cose, e quelli notare con brevi segni in questa forma su un tuo piccolo libretto, il quale tu debi sempre portar con teco, e sia di carte tinte, accio non l'abbia a scancellare ma mutare di vecchio in un novo, chè queste non sono cose da essere scancellate anzi con gran diligenza riserbate, perchè gli sono [Brizio has *perché egli è*] tante le infinite forme e atti delle cose che la memoria non è capace a ritenerle, onde queste riserberai come tua autori e maestri." See also the very similar precept in A. Philip McMahon, *Treatise on Painting (Codex Urbinas Latinus 1270) by Leonardo da Vinci* (Princeton, 1956), 2: fols. 60r–60v, (hereafter cited as McMahon); and Heinrich Ludwig, *Lionardo da Vinci: Das Buch von der Malerei* (Osnabrück, 1970), 179 (hereafter cited as Lu),

dated ca. 1492 by Pedretti, *Libro A*, 184, where Leonardo specifies that this type of record is "cosa utilissima al modo del tuo comporre."

34. The Windsor sheet (dated to ca. 1506–8 in Clark and Pedretti, *Drawings*, 1: 139) is drawn in black chalk, with groups of figures gone over in ink; it is 20.1 × 13 cm., and thus too large to qualify as the leaf from a small sketchbook.

35. McMahon 2: fols. 61v–62r (Lu 189; dated ca. 1492 by Pedretti, *Libro A*, 185).

36. On Leonardo's reference to images in the clouds, which has deep connections with the ideals of trecento and quattrocento vernacular poetry, see David Summers, *Michelangelo and the Language of Art* (Princeton, 1981), 122ff. It should be recalled that pen and ink is Cennini's ideal medium for encouraging drawing "inside your head," which in his case most likely means "in the *fantasia.*"

37. A glimpse of Leonardo practicing his own advice is given in G. Giraldi's eyewitness account from the artist's Milanese period (cited by Martin Kemp, *Leonardo da Vinci: The Marvellous Works of Man and Nature* [Cambridge, Mass., 1981], 180): "When Leonardo wished to portray a figure he first considered its quality and nature . . . and when he had decided what it was to be he went to where he knew people of that type would congregate, and observed diligently the faces, the manners, clothes and bodily movement . . . noting it down in a little book which he always kept at his belt."

38. These passages are also discussed by Gombrich in *Norm and Form*. The first is in Richter, 508 (B.N. 2038, fol. 22v; see Brizio, 211): "I shall not fail to include among these precepts a new speculative invention, which although it seems a small thing and most laughable, nevertheless is very useful in rousing [*destare*] the *ingegno* to various discoveries [*invenzioni*]. This is: if you will look at walls stained with various blots or at stones of variegated marble, if you have to invent some scene, you may see there the semblance of diverse landscapes. . . . Moreover, you may see various battles, and lively actions of figures, strange expressions on faces, costumes, and an infinity of things, which you can reduce to good, perfected form." The second is in McMahon 2: fol. 35v (Lu 66; dated to 1500 by Pedretti, *Libro A*, 180, though it is very close to that in B.N. 2038): "Do not despise my advice, which reminds you . . . to stop sometimes and look into the stains of walls, or the ashes of a fire, or clouds, or mud, or other like spots, in which, if you consider them well, you will find the most marvelous inventions; for the *ingegno* of the painter is roused to new inventions, whether of compositions of battles of animals and men, or of various compositions of landscapes and monstrous things . . . because the *ingegno* is roused to new inventions by indistinct things [*cose confuse*]. But be sure that you first know how to make all the members of those things you wish to represent [*figurare*], such as the limbs of animals, and the parts of landscapes."

39. On the Renaissance treatment of *ingegno* as a productive and associative power, see Summers, *Judgment*, 99–101. In Richter, no. 502 (B.N. 2038, fol. 26r; see Brizio, *Scritti*, 220–21), Leonardo places memory/reason in relation to composition and imagination: "The master who should pretend to be able to conserve within himself all the forms and effects of nature would certainly seem to me to be

adorned with much ignorance, since these effects are infinite, and our memory is not so capacious as to suffice. Therefore, painter . . . first you shall attend, with *disegno*, to providing the eye—through a visible form [*con dimostrativa forma*]—with the intention and the invention first made in your imaginative faculty [*imaginativa*], and then add and subtract until you are satisfied, and then arrange draped or nude men in the manner you have ordained for the work, and make sure that in proportions and size, as determined by perspective, nothing is allowed in the work that is not counseled by reason and natural effects." I translate *dimostrativa forma* as "visible form" because Leonardo is referring to the passage from a mentally conceived image/purpose to a drawn, correctable form. The deficiencies of memory are rectified by consulting live models and applying perspectival guidelines.

40. Alberti, *De Pictura*, par. 44: "There are some who in expressing over-bold movements, making the breast and the buttocks visible simultaneously in a single figure (an impossible and indecorous thing), think to be praised, because they hear that those images seem very much alive which throw about their limbs a great deal; because of this they make their figures appear like fencers and actors, with none of painting's dignity, so that not only do they lack all grace and sweetness, but, moreover, display the painter's *ingegno* as too fervid and furious." The important thing here is that animated (indeed, impossibly composite) figures are the *ingegno*'s province—no doubt because they cannot easily be copied, but must be invented, as Leonardo demonstrates.

41. See Summers, *Judgment*, chap. 10, for a discussion of the cluster of concepts (including fantasy/imagination) inherited from medieval psychology under the heading of "cogitation." For the schema of the "internal senses," see below, and n. 48.

42. Leonardo's concept of the painter's activity as a double movement—analytic/critical and synthetic/productive—is equally indebted to the discussions on scientific method that were fueled by Galenic studies in the late fifteenth and throughout the sixteenth century. I thank Claire Farago for bringing this to my attention and sharing her manuscript on "Leonardo da Vinci's Definitions of Painting and His Interpreters." Martin Kemp addresses the topic in "'Ogni dipintore dipinge se': A Neoplatonic Echo in Leonardo's Art Theory?" in *Cultural Aspects of the Italian Renaissance: Essays in Honour of Paul Oskar Kristeller* (Manchester, 1976), 319, "*Il concetto dell'anima* in Leonardo's Early Skull Studies," *Journal of the Warburg and Courtauld Institutes* 34 (1971): 129–31, and "Dissection and Divinity in Leonardo's Late Anatomies," *Journal of the Warburg and Courtauld Institutes* 35 (1972): 209ff. The Paduan contribution to the study of method in Galen is discussed by Cesare Vasoli, "La logica," *Storia della cultura veneta* (Vicenza, 1976–), vol. 3, pt. 3: 53–70.

43. Gombrich, "Leonardo's Method," 61–62, calls attention to the unprecedented associative freedom with which Leonardo passed from theme to theme while in the process of exploring particular figural combinations.

44. Codex Arundel, 190v, cited by Donald S. Strong, "Leonardo on the Eye: The MS D in the Bibliothèque de l'Institut de France," Ph.D. diss., University of California, Los Angeles, 1967, 277–78. Strong, 391 ff., discusses at length the

implications of Leonardo's analogy, which is linked to his concern with geometric schemata (spiral, helix) expressive of the temporal unfolding of mechanical forces.

45. For examples of the horse studies, see Kenneth Clark and Carlo Pedretti, *The Drawings of Leonardo da Vinci in the Collection of Her Majesty the Queen at Windsor Castle* (London, 1968), 2: nos. 12289, 12321, 12358r.

46. Paolo Giovio, in his "Leonardi vincii vita" of about 1527, wrote of Leonardo's plans (presumably at a later period than the skull drawings) to have copper engravings made from his anatomical studies "for the benefit of the art"; see Richter 1: 2–3.

47. See Kemp, *"Il concetto dell'anima,"* 118–20 and 127–29.

48. See E. Ruth Harvey, *The Inward Wits: Psychological Theory in the Middle Ages and the Renaissance* (London, 1975), passim, for an analysis of the medical and philosophical strains in the Arab and Scholastic treatment of the mental faculties. The medical path led to the localization of particular mental functions within the cavities of the brain; the philosophical was concerned with systematizing Aristotle's discussion of the relationships between the activity of the senses and the operations of the soul. H. A. Wolfson, "The Internal Senses in Latin, Arabic, and Hebrew Philosophy," in *Studies in the History of Philosophy and Religion* (Cambridge, Mass., 1973), 1: 250–314, provides a philological account of the medieval terminology for the mental operations dependent on sensory input. For a selection of medieval and Renaissance diagrams of the localized mental functions, see Edwin Clarke and Kenneth Dewhurst, *An Illustrated History of Brain Function* (Berkeley and Los Angeles, 1972), 10–48.

49. On the Aristotelian common-sensibles, which are associated with the material reality of the things perceived by sense, see Summers, *Judgment*, 78–84.

50. In the more expansive formulations of this schema (Avicenna's, for instance, or Albertus Magnus's), fantasy or imagination might span two ventricles: it would be a kind of passive sense-memory when abutting the common sense, and a source of manipulable sense-stimuli when in the vicinity of the cogitative faculty. Along with sense-impressions, memory stored the fruits of the *cogitativa*'s judgment. Summers, *Judgment*, chap. 8 ("Optics and the Common Sense") summarizes various models of postsensory activity of special relevance to Leonardo, since vision occupies a key position in them.

51. In Leonardo's later anatomies of the brain, the nerves that carry sensation and movement to the limbs consistently originate in the hindmost cavity; consequently, memory appears to preside over the mechanical activity of the body. See Keele and Pedretti, *Anatomical Studies*, 1: 326–27, on Windsor 12602r, which clearly illustrates the brain-nerve center connection. See also Kemp, "'Il concetto dell'anima,'" 126–27, for a discussion of Leonardo's early illustrations of the spinal cord as the vehicle for the generative power in humans. As the generative principle, the semen contributes vital spirits to the fetus's formation; it seems appropriate that the site of *memoria* should be somehow associated with the perpetuation of the species. (See also the concluding paragraphs of this essay.)

52. The term *imprensiva* appears to be Leonardo's adaptation of the scholastic *virtus apprehensiva*, identified with the *sensus communis* in the front of the

brain, but also with the external senses that report to it; see N. H. Steneck, "Albert the Great on the Classification and Localization of the Internal Senses," *ISIS* 65 (1974): 197–200. See, too, Farago, "Leonardo da Vinci's 'Paragone,'" note 2 (in commentary), and especially 392–93. She suggests (among other things) a source in impetus mechanics. This perhaps makes sense in light of Kenneth D. Keele, *Leonardo da Vinci's Elements of the Science of Man* (London and New York, 1983), 60–77, and chapters 8 and 10, which argues cogently for the gradual convergence of Leonardo's mechanical and physiological studies, leading him to conceive of sensory activity as a kind of percussive relay.

53. E. M. Todd, *The Neuroanatomy of Leonardo da Vinci* (Santa Barbara, 1983), 92 (but see the whole of chap. 6), cites the medieval anatomist Mundinus's placement of the *sensus communis* in the middle ventricle; in other respects, the scheme does not bear a close relation to Leonardo's. However, it was not uncommon for the *sensus communis* to become identified with the entire process of internal sensation, including judgment, rather than being confined to the preliminary integration of percepts; see Summers, *Judgment*, 71–75, but also the whole chapter, and 170–76, linking Leonardo's views to a larger tradition. I do not follow Summers's interpretation of the *imprensiva* as a term for one of the surfaces of the eye, or his view that for Leonardo the eye is in direct communication with the *senso commune*.

54. See Keele and Pedretti, *Anatomical Studies*, 1: 102–3 (pl. 42r). The ratios for the *senso commune* are one-half head from the crown, one-third head from the eye's nasolacrimal duct, two-thirds head from the nape of the neck, two fingers from the uvula (organ of taste) and one foot over the heart. These measures are ultimately derived from the study of Vitruvian proportion.

55. Windsor 19019, datable to about 1489, in Richter, 383 (see Brizio, 155–56): "The soul seems to reside in the judicial part, and the judicial part appears to be in the place where all of the senses concur, which is called the common sense. . . . The sinews, with their muscles, serve the nerves as the soldiers serve their commander, and the nerves serve the common sense as the commanders serve the captain, and the common sense serves the soul as the captain serves his lord. Therefore the joints obey the sinew, the sinew obeys the muscle, and the muscle the nerve, and the nerve the common sense, and the common sense is the soul's seat, and the memory is its ammunition, and the *imprensiva* is its watchman."

56. Kemp, "'Ogni Dipintore'": 314–15, discusses the sources of this belief, which Leonardo seems to have held throughout his life.

57. MacMahon 2, fol. 11r (Lu 23, datable ca. 1492; see Farago, "Leonardo da Vinci's 'Paragone,'" 316 and 445ff.): "In an instant, painting represents its essence in your visual virtue, and with the very means through which the *impressiva* receives the objects of nature; and furthermore, it does so in the same amount of time that it takes to compose the harmonic proportionality of the parts composing the whole that pleases the sense. And poetry conveys the same thing but by a less worthy means than the eye, for it carries the figures of the above-named things into the *impressiva* more confusedly and slowly than the eye, the true means between the object and the *impressiva*, which conveys immediately and with abso-

lute truthfulness the true surfaces and shapes of that which is presented before it. And from these is born that proportionality called harmony, which with a sweet blending of qualities (*concento*) delights the sense, not otherwise than the proportionalities of diverse voices please the sense of hearing, which is, however, less worthy than sight, since by so much as it is born, it dies." See also fols. 10r–10v (Lu 21), and 18r–18v (Lu 32), where the argument for sight's simultaneity is expanded (specifically in relation to the harmonic *composto* of the thing perceived).

58. See McMahon 2, fols. 11r–11v (continuing the citation in n. 57, above): "If you should represent to the eye a human beauty composed from a proportionality of beautiful limbs [the Zeuxian model!], those beauties are not so mortal, nor do they decay as quickly as music. Rather, it remains a long time and allows itself to be seen and contemplated by you, and is not reborn like music by being repeatedly played, nor will it satiate you. Rather, it seduces you, and makes all the senses, together with the eye, desire to possess it, so that they would seem to want to contend with the eye. The mouth would seem to want it all for itself, the ear draws pleasure from hearing of its beauties, the sense of touch would like to penetrate all of its channels, the nose, for its part, would wish to receive the air continuously exhaled from it. But time destroys the beauty of such a harmony in a few years, which does not happen to that beauty when it is imitated by the painter; for time preserves it for long, and the eye, in performing its office, draws true pleasure from that painted beauty as it would from a living beauty." The marvelous evocation of the senses contending with the eye for possession of the image strengthens the suspicion that Leonardo considers the *imprensiva* a primarily visual organ, even if it also reports to the discursive powers in the *senso commune*.

59. Kemp, "'Il concetto dell'anima,'" 131–33.

60. McMahon 2: fols. 5v–6r (Lu 15; see Farago, "Leonardo da Vinci's 'Paragone,'" 296 and 421): "Non vede la immaginatione cotal'eccellentia qual vede l'occhio, perche l'occhio riceve le spetie overo similitudini de li obbietti et dalle alla impressiva et da essa impressiva al senso commune et li è giudicata ma la immaginatione non esce fuori d'esso senso comune se non in quanto essa va alla memoria et li si ferma et li muore se la cosa immaginata non è di molta eccellentia et in questo caso si trova la poesia nella mente overo immaginativa del poeta il quale finge le medesime cose del pittore . . . adonque in tal caso de fittioni diremo con verita essere tal proportione dalla scientia della pittura alla poesia qual è dal corpo alla sua ombra derivativa, et anchora maggiore proportione concio sia che l'ombra di tal corpo almeno entra per l'occhio al senso commune, ma la immaginatione ditale corpo non entra in esso senso ma li nasce in l'occhio tenebroso o, che diferentia è a immaginarsi tal luce in l'occhio tenebroso al vederla in atto fuori delle tenebre." It is noteworthy that memory only retains such things as are of great excellence—a bias that confirms its suitability to the perfecting of style.

61. On the Weimar sheet, see Keele and Pedretti, *Anatomical Studies*, 1: 166–67, and 2: 829–30. Pedretti, *The Literary Works*, 2: 111–12, transcribes the texts on the sheet and discusses them. They are mostly memorandums on the further elucidation of the nerves issuing from the brain to the spine, and of those

moving the different features of the face. The diagram of the urogenital system, with its accompanying note, belongs with the more ambitious studies on the other side of the sheet.

62. See Kemp, "Dissection and Divinity": 200–209, and 216–25.

63. Pedretti, *Libro A*, 35 (15, no. 11).

64. For this and the following, see Kemp, "'Ogni Dipintore,'" 311–23.

65. See Keele, *Leonardo da Vinci's Elements*, 201–4.

66. See Pedretti, *The Literary Works*, 2: 110. One of these notes might almost be a reflection on Leonardo's own illegitimate conception: "And when coition is undertaken with great love and great desire between the partners, then the child will be of great intellect, and spirited, and vivacious and loving." See the notes on the sharing of souls between mother and fetus in Windsor 19115r (Richter, no. 837; see Brizio, 503), echoed in the notes to Windsor 19102r (the famous study of the fetus encased in the uterus like a seed in its pod; see Clark and Pedretti, *Drawings*, 3: 40).

67. In an essay on the painter's memory, it seems appropriate to include—if only as a postscript—the one personal reminiscence that Leonardo is known to have left. On a sheet with notes on the flight of birds datable to about 1505, Leonardo wrote: "This writing thus clearly about the kite seems to be my destiny, for in the first remembrance [*ricordazione*] from my childhood it seemed to me that, while I was in the crib, a kite came toward me and opened my mouth with its tail, and struck me repeatedly on the lips with that tail." See Richter, 1636 (C.A. 66v–b; see Brizio, 367). A provocative interpretation of this text, covering the earlier literature and giving their due to the two most famous critical contributions—Sigmund Freud's and Meyer Schapiro's—is Daniel Arasse's in "Léonard et *la culla del nibbio:* pour une approche historique du 'souvenir d'enfance,'" *Symboles de la Renaissance* (Paris, 1982), 2: 61–69. Bird flight was indeed one of Leonardo's obsessions, and the tail of the kite, with its rudderlike flexibility, occupied his attention repeatedly. Arasse agrees with Freud's purpose in interrogating the *ricordazione*, but glosses the memory with emblematic references to the Milanese state, as well as with moralized bestiary images, including fables adapted by Leonardo himself. For Arasse, these lead to multiple readings centered on the projection of the artist's childhood anxieties onto key episodes in his adult life.

The Imaginative Basis of Meaning and Cognition

1. For a general overview of the cognitive semantics orientation see George Lakoff, *Women, Fire, and Dangerous Things: What Categories Reveal about the Mind* (Chicago, 1987) and Mark Johnson, *The Body in the Mind: The Bodily Basis of Meaning, Imagination, and Reason* (Chicago, 1987).

2. Thomas Hobbes, *Leviathan*, ed. Michael Oakeshott (London, 1962; originally published 1651), pt. 1, chap. 1.

3. Ibid., chap. 2.

4. Ibid.

5. Henry L. Roediger III, "Memory Metaphors in Cognitive Psychology," *Memory and Cognition* 8, no. 3 (1980): 231–46.

6. F. C. Bartlett, *Remembering: A Study in Experimental and Social Psychology* (Cambridge, 1932), 213.

7. George Lakoff and Zoltan Kovecses, "The Cognitive Model of Anger Inherent in American English," *Berkeley Cognitive Science Report* 10 (May 1983).

8. George Lakoff and Mark Johnson, *Metaphors We Live By* (Chicago, 1980).

9. Michael Reddy, "The Conduit Metaphor—A Case of Frame Conflict in Our Language about Language," in *Metaphor and Thought*, ed, A. Ortony (Cambridge, 1979), 254–83.

10. Lakoff, *Women, Fire, and Dangerous Things*.

11. See especially Ronald Langacker, *Foundations of Cognitive Grammar* (Palo Alto, 1986); Lakoff, *Women, Fire and Dangerous Things*; Susan Linder, "A Lexico-Semantic Analysis of Verb-Particle Constructions with UP and OUT," Ph.D. diss., University of California, San Diego, 1981; Claudia Brugman, "The Use of Body-Part Terms as Locative in Chalcatongo Mixtec," *University of California, Berkeley, Report No. 4 of the Survey of California and Other Indian Languages*, 1983; Rosemary Yeagle, "The Syntax and Semantics of English Verb-Particle Constructions with *off*," M.A. thesis, Southern Illinois University, Carbondale, 1983; Eve Sweetser, *From Etymology to Pragmatics: The Mind-as-Body Metaphor in Semantic Structure and Semantic Change* (Cambridge, in press).

12. Susan Lindner, "A Lexico-Semantic Analysis."

13. The importance of malleability in schematic structure is emphasized by Ulrich Neisser, *Cognition and Reality* (San Francisco, 1976), 54. For a discussion of modeling such a flexible schema see D. Rumelhart, P. Smolensky, J. McClelland, and G. Hinton, "Schemata and Sequential Thought Processes in PDP Models," chap. 14 in David Rumelhart, James L. McClelland, and the PDP Research Group, *Parallel Distributed Processing: Explorations in the Microstructure of Cognition*, vol. 2, *Psychological and Biological Models* (Cambridge, Mass., 1986), esp. 18.

14. The most detailed treatments are Lakoff, *Women, Fire, and Dangerous Things*; Johnson, *The Body in the Mind*; Mark Turner, *Death Is the Mother of Beauty* (Chicago, 1987); and Steven Winter, "The Metaphor of Standing and the Problem of Self-Governance," *Stanford Law Review* 40, no. 6 (July 1988).

15. The primary source is Rumelhart, McClelland, and the PDP Research Group, *Parallel Distributed Processing*.

16. Clifford Geertz, *The Interpretation of Cultures* (New York, 1973).

17. Adrienne Kaeppler, "Structured Movement Systems in Tonga," in *Society and the Dance: The Social Anthropology of Process and Performance*, ed. Paul Spencer (Cambridge, 1985), 92–118.

18. Ibid., 107–8.

19. See especially, Lakoff, *Women, Fire, and Dangerous Things*, and Johnson, *The Body in the Mind*, for some of the relevant research.

20. An account of cognitive semantics—its presuppositions and relevant data—can be found in George Lakoff, "The Invariance Hypothesis: Do Metaphors Preserve Cognitive Topology?" *Cognitive Linguistics* 1, no. 1 (1990): 1–43.

21. Cf. chapter 14, on schema theory, and chapter 17, on memory, in *Parallel Distributed Processing*, 1986.

Visual Narratives, Memory, and the Medieval *Esprit du System*

This essay develops concerns first addressed in my book *Sermo corporeus: Die Erzählung der mittelalterlichen Glasfenster* (Munich, 1987) on narrative in medieval church windows. Jutta Kapf offered assistance, especially in the preparation of the scholastic texts. It was translated by Walter Melion and Alfredo Franco.

1. Aristotle, *De memoria et reminiscentia*, 2. 453a. 6–7. On Aristotle see P. Rossi, *Clavis universalis: Arte mnemoniche e logica combinatoria da Lullo a Leibniz* (Milan, 1960), 8ff. For a presentation of memory that negotiates poetically between these capabilities see book 10, chapter 8, of the *Confessions* of St. Augustine, which deals with the "involontaire," the unconscious factor, and culminates with the dictum: "For the soul is too narrow to grasp itself."
2. R. Barthes, *Die helle Kamera: Bemerkungen zur Photographie* (Frankfurt, 1985), 33ff. Even Jan Assmann's ground-breaking theory of collective and cultural memory, with its differentiation between "communicative memory" and "cultural memory," seems heir to the Aristotelian categories. See J. Assmann, "Kollektives Gedächtnis und Kulturelle Identität," in J. Assmann and T. Hoelscher, *Kultur und Gedächtnis*, (Frankfurt, 1988), 9ff.
3. On Warburg's theory of Mnemosyne see W. Kemp, "Walter Benjamin und Aby Warburg," *Kritische Berichte* 3 (1975): 5ff.
4. Relevant here is Benjamin's assimilation of Bergson, Proust, Freud, and Reik in "Über einige Motive bei Baudelaire" in *Gesammelte Schriften*, ed. R. Tiedemann and H. Schweppenhäuser (Frankfurt, 1974), 1:607ff. See also the material on this theme in *Passagenwerk*, *Gesammelte Schriften* 5:507ff. A newer complete outline of the topic can be found in H. Kilian, *Das enteignete Bewußtsein* (Berlin, 1974).
5. A recent turn for the better speaks for the overcoming of atomism, that is, for the achievement of critical reflection. See S. Settis, ed., *Memoria dell 'antico nell'arte italiana* (Turin, 1984); S. Settis, "Von *Auctoritas* zu *Vetustas*: die antike Kunst in mittelalterlicher Sicht," *Zeitschrift für Kunstgeschichte* 51(1988): 157ff.; H. Klotz, "Anmerkungen zur architekturgeschichtlichen Bedeutung des Domes von Speyer," *Marburger Jahrbuch für Kunstwissenschaft* 22 (1989): 9ff.
6. This is the fundamental tendency in R. Krautheimer, "Iconography of Medieval Architecture," *Journal of the Warburg and Courtauld Institutes* 5 (1942): 1–33. See also G. Bandmann, *Mittelalterliche Architektur als Bedeutungsträger* (Berlin, 1951).
7. F. H. Baeuml, "Varieties and Consequences of Medieval Literacy and Illiteracy," *Speculum* 55 (1980): 247ff.
8. S. Küchler, "Malangan: Art and Memory in a Melanesian Society," *Man* 22 (1987): 239.

9. For the two related works see Kemp, *Sermo corporeus*, 46ff. I treat here only the inner systematics of the Marburger tapestry's narrative. For the equally systematic relations between the cycle in the middle and the borders portraying the life of a knight, see W. Kemp, "Mittelalterliche Bildsysteme," *Marburger Jahrbuch für Kunstwissenschaft* 22 (1989): 121ff.

10. E. A. Heinemann, "The Motif of the Journey in the *Chanson de Geste*," in *The Epic in Medieval Society*, ed. H. Scholler (Tübingen, 1977), 188.

11. S. Wittig, *Stylistic and Narrative Structures in the Middle English Romances* (Austin and London, 1978), 179.

12. A. J. Greimas, "Elemente einer narrativen Grammatik," in *Strukturalismus in der Literaturwissenschaft*, ed. H. Blumensath (Cologne, 1972), 50.

13. A. Dundes, *The Morphology of North American Indian Folktales* (Helsinki, 1964). For the text by Wittig, see note 11 above. A good overview of this basic schemata is given by E. Meletinskij, "Zur strukturelltypologischen Erforschung des Volksmärchens," in *Morphologie des Märchens*, ed. V. Propp and K. Eimermacher (Frankfurt, 1975), 241ff., and W. Martin, *Recent Theories of Narrative* (Ithaca, 1986), 81ff.

14. See also Wittig, *Stylistic and Narrative Structures*, 183ff.

15. K. Stierle, *Text als Handlung: Perspektiven einer systematischen Literaturwissenschaft* (Munich, 1975), 53.

16. Cited in C. Casagrande and S. Vecchio, "L'interdizione del giullare nel vocabolario clericale del XII e del XIII secolo," in *Il contributo dei giullari alla dramaturgia italiana nelle origini* (n.p., 1978), 219.

17. For some of these areas of praxis see M. A. Rouse and R. H. Rouse, *Preachers, Florilegia and Sermons* (Toronto, 1979).

18. See the summary in Kemp, *Sermo corporeus*, 190ff, which gives particulars on the most recent literature.

19. Cited in H. Caplan, *Historical Studies of Rhetoric and Rhetoricians*, ed., R. F. Howes (Ithaca, 1960), 82.

20. D. L. D'Avray, *The Preaching of the Friars: Sermons Diffused from Paris before 1300* (Oxford, 1985), 176.

21. R. Lachmann, "Kultursemiotischer Prospekt, Vorbereitungspapier zur Tagung 'Memoria—Vergessen und Erinnern' der Gruppe 'Poetik und Hermeneutik,'" unpublished colloquium paper, 8.

22. Albertus Magnus, *De bono*, q.II, a.II, in *Opera omnia*, ed. H. Kühle, et al. (Münster, 1951), 28:248, cited in F. A. Yates, *The Art of Memory* (London, 1966), 65.

23. Yates, *Art of Memory*, 65. J. P. Antoine has recently attempted to salvage the importance of the *imagines agentes*; see Antoine, "The Art of Memory and Its Relation to the Unconscious," *Comparative Civilizations Review* 18 (1988): 1ff.

24. The treatises and passages are evaluated in Yates, *Art of Memory*, 61ff.; a shorter presentation appears in Rossi, *Clavis universalis*, 14ff.

24. The passages from R. Bacon, *Opus minus*, are given in H. Felder, *Geschichte der wissenschaftlichen Studien im Franziskanerorden* (Freiburg, 1904), 515.

26. E. Panofsky, *Gothic Architecture and Scholasticism* (Cleveland and New York, 1957), 31.

27. Yates, *Art of Memory*, 79.

28. Thomas Aquinas, *Summa theologica* II-II, q.XLIX, a.1; cited in Yates, *Art of Memory*, 75.

29. Aristotle, *De memoria et reminiscentia*, 197.

30. Ibid., 192.

31. Thomas Aquinas, *De memoria et reminiscentia*, a.371, in *Aristotelis libros De sensu et sensato, De memoria et reminiscentia commentarium*, ed., R. M. Spiazzi (Turin and Rome, 1949), 105.

32. Compare Yates, *Art of Memory*, 76: "And, particularly in Thomas, one gains the impression that the important thing is order."

33. Compare D'Avray, *Preaching*. Yates, *Art of Memory*, 85, ignores the thematic sermon, considering the preacher's aims to be founded in another, non-scholastic-philosophical *Summa*: "But the preacher needed another type of *Summae* to help him, *Summae* of examples and similitudes." Such collections of examples did exist, and were, so far as I can see, arranged likewise according to systematic points of view. See J. Berlioz, "La mémoire du predicateur: Recherches sur la mémorisation des récits exemplaires (XIII–XV siècles)," in *Temps, mémoire, tradition au Moyen-Age* (Aix-en-Provence and Marseille, 1983), 157ff.

34. A brief reference to the *artes praedicandi* in Rossi, *Clavis universalis*, 18–19. Rossi, like others after him, commits the error of conceding the ancient art of memory a constitutive role in the development of medieval rhetoric. Nor should one be persuaded by the fact that, in the fourteenth century, such treatises, while occasionally invoking ancient and contemporary authorities, themselves follow completely different principles of execution. D'Avray's *Preaching*, the standard presentation of the subject, does not acknowledge a consideration of ancient models.

35. Yates, *Art of Memory*, 85.

36. Lachmann, "Kultursemiotischer Prospekt," 9.

37. What I have written here applies to northern Europe and above all to the thirteenth century. Yates can assume with greater justification a rebirth of ancient memory rules for fourteenth-century Italy. This is confirmed by the new material and arguments in H. Belting, "Das Bild als Text: Wandmalerei und Literatur im Zeitalter Dantes," in H. Belting and D. Blume, *Malerei und Stadtkultur in der Dantezeit*, (Munich, 1989), 54ff. Belting's last example, Gaddi's *Tree of Life*, cannot be described as "the perfect example of an instruction on memory practice in accordance with ancient rhetoric," if we are to accept the further assertion that the "wall painting conveyed the textual form [of Bonaventure's "Lignum Vitae"] in the form of a diagram, illustrating its content in such a way that its order could more easily be secured in memory" (56). The diagrammatic illustration, especially that of the "Tree of Knowledge," which Bonaventure explicitly chose "in order to make it easier for the memory," does not have its origin in ancient mnemonics. From the fourteenth century on we must simply assume that there were two memory techniques: the schematic-systematic arrangement, with its tendency toward figure and diagram—which is a medieval achievement; and the

characterizing image with its tendency toward an accumulation of "pictures" around personifications—in which the ancient heritage is without doubt still vigorous. On the characterizing image (*Merkbild*) see K. A. Wirth, "Neue Schriftquellen zur deutschen Kunst des 15. Jahrhunderts," *Städel-Jahrbuch* 6 (1977): 366ff. For an example, see fig. 29, which shows a panel from an *Ars memorandi* published in 1502 in Pforzheim, with the help of which one was to memorize the events of Christ's life.

38. D'Avray, *Preaching*, 248.

39. Küchler, "Malangan," 239.

40. H. Weinrich, "Über Sprache, Leib und Gedächtnis," in *materialität der Kommunikation*, ed. H. U. Gumbrecht and K. L. Pfeiffer (Frankfurt, 1988), 92.

41. St. Augustine, *De civitate Dei*, 11. 19.

Memory and Knowledge in the Production of Dance

The twenty-two-month fieldwork on which this paper is based was supported by the Wenner-Gren Foundation for Anthropological Research, the National Institute of Mental Health, the Bishop Museum, and the Smithsonian Institution, to all of which I wish to express my warmest appreciation. I am indebted to the government of Tonga under their majesties the late Queen Sālote Tupou III and the present King Tāufa'āhau Tupou IV, and the many Tongans who helped me to understand Tongan dance and society, especially the late Vaisima Hopoate, the late Honorable Ve'ehala, Princess Pilolevu, Sister Tu'ifua, and Baron Vaea. I also wish to thank Brenda Farnell for helpful comments on a draft of this paper.

1. Drid Williams, "Introduction to the Special Issue of Semasiology," *Journal for the Anthropological Study of Human Movement* 1, no. 4 (1981): 221.

2. Adrienne L. Kaeppler, *The Structure of Tongan Dance* (Ph.D. diss., University of Hawaii, 1967); Adrienne L. Kaeppler, "Method and Theory in Analyzing Dance Structure with an Analysis of Tongan Dance," *Ethnomusicology* 16 (1972): 173–217.

3. Kaeppler, "Method and Theory," 202–4; see also below.

4. Ibid., 207.

5. Susanne Küchler, "Malangan: Art and Memory in a Melanesian Society," *Man* 22 (1987): 238.

6. This section is based on Kaeppler, "Method and Theory," 204–14, to which the reader is referred for more detail.

Finding Memories in Madagascar

This paper is based on ethnographic research in the Analalava region of northwestern Madagascar in 1971–73, 1981, and 1989. I am grateful to members of the Symposium on "Memory, Cognition, and the Production of Images," sponsored by the Program in Art History and Anthropology at The Johns Hopkins

University on 8 April, 1988, and to Susanne Küchler and Walter S. Melion for their insights and advice.

1. In practice, the representative conception of linear time-memory is hardly consistent. Conceptions of memory would surely benefit by taking into account the variability in Western cultural conceptions of time as discussed in D. J. Wilcox, *The Measure of Times Past: Pre-Newtonian Chronologies and the Rhetoric of Relative Time* (Chicago, 1987), for example.

2. W. C. Pickersgill, "Revision of North-West Place-Names: Some Curiosities of Topographical Nomenclature," *Antananarivo Annual* 12 (1888): 488–94; J. Sibree, "Malagasy Place Names," *Antananarivo Annual* 20 (1896): 401–13; G. Kling, "La toponymie malgache," *Bulletin de Madagascar* 7 (1957): 787–89; L. Molet, *Petit guide de toponymie malgache* (Tananarive-Tsimbazaza, 1957).

3. G. Fontoynont, "De quelques 'solo' célèbres en Imerina, et culte religieux de certains rois," *Bulletin de l'Académie Malgache* 12 (1913): 115–37.

4. J. C. Rakotomampiaina, "Une liturgie sacrificielle à Alsora (Tananarive)," *Journal of Religion in Africa* 2 (1969): 192–201.

5. C. Poirier, "Les '*Dady*,' '*Fibaby*' ou '*Ampagnito Be*' des anciens rois sakalava du Menabé septentrional," *Mémoires de L'Académie Malgache* 28 (1939): 13–18; S. Raharijaona and J. Valette, "Les grands fêtes rituelles des Sakalava du Menabé ou 'Fitampoha,'" *Bulletin de Madagascar* 155 (1959): 1–33, appendixes; S. Chazan-Gillig, "Le *Fitampoha* de 1968 ou l'efficacité du mythe de la royauté Sakalava dans l'actualité politique et économique malgache," in *Les Souverains de Madagascar: L'Histoire royale et ses résurgences contemporaines*, ed. F. Raison-Jourde (Paris, 1983), 451–76; Raison-Jourde, ed., *Les Souverains de Madagascar*, plates 18, 21, 23, and 28.

6. G. Feeley-Harnik, "Cloth and the Creation of Ancestors in Madagascar," in *Cloth and Human Experience*, ed. A. B. Weiner and J. Schneider (Washington, D. C., 1989), 73–116. Most of these sources include photographs. See also Raison-Jourde, ed., *Les Souverains de Madagascar*, plate 26 for photographs of Andriamanelo's tomb taken in 1958; plates 18, 19, 21, 27, and 28 for more photographs of the royal relics, relic house, and porters at the Sakalava royal shrine of Belo-sur-Tsiribihina; and plate 30 for a photograph of an enshrouded medium of a Sakalava royal ancestor, taken near Belo-sur-Tsiribihina. I was forbidden to take photographs of royal ancestors in the Analalava region, in the form of regalia, tombs, or mediums. S. Feeley-Harnik, "Dancing Battles: Representations of Conflict in Sakalava Royal Service," *Anthropos* 83 (1988): 65–85, includes photographs of the *rebiky*, a dance commemorating battles between rival branches of the Sakalava monarchy, that seems to have developed out of the practice of carrying royal relics in bundles on the back.

7. Unless otherwise indicated, the data presented here derives from my ethnographic research in northwestern Madagascar in 1971–73 and briefly in 1981. I am grateful to the Malagasy government for granting permission to do the research.

8. E.g., M. Bloch, *Placing the Dead: Tombs, Ancestral Villages, and Kinship Organization in Madagascar* (London, 1971), 124–27; J.-F. Baré, *Pouvoir des*

vivants, langage des morts: Idéologiques Sakalava (Paris, 1977), 94, 95; C. P. Kottak, *The Past in the Present: History, Ecology and Cultural Variation in Highland Madagascar* (Ann Arbor, 1980), 211.

9. *Doniány* or *doniá* derives from Swahili *dunia* (earth, the world), derived from the Arabic *al-dunya*, "the immediate here and now," in contrast to *al-akhira*, "the other [world]." L. Krapf, *A Dictionary of the Suahili Language* (Ridgewood, N.Y., 1964; first published 1882). See M. Lambek, *Human Spirits: A Cultural Account of Trance in Mayotte* (Cambridge, 1981), 26, on the expression of these ideas among Malagasy speakers in Mayotte.

10. M. Fortes, "An Introductory Commentary," in *Ancestors*, ed. W. H. Newell (The Hague, 1976), 7.

11. See G. Feeley-Harnik, *A Green Estate: Land, Labor, and Ancestry in Northwestern Madagascar* (Washington, D. C., forthcoming) for more details.

12. Poirier, "Fin de règne." See C. Poirier, "Notes d'ethnographie et d'histoire malgaches: Les Royaumes Sakalava Bemihisatra de la côte nord ouest de Madagascar," *Mémoires de l'Académie malgache* 28 (1939): 103–4.

13. A. Dandouau, "Coutumes funéraires dans le nord-ouest de Madagascar," *Bulletin de l'Académie malgache* 9 (1911): 169; Poirier, "Notes d'ethnographie," 68–76.

14. See J. Dez, "Le Retournement des morts chez les Betsileo," *Société d'Ethnographie de Paris* 51 (1956): 119; W. R. Huntington, "Death and the Social Order: Bara Funeral Customs (Madagascar)," *African Studies* 32 (1973): 64–84. Dez writes about highland Betsileo funerals in the 1950s, Huntington about funerals among the Bara people in the highlands south of the Betsileo in the late 1960s. Bloch, *Placing the Dead*, 159, and Kottak, *The Past in the Present*, 216, 221, writing about the highland Merina and Betsileo in the late sixties, do not describe the same explicitly sexual behavior, but they do mention that women fight over the scraps of old shrouds and mats from earlier burials, because sleeping on them is thought to increase fertility.

15. Dandouau, "Coutumes fúneraires," 171–72; Poirier, "Notes d'ethnographie," 104; J. V. Mellis, *Nord et nord-ouest de Madagascar: Volamena et volafotsy, suivi d'un vocabulaire de nord-ouest expliqué, commenté, et comparé au Merina* (Tananarive, 1938), 61 (photographs), 62, 67.

16. See G. Feeley-Harnik, "The Political Economy of Death: Communication and Change in Malagasy Colonial History," *American Ethnologist*, 11 (1984): 1–19.

17. E. Goffman, *Asylums: Essays on the Social Situation of Mental Patients and Other Inmates* (Garden City, N. J., 1961), xiii; see also M. Foucault, *Discipline and Punish: The Birth of the Prison* (New York, 1979; originally published 1975), 235.

18. Goffman, *Asylums*, 197.

19. Foucault, *Discipline and Punish*, 135–51.

20. Goffman, *Asylums*, 12. In Foucault's case, this is partly because he sees family forms as being incorporated into the carceral archipelago. But he does not go further to explore how kin may resist these incursions and continue to define their relationships on their own terms.

21. Ibid., 16; Foucault, *Discipline and Punish*, 151–69, 170–94.

22. Feeley-Harnik, "The Political Economy of Death"; G. Feeley-Harnik, "Issues in Divine Kingship," *Annual Review of Anthropology* 14 (1985): 273–313.

23. R. R. MacDonald, *The Burial Places of Memory: Epic Underworlds in Vergil, Dante, and Milton* (Amherst, 1987), 8.

24. K. H. Basso, "'Stalking with Stories': Names, Places, and Moral Narratives among the Western Apache," in *Text, Play and Story: The Construction and Reconstruction of Self and Society*, Proceedings of the American Ethnological Society, 1983, ed. E. M. Bruner (Washington, D. C., 1984), 43.

25. B. Malinowski, *Argonauts of the Western Pacific* (New York, 1961; originally published 1922), 408.

26. Ibid., 409.

27. Ibid., 410.

Transformations of Time and Space

The research on which this paper is based was assisted by grants from the Graduate Research Board of the University of Maryland, the Joint Committee on Latin American Studies of the American Council of Learned Societies, and the Social Science Research Council. Grants-in-aid from the Wenner-Gren Foundation for Anthropological Research and the American Council of Learned Societies also contributed to making this work possible.

Bill Hanks, Susanne Küchler, Joyce Marcus, John Paddock, and Angeles Romero all read a preliminary version of this paper and freely gave their constructive comments, some of which have been incorporated into my text and notes. While their comments have strengthened my arguments, the hypotheses and conclusions expressed here are my own responsibility. I would also like to thank my research assistant at the University of Maryland, Charles Brock, for his diligent exploration of writings on Greek and Roman maps in the Library of Congress. I am grateful for the invitation from the Ecole des Hautes Etudes en Sciences Sociales to direct a seminar in Paris on the subject of this paper during May of 1988. The comments on Serge Gruzinski, Nathan Wachtel, and Tom Zuidema were particularly useful in developing my thinking on this topic. As always, my wife and colleague, Nancy Farriss, was a constant source of constructive criticism and encouragement.

1. Our region of study clusters around the Spanish settlement of Villa Alta, situated in the midst of a densely populated mountainous region inhabited by Zapotec, Chinantec, and Mixe Indians. See Peter Gerhard, *A Guide to the Historical Geography of New Spain* (Cambridge, 1972), 367–73 for a historical geography of this large and important colonial jurisdiction, known as Villa Alta de San Ildefonso de los Zapotecas. Recently, John Chance has published a book on the colonial experience of Spaniards and Indians in the Sierra: *Conquest of the Sierras: Spaniards and Indians in Colonial Oaxaca* (Norman, Oklahoma, 1989).

2. In so doing, I am not equating the Zapotec with better-known Mesoamerican cultures. Mixtec scholars, in particular, have been sensitive to the inter-

pretation of Mixtec codices in terms of Central Mexican symbolism and ethnohistory (see, for example, Nancy P. Troike, *Current Problems in the Mixtec Codices*, Actes du XLII Congrès Internationales des Américanistes, 1979; Jill L. Furst, *Codex Vindobonensis Mexicanus I: A Commentary* [Albany, 1978]). Gordon Whittaker, in "The Hieroglyphics of Monte Albán," Ph.D. diss., Yale University, 1980, rejects the use of comparative data from outside Oaxaca to understand Zapotec texts. My view is that internal evidence is best, but lacking that, one may justify cautious comparisons with external data.

3. While there are no Zapotec pictorial manuscripts known, pre-Hispanic "calendars" do exist among other Mesoamerican groups. Perhaps the best known is the so-called Aztec calendar stone. Divinatory or ritual calendars are extant in pictorial manuscripts outside the Zapotec area. In all extant pre-Hispanic "calendars," information on the significance of day name and number combinations is lacking, and resides only in the memory of calendar specialists.

4. For a comparative example of "oral literacy," where text is read aloud to a literate audience, see Jesper Svenbro's *Phrasikleia: Anthropologie de la lecture en Grèce ancienne* (Paris, 1989). Svenbro views the isolation of writer from reader as a gradual process of separation in literate societies. He contrasts "oral literacy" with an autonomous form of literacy which he relates to the development of silent reading among late fifth-century literate elite. It is what Svenbro describes as an autonomous form of literacy that I am associating with "European literacy" in early colonial Mexico.

5. Jack Goody, ed., *Literacy in Traditional Societies* (Cambridge, 1968); Jack Goody, *The Domestication of the Savage Mind* (Cambridge, 1977); Jack Goody, *The Logic of Writing and the Organization of Society* (Cambridge, 1986); Jack Goody, *The Interface between the Written and the Oral* (Cambridge, 1987).

6. Zapotec Classic Period (Monte Albán IIIa–IIIb/IV: A.D. 250–750) glyphic forms for place (usually referred to as *place signs*), less well understood than latter Mixtec ones in pictorial manuscripts with a Western Oaxaca provenience (see, for example Mary Elizabeth Smith, *Picture Writing from Ancient Southern Mexico: Mixtec Place Signs and Maps* [Norman, Oklahoma, 1973]), are associated often with calendrical date glyphs, suggesting a special geographical function for these place/time indicators.

7. See Gillian Feeley-Harnik's paper on communication and change in Malagasy colonial history, "The Political Economy of Death: Communication and Change in Malagasy Colonial History," *American Ethnologist* 11, no. 1 (1984): 1–19, for a discussion of the process by which an indigenous political economy is hidden from colonial intrusion, by reformulating it in ways framed as shared experience. Feeley-Harnik argues that the specific example she analyzes in French-colonized Madagascar exhibit general features which may be widespread. Based on my preliminary examination of the Sierra Zapotec case, I think that the kind of colonial passive resistance Feeley-Harnik describes for Madagascar is also evident in colonial Mexico.

8. Eric R. Wolf, *Sons of the Shaking Earth: The People of Mexico and Guatemala, Their Land, History and Culture* (Chicago, 1967); Gonzalo Aguirre Beltrán, *El proceso de aculturación* (Mexico, 1982); Charles Gibson, *The Aztecs*

under Spanish Rule: A History of the Indians of the Valley of Mexico, 1519–1810(Stanford, 1964); Nancy M. Farriss, *Maya Society under Colonial Rule: The Collective Purchase of Survival* (Princeton, 1984); James Lockhart, "Some Nahua Concepts in Preconquest Guise," *History of European Ideas* 6, no. 4 (1985): 465–82; Serge Gruzinski, *La colonisation de l'imaginaire: Société indigenes et occidentalisation dans le Mexique espagnol XVI–XVIII siècle* (Paris, 1988); for publication of maps, Cecil R. Welte, "Preconquest and Early Colonial Pictorial Manuscripts of the 'Oaxaca area,'" *Welte's Ready Reference Releases*, no. 5 (Oaxaca, 1981); Donald Robertson, *Mexican Manuscript Painting of the Early Colonial Period: The Metropolitan Schools* (New Haven, 1959); Eva Hunt, *The Transformation of the Hummingbird: Cultural Roots of a Zinacantecan Mythical Poem* (Ithaca, 1977); Barbara Tedlock, *Time and the Highland Maya* (Albuquerque, 1982); Goody, *Literacy in Traditional Societies*; Goody, *The Domestication of the Savage Mind*; Goody, *The Logic of Writing*; Goody, *The Interface between the Written and the Oral*; Caroline Bledsoe and Kenneth M. Robey, "Arabic Literacy and Secrecy among the Mende of Sierra Leone," *Man* 21, no. 2 (1986): 202–26; Phillip D. Curtin, ed., *Africa and the West: Intellectual Responses to European Culture* (Madison, Wisconsin, 1972); Robin Horton and Ruth Finnegan, eds., *Modes of Thought: Essays on Thinking in Western and Non-Western Societies* (London, 1973); Feeley-Harnik, "The Political Economy of Death."

9. Arthur G. Miller, *The Mural Paintings of Teotihuacán* (Washington, D.C., 1973); Arthur G. Miller, "Captains of the Itzá: Unpublished Mural Evidence from Chichn Itzá," in *Social Process in Maya Prehistory: Studies in Honor of Sir Eric Thompson*, ed. Norman Hammond (London, 1977), 197–225; Arthur G. Miller, *On the Edge of the Sea: Mural Paintings at Tancah-Tulum, Quintana Roo, Mexico* (Washington, D.C., 1982); Arthur G. Miller, "Pre-Hispanic Mural Painting in the Valley of Oaxaca, Mexico," *National Geographic Research* 4, no. 2 (1988): 233–58. In March 1987, the Regional Center of Oaxaca (Centro Regional de Oaxaca) of the Mexican National Institute of Anthropology and History (Instituto Nacional de Antropología e Historia) asked me to record and analyze the sculptural and mural painting of a recently discovered tomb in Santiago Suchilquitongo's community lands. With the support of funds from the National Geographic Society's Committee of Research and Exploration and from the College of Arts and Humanities and the Department of Art History and Archaeology of the University of Maryland, College Park, Mexican archaeological artist Felipe Dávalos and I spent a total of sixteen months from 1988–89 in the tomb studying its rich glyphic and pictorial remains. The results of these investigations will be published in monographic form.

10. Archivo General de Indias, *Mexico 882*; José Alcina Franch, "Calendarios zapotecos prehispánicos según documentos de los siglos XVI y XVII," *Estudios de Cultura Náhuatl* 6 (1966): 119–33; José Alcina Franch, "Calendario y religión entre los zapotecos serranos durante el siglo XVII," in *Mesoamerica: Homenaje al Doctor Paul Kirchoff*, ed. Barbro Dahlgren (Mexico, 1979), 212–24.

11. Nancy M. Farriss has recently located a series of trials covering two centuries from the 1530s to the 1730s, with only the major lacuna so far of the last two decades of the sixteenth century, in Seville (Justicia section), in local Juzgado

records (Juzgado of Villa Alta), and in the Archivo General de la Nación. In addition, historical narratives incorporated into published chronicles (Relaciones geográficas) and into unedited community "titles" in The Archivo general de la Nation's Tierras section may shed light on the transition to the colonial form of calendar.

12. Welte, "Preconquest and Early Colonial Pictorial Manuscripts."

13. Alfonso Caso has been the primary student of calendar and writing systems in ancient Oaxaca. His most influential writings on the Zapotec calendar include his pioneering *Las estelas zapotecas* (Mexico, 1928); *Las exploraciones en Oaxaca, quinta y sexta temporadas, 1936–1937* Publicación 34, Instituto Pan-americano de Geografía e Historia (Mexico, 1938); "Calendario y escritura de las antiguas culturas de Monte Albán," in *Obras completas,* ed. Miguel Othón de Mendizábal (Mexico, 1946), 1:114–45; and "Zapotec Writing and Calendar," in *Archeology of Southern Mesoamerica,* part 2, ed. Gordon R. Willey, *Handbook of Middle American Indians* (Austin, Texas), 3:931–47.

14. As of this writing, Javier Urcid is completing a doctoral dissertation in the Anthropology Department of Yale University on aspects of Zapotec writing. He has identified the year bearers in the Zapotec calendar as Caso's Glyphs E,G,N, and a variant of M (M. Winter, *Oaxaca: The Archeological Record* [Mexico, 1983], 51).

15. John Paddock, personal communication, 1988.

16. Over three hundred so-called danzante carvings are extant, most of them encountered during the course of the eighteen field seasons (1931–58) of the Monte Albán Project, directed by Alfonso Caso. Known since Dupaix's 1806 expedition to Monte Albán, the carvings have been the object of much speculative writing. Caso's 1946 study securely fixed their chronology to the beginnings of Monte Albán, a period he considered to be "pre-Zapotec."

17. Miller, "Pre-Hispanic Mural Painting."

18. For an analysis of the glyph columns fronting profile figures painted on the Tomb 105 wall, enscribing rulers' genealogies expressed as a series of named male and female ancestors, see Joyce Marcus, "Stone Monuments and Tomb Murals of Monte Albán IIIa," in *The Cloud People: Divergent Evolution of the Zapotec and Mixtec Civilizations,* ed. Kent. V. Flannery and Joyce Marcus (New York, 1983), 140–43.

19. Archivo General de Indias, *Mexico 882.*

20. Juan de Córdova, *Arte del idioma zapoteca* (Mexico, 1987; facsimile of 1886 Morelia edition); AGI, *Mexico 882.* Eva Hunt, in *The Transformation of the Hummingbird: Cultural Roots of a Zinacantecan Mythical Poem* (Ithaca, 1977), 55–56, has (I think correctly) characterized this pantheistic quality of pre-Hispanic religion: "Prehispanic religion . . . was truly pantheistic. . . . Mesoamerican cultures were neither polytheistic nor monotheistic. In their view, as in those of all pantheistic cultures, reality, nature, and experience were nothing but multiple manifestations of a single unity of being. . . . Since the divine reality was multiple, fluid, encompassing the whole, its aspects were changing images, dynamic, never frozen, but constantly being recreated, redefined. This fluidity was a culturally defined mystery of the nature of divinity itself. Therefore, it was expressed in the dynamic,

ever-changing aspects of multiple 'deities' that embodied it. For didactic, artistic, and ritual purposes, however, these fluid images were carved in stone, painted into frescoes, described in prayer. It is here, at this reduced level of visualization, that the transient images of a sacralized universe became 'gods,' with names attached to them, with anthropomorphic attributes, and so on."

21. AGI, *Mexico 882*. The mediating role of a calendar priest regarding a newborn child's fate perscribed by his birth date is evident in Central Mexico (Charles E. Dibble and Arthur J. O. Anderson eds., "Book 4—The Soothsayers and Book 5—The Omens" in Fray Bernardino de Sahagun, *Florentine Codex: General History of the Things of New Spain* [Santa Fe, 1979], 113–15; Munro S. Edmonson, *The Book of Counsel: The Popol Vuh of the Quiche Maya of Guatemala*, Middle American Research Institute, Publication 35 [New Orleans], 108, n. 3436). A Mixe informant, with whom I am working in Oaxaca, reports that calendar specialists currently delay naming rituals to the nearest propitious day after the birth. For Mixe calendar use in recent times, see Frank Joseph Lipp, "The Mije Calendrical System: Concepts and Behavior" (Ph.D. diss., New School for Social Research, 1982).

22. A precondition to "see" or "visualize" experience in a culture-specific manner has been characterized recently, for art history, as the "period eye" and "cognitive style." See Michael Baxandall's analysis of the cognitive skills which generate images and are in turn exercised by them, for example, where narrative pictorial construction stimulates the Latinist's familiarity with the linguistic structure of the Latin period (Michael Baxandall, *Painting and Experience in Fifteenth-Century Italy* [Oxford, 1988]).

23. An evident example is sixteenth-century Yucatan, where several transliterated ritual cycles, known as Chilam Balams, are associated with Maya towns in the peninsula. The chronologies of these Chilam Balams differ from town to town, suggesting that locus was a factor in establishing differing time lines in colonial Maya society.

24. For a description and analysis of Mesoamerican screenfolds, see Donald Robertson's *Mexican Manuscript Painting of the Early Colonial Period* (New Haven, 1959). No screenfolds are known from the Zapotec region. Several derive from neighboring Western Oaxaca, the region known as the Mixteca Alta.

25. AGI, *Mexico 882*.

26. William Hanks, personal communication, 1988.

27. Julio de la Fuente, *Yalag: Una villa zapoteca serrana* (Mexico, 1977).

28. Hanks, personal communication, 1988.

29. For a discussion of "fetish-worshipers" and the "forgetting" found in anthropological accounts of fetishism, see W. J. T. Mitchell's "The Rhetoric of Iconoclasm in Iconology" in *Iconology: Image, Text, Ideology* (Chicago, 1987), 160–208, esp. 192–93. The magic of the fetish depends on the projection of consciousness into the object, and then a forgetting of that act of projection" (193).

30. Lewis Hanke, "The 'Requerimiento' and Its Interpretors," *Revista de Historia de América* 1 (1938): 24–25.

31. Charles Gibson, ed., *The Spanish Tradition in America* (New York, 1968), 58.

32. The origin and function of cadastral maps is the subject of major treatises on the history of cartography. Whereas Robertson, *Mexican Manuscript Painting*, draws a distinction between maps and landscapes, the Roman tradition combines the two. See, for example, O. A. W. Dilke's, *Greek and Roman Maps* (London, 1985); J. B. Harley and David Woodward, eds., *The History of Cartography: Cartography in Prehistoric, Ancient, and Medieval Europe and the Mediterranean* (Chicago, 1987); and especially James Nelson Carder's *Art Historical Problems of a Roman Land Surveying Manuscript: the Codex Arcerianus A. Wolfenbüttel* (New York, 1978).

33. Despite the vast literature on Roman cartography, the role of Roman cadastral maps in assessing the results of conquest is not well understood. Nevertheless, it seems clear that the model for sixteenth-century Spanish maps in the New World was Roman cadastral maps and landscapes.

34. The fifty queries compiled on the order of Spanish monarch Philip II form part of the *Relaciones geográficas*, considered a major source on Spain's New World territories (Howard F. Cline, "The Relaciones Geográficas of the Spanish Indies 1577–1648," in *Guide to Ethnohistorical Sources*, part 1, ed. Howard F. Cline, *Handbook of Middle American Indians* [Austin, Texas, 1972], 12:183. Three of the questions required a map or *pintura* to accompany the textual report. Specifically, local officials (*alcaldes mayores, corregidores*) were charged with complying with the questionnaire. That indigenous liasons with the local Spanish bureaucracy did in fact draw the *pintura* demanded is not generally evident in written testimony, but it is apparent on stylistic grounds.

35. The detailed analysis of the *Relaciones geográficos* by Alejandra Moreno Toscano (*Geografía económica de México*, [Mexico, 1968]) analyzes social and economic implications of conquesst as revealed in the *Relaciones*.

36. "The autochthonous styles of American art were superseded by the imported arts of Renaissance Spain" (Donald Robertson, "The Pinturas [Maps] of the Relaciones Geográficas, with a Catalog," in *Guide to Ethnohistorical Sources*, part 1, ed. Howard F. Cline, *Handbook of Middle American Indians* [Austin, Texas, 1972], 12:243). Robertson applies this view directly to the *Relaciones*: "The process is clearly demonstrated for the history of painting in Middle America by 92 *pinturas* accompanying the written texts of the *Relaciones Geográficas* of 1579–86, making up the largest single group of interrelated early colonial pictorial manuscripts which has come down to us" (243).

37. That Indian informants were gathered by the *corregidor*, a local official, to help him answer the questionnaire is clear in the Relación of Macuilxochitl in the Valley of Oaxaca, stating that an interpreter was engaged (Francisco del Paso y Troncoso, ed., *Relaciones geográficas de Oaxaca* [Mexico, 1981; originally published 1579], 100). Two questions in particular (13 and 14) would have required access to Indian informants: "13 Item. lo que quiere decir en lengua de Indios el nombre del dicho pueblo de Indios, y porque se llama assi, si huuiere que saber en ello, y como se llama la lengua que, los Indios de los dichos pueblos hablan" (Moreno Toscano, *Geografía económica*, 129). ["What does the name of this Indian town mean in the language of the Indians; why is it so called, if known; and what is the name of the language spoken by the Indians of this town?" (translation

by Clinton R. Edwards in Cline "The Relaciones Geográficas," 235)]; question 14: "Cuyos eran en tiempo de su gentilidad, y el Señorio que sobre ellos tenian sus señores, y lo que tributauan, y las adoraciones, ritos, y costumbres buenas o malas que tenian" (Moreno Toscano, *Geografía económica*, 129). ["To whom were they subject when they were heathens; what power did their rulers have over them; what did they pay in tribute; what forms of worship, rites, and good or evil customs did they have?" (translation by Clinton R. Edwards in Cline, "The Relaciones Geográficas," 235)].

38. See John Paddock's 1982 paper on the *Relación de Macuilxochitl* for an example of "self-censorship by the Indians to conceal certain facts from the Spanish" ("Confluence in Zapotec and Mixtec Ethnohistories: The 1580 Mapa de Macuilxochitl," *Papers in Anthropology: Native American Ethnohistory* 23, no. 2 [1982]: 347).

39. *Pinturas* (paintings, maps) were drawn in response to three of the fifty questions posed by the *Relaciones*. Question 10: "El sitio y asiento donde los dichos pueblos estuuieren, si es en alto, o en baxo, o llano, con la traça y designo en pintura de las calles, y plaças, y otros lugares señalados de monesterios como quiera que se pueda rascuñar facilmente en un papel, en que se declare, que parte del pueblo mira al medio dia o al norte" (Moreno Toscano, *Geografía económica*, 129). ["Describe the site upon which each town is established; whether it is on a height, or low-lying, or on a plain. Make a plan in color of the streets, plazas, and other significant features such as monasteries, as well as can be sketched easily on paper, indicating which part of the town faces south or north" (translation by Clinton R. Edwards in Cline, "The Relaciones Geográficas," 235)]; question 42. "Los puertos y desembarcaderos que huuiere en la dicha costa y la figura y traça de ellos en la pintura como quiera que sea en un papel, por donde se pueda ver la forma y talle que tienen" (Moreno Toscano, *Geografía económica*, 132). ["Note the ports and landings that occur on the coast, making a plan of each in color, as can be drawn on a sheet of paper, by which their form and shape can be seen" (translated by Clinton R. Edwards in Cline, "The Relaciones Geográficas," 237)]; question 47. "Los nombres de las Islas pertenecientes a la costa, y porque se llaman assi, la forma, y figura dellas en pintura, si pudiere ser y el largo, y ancho y lo que boxan, el suelo, pastos, arboles y aprouechamientos que tuuieren las aves, y animales que ay en ellas y los rios, y fuentes señaladas. (Moreno Toscano, *Geografía económica*, 132.) ["Note the names of the islands along the coast; why they are so called; their form and shape in color, if possible; their length, width, and area; the soil, pastures, trees, and resources they may have; the birds and animals; and the significant rivers and springs" (translation by Clinton R. Edwards in Cline, "The Relaciones Geográficas," 237)].

40. Robertson, "The Pinturas," 260.

41. In his survey of native Middle American pictorial manuscripts, John Glass classes the extant corpus into four major groups (preconquest survivals, Spanish patronage, native colonial, mixed colonial), the last of which includes maps or "pictorial manuscripts" produced as proof of land titles before Spanish courts. ("A survey of Middle American Pictorial Manuscripts," in *Guide to Ethnohistorical Sources*, part 3, ed. Howard F. Cline, *Handbook of Middle American Indians* [Austin, Texas], 14: 3–80).

42. Mary Elizabeth Smith, *Picture Writing from Ancient Southern Mexico: Mixtec Place Signs and Maps* (Norman, Oklahoma, 1973), 166.

43. Donald Robertson, *Mexican Manuscript Painting of the Early Colonial Period: The Metropolitan Schools* (New Haven, 1959); Glass, "A Survey of Middle American Pictorial Manuscripts." Glass is quite definite about the existence of pre-Hispanic maps: "Mexican Indian maps were one of the categories of manuscripts that most impressed the earliest Spaniards in the New World. References to maps will be found in the letters of relation of Cortés, the writings of Bernal Díaz and Peter Martyr, and in other sources" (33).

44. Richard E. Blanton, *Monte Albán: Settlement Patterns at the Ancient Zapotec Capital* (New York, 1978), 38–40.

45. Tatiana Proskouriakoff, *Civic and Religious Structures of Mayapan.* Carnegie Institution of Washington Publication 619 (Washington, 1962), 90.

46. David A. Freidel and Jeremy A. Sabloff, *Cozumel: Late Maya Settlement Patterns* (New York, 1984), 160–61; Robert M. Carmack, *The Quiche Maya of Utatlan* (Norman, Oklahoma, 1981), 76, 166–68, 225–56.

47. Olivier de Montmollin, "Tenam Rosario—A Political Microcosm," *American Antiquity* 53, no. 2 (1988): 364.

48. These examples are not only suggestions that significant information in Mesoamerica was recorded in the huge scales of site planning. Michael D. Coe, "A Model of Ancient Community Structure in the Maya Lowlands," *Southwestern Journal of Anthropology* 21, no. 2 (1965): 111, argues that elevated, stuccoed causeways forming intra- and intercity communication systems (*sacbeob* in Yucatec Maya) served to tie together symbolically royal partilineages in the Classic Maya site of Tikal. C. Antonio Benavides, *El Sistema prehispánico de communicaciones terrestres en la región de Cobá, Quintana Roo y sus implicaciones sociales* (Mexico, 1976), sees such *sacbeob* as expressive of relative intra- and intersite rankings. Clemency Coggins, *The Stucco Decoration and Architectural Assemblage of Structure 1-Sub, Dzibilchaltun, Yucatan, Mexico,* Middle American Research Institution, Publication 49 (New Orleans, 1983), interprets Structure 1-sub at the northern Yucatecan Maya site of Dzibilchaltun (with its radial symmetry, intercardinal inset corners and sculptured embellishment) as forming an architectural symbol for cyclical completion within the Mesoamerican fifty-two-year calendar round.

49. The first quotation is from Joyce Marcus, "Mesoamerican Territorial Boundaries: Reconstructions from Archeology and Hieroglyphic Writing," *Archeological Review from Cambridge* 3, no. 2 (1984): 56. The other two are from Marcus, "Stone Monuments and Tomb Murals," 304. Marcus finds "the delimitation of Zapotec territory by named natural landmarks interesting, because it calls to mind the carved stones of Building J at Monte Albán, which list 40-odd places associated with 'hill' or 'mountain' glyphs. It reinforces my suspicion that Building J records the territorial boundaries of the Zapotec state in Monte Albán II by reference to a series of named landmarks" (Joyce Marcus, "The Reconstructed Chronology of the Later Zapotec Rulers, A.D. 1415–1563," in *The Cloud People: Divergent Evolution of the Zapotec and Mixtec Civilizations,* ed. Kent V. Flannery and Joyce Marcus [New York, 1983], 304).

50. The *lienzo,* a loosely woven cotton cloth of local manufacture depicting territorial boundaries and genealogy, pertains to Santiago Guevea de Humbolt,

located to the north of the Isthmus of Tehuantepec. It was first reported by Eduard Seler in "Das Dorfbuch von Santiago Guevea," in *Gesammelte Abhandlungen* (Graz, 1960), 157–93. The original, said to be in Guevea, has never been published. Two extant copies, both of which have glosses in Zapotec, have been published recently (Joyce Marcus, "Zapotec Writing," *Scientific American* 242 *[1980]: 50–64; Marcus, "Reconstructed Chronology"; John Paddock, "Comments on the Lienzos of Huilotepec and Guevea," in The Cloud People: Divergent Evolution of the Zapotec and Mixtec Civilizations,* ed. Kent V. Flannery and Joyce Marcus [New York, 1983], 308–13); John Paddock, *Lord 5 Flower's Family: Rulers of Zaachila and Cuilapan,* Publications in Anthropology, 29 [Nashville, Tennessee, 1983]). Photographs of the original are reported in the University of Texas Library, Austin (Paddock, "Comments on the Lienzos," 313).

51. Probably drawn around 1550, the Lienzo de Jicayán is a pictographic map of the town of San Pedro Jicayán, where it is currently kept. See Smith, *Picture Writing,* 122–61 for an extensive and intensive analysis of this important document.

52. The number of places depicted surrounding Jicayán corresponds with the Mesoamerican calendar round of fifty-two years, i.e., the complete permutation of the *pije* (260 days) and *yza* (360+5 days).

53. Furst, *Codex Vindobonensis,* 315, 313.

54. See note 9.

55. Animal skin screenfold pictorial manuscripts, referred to as codices, include an uncertain number of pre-Hispanic examples from the Mixteca Alta. Usually considered preconquest are those of the Nuttall Group: Codices Becker no. 1, Bodley, Colombino, Zouche-Nuttall, and Vienna. For a discussion of these in the context of known Mesoamerican manuscripts, see Glass, "*A Survey of Middle American Pictorial Manuscripts,*" 3–80, esp. 11–13.

56. Robertson classifies the rendering of territories into two broad categories: maps and landscapes: "A map to the twentieth century is a diagram of nature essentially dependent upon measuration and proportion. A landscape is a picture of nature essentially dependent upon what the viewer sees, whether from one or more points of view. One can suggest here the distinction already made between sign and image. The map is a sign of nature; the landscape is the image" (Robertson, "Mexican Manuscript Painting," 183).

57. Ibid.

58. Cotty Burland, "The Map as a Vehicle of Mexican History," *Imago Mundi* 15 (1960): 11–18. Maarten E. R. G. N. Jansen, "Apoala y su importancia para la interpretacíon de los códices vindobonensis y Nuttall," in *Actes du XLII Congrès International des Américanistes,* ed. Jacques La Faye (Paris, 1979).

59. Furst, *Codex Vindobonensis,* 313. Furst further states "In *Fonds Mexicanus 20* and on page 33 of Codex Porfirio Díaz, the four cardinal points are shown as real sites that are also associated with gods and day signs. This is less of an abstraction, but still gives us little idea of spatial relationships. In representing the concept of the world directions, each of these documents projects essentially a bird's-eye view of a delineated universe (313)."

60. Jansen, "Apoala," 167–68, identifies the wedding scene depicted on Nuttall page 19 as an actual place in the Mixteca Alta known today as Apoala; Furst, *Codex Vindobonensis*, 180, discusses the identity of the male "wearing the costume of the Fire Serpent" entering the large hill occupying two pages of the manuscript.

61. Discussing the Vienna screenfold, Jansen makes a similar observation: "Por lo tanto, yo opino que el Vindobonensis en parte representa un conjunto geográfico y que el orden geográfico de los lugares alteró el orden histórico de las fechas. Diferentes personas ocuparon durante más o menos el mismo tiempo diferentes lugares, aparentemente en las cuatro direcciones, pero el códice por su forma, a diferencia de los maps, no puede expresar una sincronía, sino sólamente una diácronía" ("In any case, I suggest that the Vindobonensis represents in part a geographic ensemble, and that the geographic order of places altered the historical order of the dates. Different personages occupy during more or less the same time different places, apparently in four directions. However, the codex by its form, in contrast to the map, is not able to express synchronically, but only diachronically"; Jansen, "Apoala," 167).

62. A. Zorita, *Life and Labor in Ancient Mexico: The Brief and Summary Relation of the Lords of New Spain*, trans. B. Keen (New Brunswick, 1963), 110.

63. Nancy M. Farriss, personal communication, 1988.

64. Francisco Antonio Lorenzana, ed., *Historia de Nueva España, escrita por su esclarecido conquistador Hernán Cortes, aumentada con otros documentos, y notas* (Mexico, 1770), 91; Bernal Díaz del Castillo, *Historia verdadera de la conquista de la Nueva España por Bernal Díaz del Castillo, uno de sus conquistadores, única edición hecha según el códice autógrafo,* ed. Genara Garcia, (Mexico, 1904), 334.

65. Robertson, *Mexican Manuscript Painting*, 32.

66. "The retention of substantial land-holdings and high social status by the hereditary native chieftains is a distinguishing feature of colonial society in the Valley of Oaxaca" (William B. Taylor, *Landlord and Peasant in Colonial Oaxaca* [Stanford, 1972], 35).

67. Smith, *Picture Writing*, 168.

68. H. R. Harvey, "Techialoyan Codices: Seventeenth-Century Indian Land Titles in Central Mexico," in *Supplement to the Handbook of Middle American Indians: Ethnohistory*, ed. Ronald Spores (Austin, Texas, 1986), 154.

69. AGI, *Mexico 882.*

70. Joyce Marcus, "The Origins of Mesoamerican Writing," *Annual Review of Anthropology* 5 (1976): 35–67, effectively criticizes ethnocentric evaluations of writing's "development," demonstrating that Old World paradigms do not take into account the diverse purposes of texts in differing cultural traditions.

71. Henige observes that in Ganda and Myoro kinglists, the "oral mode . . . allows for inconvenient parts of the past to be forgotten because of the exigencies of the continuing present" (David Henige, "'The Disease of Writing': Gando and Nyoro Kinglists in a Newly Literate World," in *The African Past*, ed. Joseph C. Miller [London and Hampden, Connecticut, 1980], 225). Similarly, memory

stored as pictures permits more variation in the future because meaning in images is less arbitrary than in texts.

Private Art and Public Knowledge in Later Chinese Painting

1. Cf. Michael Baxandall, "The Language of Art History," *New Literary History* (1979): 453–65.

2. See Clifford Geertz, "Art as a Cultural System," in *Local Knowledge: Further Essays in Interpretive Anthropology* (New York, 1983), 94–120.

3. For an adumbration of literati painting theory during the Song dynasty, and selections from critical and theoretical texts of this school through the late Ming dynasty, see Susan Bush, *The Chinese Literati on Painting: Su Shih (1037–1101) to Tung Ch'i-ch'ang (1555–1636),* Harvard-Yenching Institute Studies 27 (Cambridge, Mass., 1971).

4. Erwin Panofsky, "Jan van Eyck's Arnolfini Portrait," in *Modern Perspectives in Western Art History*, ed. W. E. Kleinbauer (New York, 1971), 193–204.

5. For cogent and broad-ranging discussions of issues of representation in painting, see Svetlana Alpers, *The Art of Describing: Dutch Art in the Seventeenth Century* (Chicago, 1983).

6. For Western painting as a medium of erasure, see Norman Bryson, *Vision and Painting* (London, 1983), 87–96.

7. For a full record and partial translation of the inscriptions on the painting by the artist and later viewers, see Kojiro Tomita and Hsien-chi Tseng, *Portfolio of Chinese Paintings in the Museum (Yuan to Ch'ing Periods): A Descriptive Text* (Museum of Fine Arts, Boston, 1961), 8–9.

8. Ibid.

9. Richard Vinograd, "Situation and Response in Traditional Chinese Scholar-Painting," *The Journal of Aesthetics and Art Criticism* 46 (1988): 365–74.

10. For the concept of *shen-hui*, see Bush, *The Chinese Literati on Painting*, 44, 49–50, 64–66.

11. See Chad Hansen, *Language and Logic in Ancient China* (Ann Arbor, 1983), 55–67, for the relationship of early Chinese language to concepts of knowledge.

12. For the extended concept of *xie* as *xie yi* (sometimes rendered *hsieh-i*), see Bush, *The Chinese Literati*, 66–70, 126, where the phrase is rendered "to sketch, or write, ideas."

13. The commonest character for "portrait-painting" is closely related in graphic form and pronunciation to the character *hsiang*, "image" in a semantic cluster that includes the concepts of "resemblance," "portents," "constellations," and "appearance."

14. For a selection of comments on portraiture in early Chinese painting criticism, see Susan Bush and Hsio-yen Shih, eds., *Early Chinese Texts on Painting* (Cambridge, Mass., 1985), 230, 243.

15. My use of "descriptive painting" requires some qualification, because of the loaded status of the term in recent Western art-historical and theoretical

writing. I would sharply differentiate my usage of "descriptive" from that found in Alpers, *The Art of Describing*, xxi–xxv, where "descriptive" is used as a rough analogue of "visually realistic," and contrasted with "narrative." I mean instead to point to the verbal, durational implications of description in my account; compare the review of *The Art of Describing* by Nancy Marmer in *Art in America* 72 (September 1984): 25, where the textual implications of "description" are noted. Michael Baxandall, in *Patterns of Intention: On the Historical Explanation of Pictures* (New Haven, 1985), 1–11, uses "descriptive" to refer to verbal explanations or accounts of pictures. My usage here emphasizes, rather, the descriptive status of Chinese literati paintings themselves, but it points also to the possibilities of the close implication of such paintings with textual accounts of them.

16. For the "second reality" of Chinese paintings see Victoria Contag, "The Unique Characteristics of Chinese Landscape Pictures," *Archives of the Chinese Art Society of America* 6 (1952): 45–63.

17. See Michael Fried's analysis of Pollock's nonobjective painting of 1947 through 1950, quoted in Bernice Rose, *Jackson Pollock: Drawing into Painting* (Museum of Modern Art, New York, 1980), 19.

18. See Bernice Rose, "Sol LeWitt and Drawing," in *Sol LeWitt*, ed. Alicia Legg (Museum of Modern Art, New York, 1978).

19. See James Cahill, *Hills Beyond a River: Chinese Painting of the Yuan Dynasty, 1279–1368* (New York, 1976), 4–6; Wen C. Fong, *Images of the Mind* (Princeton, 1984), 94–129.

20. See Sherman E. Lee, "Chinese Painting from 1350 to 1650," in *Eight Dynasties of Chinese Painting*, ed. Wai-kam Ho, Sherman E. Lee, Laurence Sickman, and Marc F. Wilson (Cleveland, 1980), xxxv–xxxviii.

21. There were a number of important painters, especially among the monumental landscapists of the Five Dynasties and Northern Song periods, who remained apart from court art circles throughout their careers, but for the most part their paintings were collected and appreciated at the court and their approaches absorbed into the world of court taste and criticism. In some cases, followers after the styles of such independent artists were proper members of the court academies. For examples, and an accessible summary of the careers of the most important painters of the Tang, Five Dynasties, and Song periods, see Max Loehr, *The Great Painters of China* (New York, 1980), 31–230.

22. See Jan Fontein and Money L. Hickman, *Zen Painting and Calligraphy* (Museum of Fine Arts, Boston, 1970), xxxii–xxxvi.

23. See Fu Shen, "Yuan-tai Huang-shih shu-hua shou-ts'ang shih-lueh" [A history of the Yuan imperial art collections], *National Palace Museum Quarterly* 13, no. 1 (autumn 1978): 25–52 (pt. 1); no. 2 (winter 1978): 1–24 (pt. 2); no. 3 (spring 1979): 1–12 (pt. 3).

24. See Bush, *The Chinese Literati on Painting*, 118–45.

25. See Lee, "Chinese Painting," in *Eight Dynasties of Chinese Painting*, xxxv–xxxviii.

26. See, for example, the recorded activities and commissions of the eighth-century court painter Wu Tao-tzu, including paintings for palace buildings, and Buddhist and Taoist temple commissions, for which Wu's painting took

on the character of a public performance or spectacle, documented in translated quotations in Bush and Shih, eds., *Early Chinese Texts on Painting*, 55–56, 66–68.

27. See Wai-kam Ho, "Aspects of Chinese Painting from 1100 to 1350: The Sung Academy of Painting," in *Eight Dynasties of Chinese Painting,* xxv–xxx.

28. See Richard Barnhart, "The 'Wild and Heterodox School' of Ming Painting," in *Theories of the Arts in China*, eds. Susan Bush and Christian Murck (Princeton, 1983), 365–96.

29. See the extensive sections concerned with critical standards from painting texts of the pre-Tang, Tang, and Song periods, quoted in Bush and Shih, eds., *Early Chinese Texts on Painting*, 39–42, 71–84, 94–103.

30. See the selections from their texts in ibid., 155–56, 160–62, 177–86.

31. Theoretical treatises continued to be written after the Song, and the Yuan period, transitional in this regard, saw some focus on technically specialized treatises on subjects like portraiture, bamboo and plum painting, and the faults and techniques of landscape painting; ibid., 241–88.

32. See the sections on Yuan and Ming literati art theory in Bush, *The Chinese Literati*, 118–79.

33. A nice example of the mnemonic functions of such painting is Dong Qichang's (1555–1636) "Landscape in the Manner of Zhao Mengfu" album leaf of 1624, where Dong's accompanying inscription notes that he had owned both Zhao's "Village by the Water" handscroll of 1302, and a direct copy of the latter work by Wen Zhengming (1470–1559), both of which in turn followed the brush manner of the "Wangquan Villa" scroll of the ancient master Wang Wei (699–759). Dong then states that both formerly owned scrolls had long been lost from his household collection; they looked, he concludes, more or less like the present album leaf. See the reproduction of this album leaf in James Cahill, *The Compelling Image: Nature and Style in Seventeenth-Century Chinese Painting* (Cambridge, Mass., 1982), 50, fig. 2.16, and fig. 2.15 for Zhao Mengfu's original.

34. See Chu-tsing Li, "The Literati Life," in *The Chinese Scholar's Studio*, eds. Chu-tsing Li and James C. Y. Watt (The Asia Society, New York, 1987), 37–40, for examples of the importance of access to painting collections.

35. See Lee, "Chinese Painting," in *Eight Dynasties*, xli.

36. See Bush, *The Chinese Literati*, 151–79.

37. For an overview of these artists and representative examples of their works, see James Cahill, *Fantastics and Eccentrics in Chinese Painting* (Asia House Gallery, New York, 1967).

38. See James Cahill, *The Compelling Image: Nature and Style in Seventeenth Century Chinese Painting* (Cambridge, Mass., 1982).

39. See Jao Tsung-i, *Chih-lo Lou ts'ang Ming i-min shu-hua* [Painting and calligraphy by Ming loyalists from the Chih-lo Lou collection] (Chinese University of Hong Kong Art Gallery, Hong Kong, 1975).

40. See Marc F. Wilson, "Continuity and Change in Chinese Painting from 1650 to 1850," in *Eight Dynasties of Chinese Painting*, xlvii–xlviii.

41. See A. K'ai-ming Ch'iu, "The Chieh Tzu Yuan Hua Chuan [Mustard Seed Garden Painting Manual]: Early Editions in American Collections," *Archives of the Chinese Art Society of America* 5 (1951): 55–70; also Mai-mai Sze, *The*

Mustard Seed Garden Manual of Painting (Princeton, 1956), for an accessible facsimile of a late nineteenth-century reprint edition of the *Mustard Seed Manual*, with English translations of the accompanying text.

42. Cf. the original preface to the color prints of the *Ten Bamboo Studio Treatise on Calligraphy and Painting* by Wang Sande, quoted in Jan Tschichold, *Chinese Color Prints from the Ten Bamboo Studio* (New York, 1972), 27, where the low cost and availability of the woodblock-print designs are specifically contrasted with the practice of earlier artists of hiding their works away to increase their value.

43. See the discussion of seventeenth- and eighteenth-century painting catalogues in the individual entries in Hin-cheung Lovell, *An Annotated Bibliography of Chinese Painting Catalogues and Related Texts*, Michigan Papers in Chinese Studies, no. 16 (Ann Arbor, 1973), especially nos. 47, 49, 54, 57.

44. Wang Yuan-ch'i et al., eds., *Pei-wen-chai shu hua p'u* [Encyclopedia of calligraphy and painting commissioned by the K'ang-hsi emperor], (Shanghai, compiled 1708; reprint, 1883).

45. See Wilson, "Continuity and Change," in *Eight Dynasties*, xlvii–xlviii.

46. See Cahill, *Compelling Image*, 70–105, 168–83.

47. See Hiromitsu Kobayashi and Samantha Sabin, "The Great Age of Anhui Printing," in *Shadows of Mt. Huang: Chinese Painting and Printing of the Anhui School*, ed. James Cahill (University Art Museum, Berkeley, 1981), 25–28.

48. See the summary account in Cahill, *The Compelling Image*, chap. 3; also the fuller translations and documentation of Chinese viewers' responses to European pictures in Hsiang Ta, "European Influences on Chinese Art in the Later Ming and Early Ch'ing Period," in *The Translation of Art: Essays on Chinese Painting and Poetry*, trans. Wang Teh-chao (Hong Kong, 1976), 152–60.

49. Cahill, *Compelling Image*, 72.

50. See ibid., figs. 3.20–3.22.

51. Ibid., 92–105; 168–83.

52. See James Cahill, *The Distant Mountains: Chinese Painting of the Late Ming Dynasty, 1570–1644* (New York, 1982), 244–66.

53. See ibid. for examples of this approach.

54. Wilson, "Continuity and Change," in *Eight Dynasties*, xlvii.

55. See William Wu, "Kung Hsien's Style and His Sketchbooks," *Oriental Art* 16, no. 1 (spring 1970): 72–80, where the surviving copies of two versions of the sketchbooks are said to reflect Gong Xian's styles in the 1660s and 1680s, bracketing the period of publication of the *Mustard Seed Manual*.

56. For possible instances of painted albums and scrolls with appended instructional texts from the Yuan dynasty (1279–1368), see Bush and Shih, eds., *Early Chinese Texts*, 240–45; note that printed manuals appeared at this time, though confined to specialized subjects such as bamboo and prunus.

57. See Cahill, *The Compelling Image*, 176–83, where the combination of European pictorial influence and texture and tonality-based rendering leads to images characterized as at once natural and visionary.

58. See Marilyn Fu and Shen Fu, *Studies in Connoisseurship* (Princeton, 1973), 36–37.

59. In an inscription for a leaf from a "Ten-leaf Album of Landscapes," dated 1682; the translation is adapted from Fu, *Studies in Connoisseurship*, 44–45, where the album leaf in question is reproduced as fig. 7.

60. See Sze, *The Mustard Seed Garden Manual*, 133, 138, 166, 181 for illustrated examples.

61. Translation after Fu, *Studies in Connoisseurship*, 46.

62. See Wen C. Fong, *Images of the Mind* (Princeton, 1984), 204–6, for a summary and characterization of Shi'tao's late major theoretical treatise.

63. See Richard Vinograd, "Reminiscences of Ch'in-huai: Tao-chi and the Nanking School," *Archives of Asian Art* 31 (1977–78): 6–31.

64. See Richard Edwards, *The Painting of Tao-chi* (Museum of Art, University of Michigan, 1967), 22–23. For the appearance of the theme of the Peach Blossom Spring—with its associations of a return to a natural simplicity, escape from history, and forgetting—in the late art of Shitao around 1700–1702, see Nakamura Shigeo, *Sekito—hito to geijutsu* (Tokyo, 1985), 282–85; for a translation of the legend of the Peach Blossom Spring, as recorded in a classic fifth-century text by Tao Yuanming, see Cyril Birch, ed., *Anthology of Chinese Literature: From Early Times to the Fourteenth Century* (New York, 1965), 167–68.

65. See Cahill, *Fantastics and Eccentrics*, 76–80.

66. The sections of the *Mustard Seed Garden Manual of Painting* illustrating subjects such as flowers, plants, birds, and animals that have most in common with Zhu Da's innovative compositions did not appear until the second, complete edition of 1701, late in Zhu Da's life. However, bird-and-flower compositions were included in the woodblock-printed *Ten Bamboo Studio Painting Manual* from the 1640s. See Wen Fong, "Stages in the Life and Art of Chu Ta (1626–1705)," *Archives of Asian Art* 40 (1987): 9–10, for a discussion of the influence of *Ten Bamboo Studio Stationery Designs* of 1644 on the early works of Zhu Da, in an article that came to my attention after this paper was prepared.

Selected Bibliography

Introduction

Alpers, S. *The Art of Describing*. Chicago, 1983.

_____. *Rembrandt's Enterprise: The Studio and the Market*. Chicago, 1988.

Bartlett, F. C. *Remembering: A Study in Experimental and Social Psychology*. Cambridge, 1932.

Baxandall, M. *Giotto and the Orators*. Oxford, 1971.

_____. *Painting and Experience in Fifteenth-Century Italy*. Oxford, 1972.

_____. *The Limewood Sculptors of Renaissance Germany*. New Haven and London, 1980.

Belting, H. *Giovanni Bellini, "Pieta": Ikone und Bildererzählungen in der venezianischen Malerei*. Frankfurt am Main, 1985.

_____. *The End of Art History?* Chicago, 1987.

Bourdieu, P. *Outline of a Theory of Practice*. Cambridge, 1977.

Feeley-Harnik, G. "Divine Kingship and the Meaning of History among the Saklava (Madagaskar)." *Man* 13 (1978): 402–17.

_____. "The Political Economy of Death: Communication and Change in Malagasy Colonial History." *American Ethnologist* 11 (1984): 1–19.

_____. "Cloth and the Creation of Ancestors in Madagascar." In *Cloth and Human Experience*. Ed. J. Schneider and A. B. Weiner. Washington, 1988.

Fried, M. "Painting Memories: On the Containment of the Past in Baudelaire and Manet." In *Canons*. Ed. R. von Hallberg. Chicago and London, 1983.

Gombrich, E. *Art and Illusion*. Princeton, 1960.

Jewsiewicki, B. "Collective Memory and Its Images: Popular Urban Painting in Zaire—A Source of 'Present Past.'" *History and Anthropology* 2 (1986): 389–96.

_____. "Collective Memory and the Stakes of Power: A Reading of Popular Zairian Historical Discourses." *History in Africa* 13 (1986): 195–223.

Johnson, M. *The Body in the Mind: The Bodily Basis of Meaning, Imagination, and Reason.* Chicago, 1987.

Kaeppler, A. "Structured Movement Systems in Tongga." In *Society and the Dance.* Ed. P. Spencer. Cambridge, 1985.

Küchler, S. "Malangan—Art and Memory in a Melanesian Society." *Man* 22 (1987): 238–55.

Lakoff, G., and M. Johnson. *Metaphors We Live By.* Chicago, 1980.

MacDonald, R. R. *The Burial Places of Memory: Epic Underworlds in Vergil, Dante, and Milton.* Amherst, 1987.

Melion, W. "Karel van Mander's 'Life of Goltzius': Defining the Paradigm of Protean Virtuosity in Haarlem around 1600." *Studies in the History of Art* 27 (1989): 113–33.

Miller, A. "Text and Image in Pre-Columbian Art." In *Proceedings of the 44th International Congress of Americanists.* Manchester, 1983, 41–55.

_____. *Maya Rulers of Time: A Study of Architectural Sculpture at Tikal, Guatemala.* Philadelphia, 1986.

Pardo, M. *Paolo Pino's "Dialogo di pittura": A Translation with Commentary.* Ph.D. dissertation, University of Pittsburgh, 1984.

Roy, B., and P. Zumthor, eds. *Jeux de memorie: Aspects de la mnémotechnie médiévale.* Vrin, 1985.

Sperber, D. *Rethinking Symbolism.* Cambridge, 1975.

_____. "Anthropology and Psychology: Toward an Epidemiology of Representations." *Man* 20 (1985): 73–89.

Vinograd, R. "Family Properties: Personal Context and Cultural Patterns in Wang's 'Pien Mountains' of 1366." *Ars Orientalis* 13 (1987): 1–29.

Yates, F. *The Art of Memory.* Chicago, 1966.

Zuidema, R. T. "Bureaucracy and Systematic Knowledge in Andean Civilization." In *The Inca and Aztec States, 1400–1800.* Ed. G. Collier, R. Rosaldo, and J. Wirtz. New York, 1982.

Memory, Imagination, Figuration

Alberti, Leon Battista. *De pictura.* Ed. Cecil Grayson. Rome and Bari, 1975.

Ames-Lewis, Francis. *Drawing in Early Renaissance Italy.* New Haven, 1981.

Baxandall, Michael. *Giotto and the Orators.* Oxford, 1971.

_____. *Painting and Experience in Fifteenth-Century Italy.* London, 1972.

Brizio, Anna Maria. *Scritti scelti di Leonardo da Vinci.* 2d ed., Turin, 1968.

Cennini, Cennino. *Il libro dell'arte.* Ed. Franco Brunello. Vicenza, 1971.

Children of Mercury: The Education of Artists in the Sixteenth and Seventeenth Centuries. Providence, R. I., 1984.

Clark, Kenneth, and Carlo Pedretti. *The Drawings of Leonardo da Vinci in the Collection of Her Majesty the Queen at Windsor Castle.* 3 vols. London, 1968.

Farago, Claire. "Leonardo da Vinci's 'Paragone,' a Critical Interpretation: The 'Parte Prima' of 'Codex Vaticanus Urbinus 1270.'" Ph.D. dissertation, University of Virginia, 1988.

Gombrich, Ernst H. "Leonardo's Method of Working Out Compositions." In *Norm and Form,* 58–63. London, 1966.

Harvey, E. Ruth. *The Inward Wits: Psychological Theory in the Middle Ages and the Renaissance.* London, 1975.

Keele, Kenneth D. *Leonardo da Vinci's Elements of the Science of Man.* London and New York, 1983.

_____, and Carlo Pedretti. *Leonardo da Vinci: Corpus of the Anatomical Studies in the Collection of Her Majesty the Queen at Windsor Castle.* 3 vols. London, 1979.

Kemp, Martin. "*Il concetto dell'anima* in Leonardo's Early Skull Studies." *Journal of the Warburg and Courtauld Institutes* 34 (1971): 115–34.

_____. "Dissection and Divinity in Leonardo's Late Anatomies." *Journal of the Warburg and Courtauld Institutes* 35 (1972): 200–25.

_____. "'Ogni dipintore dipinge se': A Neoplatonic Echo in Leonardo's Art Theory?" In *Cultural Aspects of the Italian Renaissance: Essays in Honour of Paul Oskar Kristeller.* Manchester, 1976.

_____. *Leonardo da Vinci: the Marvellous Works of Man and Nature.* Cambridge, Mass., 1981.

Ludwig, Heinrich. *Lionardo Da Vinci: Das Buch von der Malerei.* 3 vols. 1882. Reprint, Osnabrück, 1970.

McMahon, A. Philip, ed. and trans. *Treatise on Painting (Codex Urbinas Latinus 1270) by Leonardo da Vinci.* 2 vols. Princeton, 1956.

Pedretti, Carlo. *Leonardo da Vinci on Painting: A Lost Book (Libro A).* Berkeley, 1964.

_____. *The Literary Works of Leonardo Da Vinci: A Commentary to Jean Paul Richter's Edition.* 2 vols. Berkeley, 1977.

Richter, Jean Paul. *The Literary Works of Leonardo da Vinci.* 2 vols. London, 1939.

Strong, Donald S. "Leonardo on the Eye: The MS D in the Bibliothèque de l'Institut de France . . ." Ph.D. dissertation. University of California, Los Angeles, 1967.

Summers, David. *The Judgment of Sense: Renaissance Naturalism and the Rise of Aesthetics*. Cambridge, 1987.

Vasari, Giorgio. *La vita di Michelangelo nelle redazioni del 1550 e del 1568*. Ed. P. Barocchi. 5 vols. Milan, 1962.

Yates, Frances A. *The Art of Memory*. Chicago, 1966.

Memory and Knowledge in the Production of Dance

Kaeppler, Adrienne L. *The Structure of Tongan Dance*. Ph.D. dissertation, University of Hawaii, 1967.

_____. "Method and Theory in Analyzing Dance Structure with an Analysis of Tongan Dance." *Ethnomusicology* 16, no. 2 (1972): 173–217.

_____. "Structured Movement Systems in Tonga." In *Society and the Dance*. Ed. Paul Spencer, 92–118. Cambridge, 1985.

Küchler, Susanne. "Malangan: Art and Memory in a Melanesian Society." *Man* 22, no. 2 (1987): 238–55.

Sperber, Dan. "Anthropology and Psychology: Towards an Epidemiology of Representations." *Man* 20, no. 1 (1985): 73–89.

Williams, Drid. "Introduction to the Special Issue of Semasiology." *Journal for the Anthropological Study of Human Movement*, New York University 1, no. 4 (1981): 207–25.

Finding Memories in Madagascar

Baré, J.-F. *Pouvoir des vivants, langage des morts: Idéologiques sakalava*. Paris, 1977.

Basso, K. H. "'Stalking with Stories': Names, Places, and Moral Narratives among the Western Apache." In *Text, Play and Story: the Construction and Reconstruction of Self and Society*, Proceedings of the American Ethnological Society, 1983. Ed. E. M. Bruner, 19–55. Washington, D. C., 1984.

_____. "'Speaking with Names': Language and Landscape among the Western Apache." *Cultural Anthropology* 3 (1988): 99–130.

Bloch, M. *Placing the Dead: Tombs, Ancestral Villages, and Kinship Organization in Madagascar*. London, 1971.

Chazan-Gillig, S. "Le *Fitampoha* de 1968 ou l'efficacité du mythe de la royauté sakalava dans l'actualité politique et économique malgache." In *Les Souverains de Madagascar: L'Histoire royale et ses résurgences contemporaines*. Ed. F. Raison-Jourde, 451–76. Paris, 1983.

Dandouau, A. "Coutumes funéraires dans le nord-ouest de Madagascar." *Bulletin de l'Académie malgache* 9 (1911): 165–77.

Dez, J. "Le Retournement des morts chez les Betsileo." *Société d'Ethnographie de Paris* 51 (1956): 115–22.

Feeley-Harnik, G. "The Political Economy of Death: Communication and Change in Malagasy Colonial History." *American Ethnologist* 11 (1984): 1–19.

_____. "Issues in Divine Kingship." *Annual Review of Anthropology* 14 (1985): 273–313.

_____. "Dancing Battles: Representations of Conflict in Sakalava Royal Service." *Anthropos* 83 (1988): 65–85.

_____. "Cloth and Creation of Ancestors in Madagascar." In *Cloth and Human Experience*. Ed. A. B. Weiner and J. Schneider, 73–116. Washington, D. C., 1989.

_____. *A Green Estate: Land, Labor, and Ancestry in Northwestern Madagascar*. Washington, D. C., 1991, in press.

Fontoynont, G. "De quelques 'solo' célèbres en Imerina, et culte religieux de certains rois." *Bulletin de l'Académie Malgache* 12 (1913): 115–37.

Fortes, M. "An Introductory Commentary." In *Ancestors*. Ed. W. H. Newell, 1–16. The Hague, 1976.

Foucault, M. *Discipline and Punish: The Birth of the Prison*. New York, 1979; originally published 1975.

Fox, J. J. "'Standing' in Time and Place: The Structure of Rotinese Historical Narratives." In *Perceptions of the Past in Southeast Asia*. Ed. A. Reid and D. Marr, 10–25. Singapore and London, 1973.

Gennep, A. van. *The Rites of Passage*. Chicago, 1960.

Goffman, E. *Asylums: Essays on the Social Situation of Mental Patients and Other Inmates*. Garden City, N. J., 1961.

Huntington, W. R. "Death and the Social Order: Bara Funeral Customs (Madagascar)." *African Studies* 32 (1973): 65–84.

Kling, G. "La Toponymie malgache." *Bulletin de Madagascar* 7 (1957): 787–89.

Kottak, C. P. *The Past in the Present: History, Ecology and Cultural Variation in Highland Madagascar*. Ann Arbor, 1980.

Krapf, Ludwig. *A Dictionary of the Suahili Language*. Ridgewood, N. Y., 1964; originally published 1882.

Küchler, S. "*Malangan*: Art and Memory in a Melanesian Society." *Man* n.s. 22 (1987): 238–55.

Kuipers, J. C. "Place, Names, and Authority in Weyéwa Ritual Speech." *Language and Society* 13 (1984): 455–66.

Lambek, M. *Human Spirits: A Cultural Account of Trance in Mayotte*. Cambridge, 1981.

Lombard, J. "Le Royaume Sakalava-Menabe: Résultat d'une enquête et présentation d'un corpus de traditions et de littérature orales." *Cahiers O.R.S.T.O.M.*, série Sciences humaines 13 (1976): 173–202.

MacDonald, R. R. *The Burial Places of Memory: Epic Underworlds in Vergil, Dante, and Milton.* Amherst, 1987.

Malinowski, B. *Argonauts of the Western Pacific.* New York, 1961; originally published 1922.

Mellis, J. V. *Nord et nord-ouest de Madagascar: Volamena et volafotsy, suivi d'un vocabulaire du nord-ouest expliqué, commenté, et comparé au Merina.* Tananarive, 1938.

Molet, L. *Petit guide de toponymie malgache.* Tananarive-Tsimbazaza, 1957.

Pickersgill, W. C. "Revision of North-West Place-Names: Some Curiosities of Topographical Nomenclature. *Antananarivo Annual* 12 (1888): 488–94.

Poirier, C. "Fin de règne et de légende . . . Rapport à Monsieur le Gouverneur Général de Madagascar et Dépendances, Cabinet, Tananarive, le 27 Décembre 1926. Annexe des Archives d'Outre-mer, Aix-en-Provence, MAD 6(2)D121." Published with revisions, including the addition of funeral songs and details concerning Tondroko's burial recorded in 1926 as "Notes d'ethnographie et d'histoire malgaches."

_____. "Les '*Dady,*' '*Fibaby*' ou '*Ampagnito Be*' des anciens rois Sakalava du Menabé septentional." *Mémoires de l'Académie Malgache* 28 (1939): 13–18.

_____. "Notes d'ethnographie et d'histoire malgaches: Les Royaumes Sakalava Bemihisatra de la côte nord-ouest de Madagascar." *Mémoires de l'Académie Malgache* 28 (1939): 41–104.

Raharijaona, S., and J. Valette. "Les Grands fêtes rituelles des Sakalava du Menabé ou 'Fitampoha.'" *Bulletin de Madagascar* 155 (1959): 1–33, appendixes.

Raison-Jourde, F., ed. *Les Souverains de Madagascar: L'Histoire royale et ses résurgences contemporaines.* Paris, 1983.

Rakotomampiaina, J. C. "Une liturgie sacrificielle à Alasora (Tananarive)." *Journal of Religion in Africa* 2 (1969): 192–201.

Sibree, J. "Malagasy Place Names." *Antananarivo Annual* 20 (1896): 401–13.

Warnock, M. *Memory.* London, 1987.

Wilcox, D. J. *The Measure of Times Past: Pre-Newtonian Chronologies and the Rhetoric of Relative Time.* Chicago, 1987.

Yates, F. *The Art of Memory.* London, 1966.

Transformations of Time and Space

Aguirre Beltrán, Gonzalo. *El proceso de aculturación.* Mexico, 1982.

Alcina Franch, José. "Calendarios zapotecos prehispánicos según documentos de los siglos XVI y XVII." *Estudios de Cultura Náhuatl* 6 (1966): 119–33.

_____. "Calendario y religión entre los zapotecos serranos durante el siglo XVII." In *Mesoamerica: Homenaje al Doctor Paul Kirchoff.* Ed. Barbro Dahlgren, 212–24. Mexico, 1979.

Archivo General de Indias (AGI). *Mexico 882.*

Baxandall, Michael. *Painting and Experience in Fifteenth-Century Italy.* Oxford, 1988.

Benavides, C. Antonio. *El sistema prehispánico de comunicaciones terrestres en la región de Cobá, Quintana Roo y sus implicaciones sociales.* Escuela Nacional de Antropología de Historia. Mexico, 1976.

Blanton, Richard E. *Monte Albán: Settlement Patterns at the Ancient Zapotec Capital,* New York, 1978.

Bledsoe, Caroline, and Kenneth M. Robey. "Arabic Literacy and Secrecy among the Mende of Sierra Leone." *Man* 21, no. 2 (1986): 202–26.

Carder, James Nelson. *Art Historical Problems of a Roman Land Surveying Manuscript: The Codex Arcerianus A. Wolfenbüttel.* New York, 1978.

Carmack, Robert M. *The Quiche Maya of Utatlan.* Norman, Okla., 1981.

Caso, Alfonso. *Las estelas zapotecas.* Mexico, 1928.

_____. *Las Exploraciones en Oaxaca, quinta y sexta temporadas, 1936–1937.* Publicación 34, Instituto Panamericano de Geografía e Historia. Mexico, 1938.

_____. "Calendario y escritura de las antiguas culturas de Monte Albán." In *Obras completas.* Ed. Miguel Othón de Mendizábal, 1: 114–45. Mexico, 1946.

_____. "Zapotec Writing and Calendar." In *Archaeology of Southern Mesoamerica,* part 2. Ed. Gordon R. Willey, 931–47. Vol. 3 of the *Handbook of Middle American Indians.* Austin, Tex., 1965.

Chance, John K. *Conquest of the Sierra: Spaniards and Indians in Colonial Oaxaca.* Norman, Okla., 1989.

Cline, Howard F. "The Relaciones Geográficas of the Spanish Indies 1577–1648." In *Guide to Ethnohistorical Sources,* part 1. Ed. Howard F. Cline, 183–242. Vol. 12 of the *Handbook of Middle American Indians.* Austin, Tex., 1972.

Coe, Michael D. "A Model of Ancient Community Structure in the Maya Lowlands." *Southwestern Journal of Anthropology* 21, no. 2 (1965): 97–114.

Coggins, Clemency. *The Stucco Decoration and Architectural Assemblage of Structure 1-Sub, Dzibilchaltun, Yucatan, Mexico.* Middle American Research Institution, Publication 49. New Orleans, 1983.

Córdova, Juan de. *Arte del idioma zapoteca.* Mexico, 1987; facsimile of 1886 Morelia edition.

Curtin, Phillip D., ed. *Africa and the West: Intellectual Responses to European Culture.* Madison, Wis., 1972.

Díaz del Castillo, Bernal. *Historia verdadera de la conquista de la Nueva España por Bernal Díaz del Castillo, uno de sus conquistadores, única edición hecha según el códice autógrafo.* Ed. Genaro García. Mexico, 1904.

Dibble, Charles E., and Arthur J. O. Anderson. "Book 4—The Soothsayers and Book 5—The Omens." In *Florentine Codex: General History of the Things of New Spain.* Ed. Fray Bernardino de Sahagun. Santa Fe, 1979.

Dilke, O. A. W. *Greek and Roman Maps.* London, 1985.

Diringer, David. *Writing.* New York, 1962.

Edmonson, Munro S. *The Book of Counsel: The Popol Vuh of the Quiche Maya of Guatemala.* Middle American Research Institute, Publication 35. New Orleans, 1971.

Farriss, Nancy M. *Maya Society under Colonial Rule: The Collective Purchase of Survival.* Princeton, 1984.

Feeley-Harnik, Gillian. "The Political Economy of Death: Communication and Change in Malagasy Colonial History." *American Ethnologist* 11, no. 1 (1984): 1–19.

Freidel, David A., and Jeremy A. Sabloff. *Cozumel: Late Maya Settlement Patterns.* New York, 1984.

Fuente, Julio de la. *Yalalag: Una villa zapoteca serrana.* Mexico, 1977.

Furst, Jill L. *Codex Vindobonensis Mexicanus I: A Commentary.* Albany, 1978.

Gelb, I. J. *A Study of Writing.* Chicago, 1974.

Gerhard, Peter. *A Guide to the Historical Geography of New Spain.* Cambridge, 1972.

Gibson, Charles. *The Aztecs under Spanish Rule: A History of the Indians of the Valley of Mexico, 1519–1810.* Stanford, 1964.

———, ed. *The Spanish Tradition in America.* New York, 1968.

Glass, John B. "A Survey of Middle American Pictorial Manuscripts." In *Guide to Ethnohistorical Sources*, part 3. Ed. Howard F. Cline, 3–80. Volume 14 of the *Handbook of Middle American Indians.* Austin, Tex., 1975.

Goody, Jack. *The Domestication of the Savage Mind.* Cambridge, 1977.

_____. *The Logic of Writing and the Organization of Society.* Cambridge, 1986.

_____. *The Interface between the Written and the Oral.* Cambridge, 1987.

_____, ed. *Literacy in Traditional Societies.* Cambridge, 1968.

Gruzinski, Serge. *La colonisation de l'imaginaire: Société indigenes et occidentalisation dans le Mexique espagnol XVI–XVIII siècle.* Paris, 1988.

Hanke, Lewis. "The 'Requerimiento' and Its Interpreters." *Revista de Historia de América* 1 (1938): 25–34.

Harley, J. B., and David Woodward, eds. *The History of Cartography: Cartography in Prehistoric, Ancient, and Medieval Europe and the Mediterranean.* Chicago, 1987.

Harvey, H. R. "Techialoyan Codices: Seventeenth-Century Indian Land Titles in Central Mexico." In *Supplement to the Handbook of Middle American Indians: Ethnohistory.* Ed. Ronald Spores, 153–64. Austin, Tex., 1986.

Henige, David. "'The Disease of Writing': Ganda and Nyoro Kinglists in a Newly Literate World." In *The African Past Speaks.* Ed. Joseph C. Miller, 240–61. London and Hamden, Conn., 1980.

Horton, Robin, and Ruth Finnegan, eds. *Modes of Thought: Essays on Thinking in Western and Non-Western Societies.* London, 1973.

Hunt, Eva. *The Transformation of the Hummingbird: Cultural Roots of a Zinacantecan Mythical Poem.* Ithaca, 1977.

Jansen, Maarten E. R. G. N. "Apoala y su importancia para la interpretación de los códices Vindobonensis y Nuttall." In *Actes du XLII Congrès International des Américanistes.* Ed. Jacques LaFaye. Paris, 1979.

Lipp, Frank Joseph. "The Mije Calendrical System: Concepts and Behavior." Ph.D. dissertation, New School for Social Research, 1982.

Lockhart, James. "Some Nahua Concepts in Postconquest Guise." *History of European Ideas* 6, no. 4 (1985): 465–82.

Lorenzana, Francisco Antonio, ed. *Historia de Nueva España, escrita por su esclarecido conquistador Hernán Cortes, aumentada con otros documentos, y notas.* Mexico, 1770.

Marcus, Joyce. "The Origins of Mesoamerican Writing." *Annual Review of Anthropology* 5 (1976): 35–67.

_____. "Zapotec Writing." *Scientific American* 242 (1980): 50–64.

_____. "The Reconstructed Chronology of the Later Zapotec Rulers, A.D. 1415–1563." In *The Cloud People: Divergent Evolution of the Zapotec and Mixtec Civilizations.* Ed. Kent V. Flannery and Joyce Marcus, 301–8. New York, 1983.

_____. "Stone Monuments and Tomb Murals of Monte Albán IIIa." In *The Cloud People: Divergent Evolution of the Zapotec and Mixtec*

Civilizations. Ed. Kent V. Flannery and Joyce Marcus, 137–43. New York, 1983.

_____. "Mesoamerican Territorial Boundaries: Reconstructions from Archaeology and Hieroglyphic Writing." *Archaeological Review from Cambridge*, 3, no. 2 (1984): 48–62.

Miller, Arthur G. *The Mural Paintings of Teotihuacán*. Washington, D. C., 1973.

_____. "Captains of the Itzá: Unpublished Mural Evidence from Chichn Itzá." In *Social Process in Maya Prehistory: Studies in Honor of Sir Eric Thompson*. Ed. Norman Hammond, 197–225. London, 1977.

_____. *On the Edge of the Sea: Mural Painting at Tancah-Tulum, Quintana Roo, Mexico*. Washington, D. C., 1982.

_____. "Pre-Hispanic Mural Painting in the Valley of Oaxaca, Mexico." *National Geographic Research*, 4, no. 2 (1988): 233–58.

_____. "Living with Death: Painted Tombs from Ancient Oaxaca." n.d.

Mitchell, W. J. T. *Iconology: Image, Text, Ideology*. Chicago, 1987.

Montmollin, Olivier de. "Tenam Rosario—A Political Microcosm." *American Antiquity*, 53, no. 2 (1988): 351–70.

Moreno Toscano, Alejandra. *Geografía económica de México*. Mexico, 1968.

Nuttall, Zelia. *The Codex Nuttall*. Ed. Arthur G. Miller. New York, 1975.

Paddock, John. "Confluence in Zapotec and Mixtec Ethnohistories: The 1580 Mapa de Macuilxochitl." *Papers in Anthropology: Native American Ethnohistory* 23, no. 2 (1982): 345–53.

_____. "Comments on the Lienzos of Huilotepec and Guevea." In *The Cloud People: Divergent Evolution of the Zapotec and Mixtec Civilizations*. Ed. Kent V. Flannery and Joyce Marcus, 308–13. New York, 1983.

_____. *Lord 5 Flower's Family: Rulers of Zaachila and Cuilapan*. Publications in Anthropology, 29, Vanderbilt University, Department of Anthropology. Nashville, Tenn., 1983.

Paso y Troncoso, Francisco del, ed. *Relaciones geográficas de Oaxaca*. Mexico, 1981; originally published 1579.

Proskouriakoff, Tatiana. *Civic and Religious Structures of Mayapan*. Carnegie Institution of Washington Publication 619, 87–164. Washington, D. C., 1962.

Reko, Blas Pablo. *Mitobotánica zapoteca*. Tacubaya, 1945.

Robertson, Donald. *Mexican Manuscript Painting of the Early Colonial Period: The Metropolitan Schools*. New Haven, 1959.

_____. "The Pinturas (Maps) of the Relaciones Geográficas, with a Catalog." In *Guide to Ethnohistorical Sources*, part 1. Ed. Howard F.

Cline, 243–78. Vol. 12 of the *Handbook of Middle American Indians.* Austin, Tex., 1972.

Saussure, Ferdinand de. *Course in General Linguistics.* New York, 1959.

Seler, Eduard. "Das Dorfbuch von Santiago Guevea." In *Gesammelte Abhandlungen,* 157–93. Graz, 1960.

Smith, Mary Elizabeth. *Picture Writing from Ancient Southern Mexico: Mixtec Place Signs and Maps.* Norman, Okla., 1973.

Svenbro, Jesper. *Phrasikleia: Anthropologie de la lecture en Grèce ancienne.* Paris, 1989.

Taylor, William B. *Landlord and Peasant in Colonial Oaxaca.* Stanford, 1972.

Tedlock, Barbara. *Time and the Highland Maya.* Albuquerque, 1982.

Troike, Nancy P. "Current Problems in the Mixtec Codices" in *Actes du XLII Congrès International des Américanistes.* Paris, 1979.

Weber, Max. *On Charisma and Institution Building: Selected Papers.* Ed. S. N. Eisenstadt. Chicago and London, 1977.

Welte, Cecil R. *Welte's Ready Reference Releases,* 1–5. Oaxaca, 1973–81. See especially no. 5, "Preconquest and Early Colonial Pictorial Manuscripts of the 'Oaxaca Area,'" 1981.

Whitecotton, Joseph W. "Zapotec Pictorials and Zapotec Naming: Towards an Ethnohistory of Ancient Oaxaca." *Papers in Anthropology* 23, no. 2 (1982): 285–343.

Whittaker, Gordon. "The Hieroglyphics of Monte Albán." Ph.D. dissertation, Yale University, 1980.

Winter, Marcus. *Oaxaca: The Archaeological Record.* Mexico, 1989.

Wolf, Eric R. *Sons of the Shaking Earth: The People of Mexico and Guatemala, Their Land, History and Culture.* Chicago, 1967.

Zilberman, María Cristina. "Idolatrías de Oaxaca en el siglo XVIII." In *Actas y Memorias del Congreso Internacional de Americanistas (Sevilla, 1964),* 111–23. Seville, 1966.

Zorita, A. *Life and Labor in Ancient Mexico: The Brief and Summary Relation of the Lords of New Spain.* Trans. B. Keen. New Brunswick, 1963.

Index